ROUTLEDGE LIBRARY EDITIONS:
LIBRARY AND INFORMATION SCIENCE

Volume 49

INTERNATIONAL ASPECTS OF REFERENCE AND INFORMATION SERVICES

INTERNATIONAL ASPECTS OF REFERENCE AND INFORMATION SERVICES

Edited by
BILL KATZ AND RUTH FRALEY

Taylor & Francis Group
LONDON AND NEW YORK

First published in 1987 by The Haworth Press, Inc.

This edition first published in 2020
by Routledge
2 Park Square, Milton Park, Abingdon, Oxon OX14 4RN

and by Routledge
52 Vanderbilt Avenue, New York, NY 10017

Routledge is an imprint of the Taylor & Francis Group, an informa business

© 1987 The Haworth Press, Inc.

All rights reserved. No part of this book may be reprinted or reproduced or utilised in any form or by any electronic, mechanical, or other means, now known or hereafter invented, including photocopying and recording, or in any information storage or retrieval system, without permission in writing from the publishers.

Trademark notice: Product or corporate names may be trademarks or registered trademarks, and are used only for identification and explanation without intent to infringe.

British Library Cataloguing in Publication Data
A catalogue record for this book is available from the British Library

ISBN: 978-0-367-34616-4 (Set)
ISBN: 978-0-429-34352-0 (Set) (ebk)
ISBN: 978-0-367-37406-8 (Volume 49) (hbk)
ISBN: 978-0-367-37409-9 (Volume 49) (pbk)
ISBN: 978-0-429-35364-2 (Volume 49) (ebk)

Publisher's Note
The publisher has gone to great lengths to ensure the quality of this reprint but points out that some imperfections in the original copies may be apparent.

Disclaimer
The publisher has made every effort to trace copyright holders and would welcome correspondence from those they have been unable to trace.

International Aspects of Reference and Information Services

Edited by
Bill Katz and Ruth Fraley

The Haworth Press
New York • London

International Aspects of Reference and Information Services has also been published as *The Reference Librarian,* Number 17, Spring 1987.

© 1987 by The Haworth Press, Inc. All rights reserved. No part of this book may be reproduced or utilized in any form or by any means, electronic or mechanical, including photocopying, microfilm and recording, or by any information storage and retrieval system, without permission in writing from the publisher. Printed in the United States of America.

The Haworth Press, Inc., 12 West 32 Street, New York, NY 10001
EUROSPAN/Haworth, 3 Henrietta Street, London WC2E 8LU England

Library of Congress Cataloging-in-Publication Data

International aspects of reference and information services.

    Published also as no. 17 of The Reference librarian.
    Bibliography: p.
    1. Reference services (Libraries)—International cooperation. 2. Information services—International cooperation. 3. International librarianship. 4. Bibliography, International. I. Katz, William A., 1924-   . II. Fraley, Ruth A.
Z711.I59   1987   025.5'2   87-11846
ISBN 0-86656-573-6

International Aspects of Reference and Information Services

The Reference Librarian
Number 17

CONTENTS

Introduction: The World of Reference and Information
    Services   1
        Bill Katz

THE WORLD

Information Counseling and Policies   7
        Marta L. Dosa
        Darla Holt

The Environment of International Information Use   9

International Comparison and Problems in the
Application of Information Technology to Information
Services   23
        Esther E. Horne

Western Europe	24
United States	25
Mexico	27
Asia	28
Developing Countries	29
Canada	33
Some Trends in Information Technology	34
Newer Technologies	36
Conclusion	39

Reference Services and Global Awareness   45
     Mohammed A. Aman
     Mary Jo Aman

Decline of Foreign Library Acquisitions   45
Weak Bibliographic Control   47
Foreign Reference Tools in Library School Curriculum   48

Information Service: Supporting the Educational Program Around the World   51
     Jean E. Lowrie

Two International Programs   53
Development of Information Service   54
Anecdotal Illustrations   55

Integrating a Central Reference Service in an International Studies Program   59
     W. Daviess Menefee

First Task   60
Training Staff   61

UNITED STATES

Hospitable Harvard: Five International Libraries and Their Services to International Readers   65
     Barbara Mitchell

Pravda, Le Monde and the CIA   67
Color TV in China   68
Mom and Pop Library   72

Overseas Publications of the Library of Congress: Their History and Use as Reference Resources   77
     Jack C. Wells

Areas of Coverage   77
The PL-480 Program   79
National Program for Acquisitions and Cataloging   80
Current Accessions Lists   81
Information Provided by the Accessions Lists   85
Accessions Lists as Reference Tools   87

International Information Activities of the U.S. Geological Survey   93
   Gary W. North
   Nancy B. Faries

International Earth Science Technical Assistance and
   Cooperative Scientific Programs   93
U.S. Geological Survey Library   95
Geological Survey Participation in International
   Organizations   96
U.S. Geological Survey Information Offices   98

A Viewpoint for Successful International Marine Data/Information Transfer   107
   Steven J. Tibbitt

Aquatic Sciences and Fisheries Information System
   (ASFIS)   108
Marine Environmental Data Information Referral
   System (MEDI)   109
Marine Data/Information Transfer Program Development   110
Conclusion   112

Scientific/Technical Translations in a Research Library   113
   Ted Crump

The Library and the Translator   115

Indexing and Abstracting Services' Coverage of Soviet English Language Periodicals   123
   Gloria Jacobs

Introduction   123
Methodology   124
Findings   125
Conclusion   127

AFRICA

Resources for the Study of Africa and the Middle East: An Overview   131
   Julian W. Witherell

Area Collections   133

Wide Coverage	136
Other Centers	138

AUSTRALIA

On-Line Information Services in Australia   143
Howard Coxon

Two Systems	145
The Impact of On-Line Systems on Australian Libraries	150
Conclusion	152

UNITED KINGDOM

The International Component of Reference Work at the Science Reference and Information Service, The British Library   155
M. W. Hill

Organisational Position	156
Clientele	158
New Activity	160

BBC Data As an Information Provider and Publisher   161
David Stoker

The BBC and Its Information Needs	161
BBC Data As an Information Provider	165
Programme Research and Information Services	166
Paper-Keeping and Documentation Services	171
Commercial Services	172
The Future	174

GERMANY

Automated Information Services for Supreme National Authorities: The Libraries' Contribution—The Example of the Federal Republic of Germany   177
Ernst Kohl

Information Requirements of Supreme National Authorities	178
Automated Documentations of Press Releases — A Challenge to Libraries	179

The Rationale of Automating Libraries in Supreme Authorities	181
Network Development	193

ISRAEL

Information Services in Industry: Difficulties in Less Developed and Small or Peripheral Countries — 199
Beth Krevitt Eres

Manpower Difficulties	200
Financial Difficulties	201
Discussion and Recommendations	202

LATIN AMERICA

The Most Useful Reference Sources on Latin America: Results of a Survey of Those Who Use Them Most — 203
Edwin S. Gleaves

Asking the Experts: The Survey	206
Reference Sources on Latin America: The Top 24 (Or So) Titles	209
Publishers' Series to Look (Out) For	220
Desiderata: What Else We Need on Latin America	225
Tentative Conclusions—And One More List (For the Small and Medium-Sized Library)	229
Latin American Specialists Who Responded to the Survey	231

Foreign Trade & Econ Abstracts Measures Up Internationally — 235
R. A. J. Van Loen

Library Division	236
Subject Coverage	238
Article Selection	240
Abstracting and Indexing Procedures	240
Cooperation	242
Future	243
Conclusion	244

Introduction:
The World of Reference and Information Services

Bill Katz

All reference librarians at one time or another use a few basic international reference works, if only the *Statesman's Yearbook* or *PAIS International*. A cursory glance at *Guide to Reference Books,* or at the latest edition of Walford indicates the impressive number of reference books published abroad. On the whole, though, most foreign reference books are not much used by the average reference librarian.

The perspective of the reference/information world is limited for American librarians. While there is talk, and some action, regarding regional and even national cooperation, that is about as far as it goes. Few librarians, other than those fortunate enough to be on committees which meet abroad as much for constructive talk as for travel, are aware of the implications of reference services beyond the boundaries of North America.

If one looks to the standard indexes for material, such as *Library Literature,* there is much less than one might expect. Of the five pages in the 1984 cumulation of that index, a good four are concerned only with IFLA (International Federation of Library Associations), and most of the fifth with the International Federation for Documentation. There are, to be sure, subheadings of major topics which cover international interests, but on the whole the representation is poor. One strongly suspects that international reference services are the concern of a limited few, most of whom, in one way or another, are connected with IFLA or IFD.

It's not encouraging to realize that the articles in this field are published in a few journals. Of first rank, and worth considering by anyone involved with international aspects of information: *IFLA Journal*, International Library Review, followed by the *Electronic Publishing Review* which rightfully classes itself "the international journal for the transfer of published information via videotext and online media." *Libri, International Forum of Information Documentation, The Library of Congress Information Bulletin* and a number of European journals cover the field. Except, though, for an odd article now and again, the more general library periodicals rarely turn to the international scene. This is understandable in view of limited pages and the expanding complexity of American library/information. Still, one might hope for at least an ongoing column on international affairs in the larger library journals.

Some of this noninvolvement is changing, primarily because of the rapid communications offered by database vendors and publishers scouting the world for perspective customers. Dialog is available in many parts of the globe, and the British and French are invading America with equally promising efforts. Another aspect of change is reflected in the concerns of IFLA which shows a refreshing interest in Africa and third world countries in Asia and Latin America. And there are various international organizations of librarians from those involved with sound archives to others turned to scientific advancement.

In special libraries and national libraries the international reference services situation is better. Here, as in large research and academic libraries, there is a well defined group who is not only interested in matters international, but depends on a world view for development of everything from research on astronomy to the care of zebras. The most concerned group is business where the international conglomerate is as much a part of the daily scene as the shades of Morgan and Frick in the history of American industrial development. And if one turns to politics, to government, there is an understandable interest in everything from the number of Soviet troops and tanks to the agricultural possibilities of growing rice in some distant third world country.

There are several well defined patterns of international reference and information services which do touch each and every librarian. First, and foremost, the volume of literature is so great, even in English speaking countries, that there has to be bibliographic control, as well as means and methods of mining the material from libraries in other countries. Resource sharing, interlibrary loan and countless other measures can bring the world's literature to even the smallest of libraries.

The need for control, for comprehensive access to scientific, political and business materials is self-evident, at least to the pragmatists who operate in these areas. And for that reason most of the attention, as the papers in this number indicate, tend to concentrate on the sciences and social sciences. One can fervently hope that the humanities will shortly receive more attention, as, indeed they are in some areas from history to art.

Be that as it may, at this point the dominant aspect of international reference and information services is the prominent role of government. To gain some idea of this role, simply look at the articles in this issue, organized under representative government headings.

The government's influence is useful, particularly in terms of coordination and funding, but in Europe and most of the Third World there has been little success in coordination. There is no real cooperation between individual countries. An obvious reason for this, too often overlooked, is a matter of languages. And while this may be overcome in science, it remains a tremendous barrier in other sectors. Unfortunately, too, there is a given lack of trust between the world's countries, even those who are allies, and each has tended to develop its own bibliographic, its own information system. The lack of standardization only adds to the confusion.

Commercialization of what heretofore has often been government dominated services may be one answer, and several critics see this as the configuration of the future. New technologies such as CD-Rom may make it possible to penetrate areas and markets now out of reach because of the cost of transmission. The information industry, which has done rather well in America, may be able to extend itself to most of Europe and developing countries. When that is done there will be more real than promised linkups between the librarian at the local college and one in southern Europe with much the same problems.

The extent of private interests in international information services is given by Horne who points out that "It is now possible to make online database searches in practically any part of Europe." She then considers services here, and in Mexico, Asia, and other parts of the globe from Pakistan to Canada. The new technologies offer the promise of hope for all, but only if they are accompanied by "leadership and vision." The Amans point out the problems associated with lack of language skills, decrease in purchase of foreign titles and the need for instructors to include international reference as part of their courses. Without this they believe "no international thrust in the library/information profession can reach full potential." Lowrie, examining school libraries, is somewhat more optimistic, and sees the world wide trend working towards a new "understanding among students of many cultures." Menefee carries this theme forward with an explanation and exploration of international studies programs.

When one examines the role of the United States in international bibliography, the first place to consider, as Wells reminds us, is the Library of Congress. The areas of coverage are impressive and he shows how the average librarian may benefit from the variety of LC programs. Accession lists are a major tool in international understanding and bibliographic control. At a specific level, North and Faries point out the activities of the U.S. Geological Survey, while Tibbitt turns to marine data and information from his agency. Scientific and technical translation is considered by Crump. These last papers cover the more familiar ground of science and technology, but it must be remembered that the U.S. government, through its libraries and services, does offer a wider spectrum of interests . . . as do other governments.

In Australia, for example, Coxon shows how newly developed online services are linked and bring the country in constant contact with American resources, as well as those in other parts of the world. The British Library, as the Library of Congress, plays a major role in international cooperation and Hill examines several programs and services. Kohl demonstrates the impressive control of information exercised by the Federal Republic of Germany. The various libraries of the Supreme Federal Authorities offer various bibliographic services which aid particular user groups, both there and abroad.

Latin America is probably closer to the average reference librarian than even Europe, if only because of the geographical proximity and, most important, the number of people from Latin America in the United States. Gleaves gives a summary of the basic "reference tools on Latin America" based on a ranking of a survey of Latin American specialists. Each is explained, and many will be of great use to those outside of academic, or special libraries. The article ends with "one more list for the small and medium sized library." The author's guidelines are impressive and, it is to be hoped, will do much to improve at least this aspect of international reference services in American libraries.

Returning to the esoteric, area of specialized reference services, Van Loen explains the activities of the Netherlands Foreign Trade Agency, and its well developed reference services, including the Foreign Trade and Econ Abstracts.

Essentially all authors agree on one point—this is no longer a parochial information world. Each country depends on the other, and if there ever is going to be true bibliographic control of information, true exchange of information around this world, then it is necessary to do much to improve international reference services. It seems a first step is to at least indicate the problems and a few of the answers one should consider in international librarianship. To that end this issue is dedicated.

THE WORLD

Information Counseling and Policies

Marta L. Dosa
Darla Holt

There are deeply seated differences in the ways various people interpret the role of information in society and in individual life. For some, the acquisition of new information opens the door to opportunities and achievements. Others get discouraged by the barriers they encounter when searching for relevant facts or opinions they will trust. Moreover, the same person may react to an announcement, a graph or a journal article differently under different circumstances. In small neighborhoods and in multinational corporations, in legislative bodies and on farms, people are using some kind of information all along and we still know very little about their preferences and habits although volumes have been written about information as a commodity and about the process of informing and being informed.

At the crossroads of efforts to grasp the nature and impact of "good" information, reference librarians and online searchers must depend on ingenuity, on finely honed skills and on their capacity to adapt to new situations. In the wake of rapid social

The authors are at the School of Information Studies, Syracuse University, Syracuse, NY 13210.

and technological changes, new information handling roles have emerged in many organizational and social settings outside of libraries. In the library, too, we can observe the application of new technologies to a multiplicity of resources and processes.[1] The scope of interest and requirements of information users have been steadily expanding from facts in well defined fields of knowledge to complex multidisciplinary research and from passive reading in public libraries to active involvement in public policy making.[2,3,4] In terms of the user-librarian relationship, probably the most powerful change—whose influence on reference and online work is still a matter of speculation—is the proliferation of online public access catalogs and microcomputer-based gateway systems. In addition, more and more journals and newspapers are available for electronic document access by the end-user.[5,6]

We have a wide spectrum of services ranging from libraries subsidized by public or private funds to market-based information provision. Similarly, the continuous debate over national information policies encompasses issues from information equity of access to the role of the private sector in encouraging innovation through competition. The increasingly diversified options in information transmission and use have become a global phenomenon.

These characteristics of the information society are also evident in every situation where international information is being pursued. Users, searching either for a description of the work of international organizations or for data on social and economic conditions in developing countries, face a maze of overlapping and often badly lacking resources. Without the help of intermediaries, and sometimes in spite of it, they might be overloaded by irrelevant materials or they might find that even the best sources can rapidly become obsolete. N. W. Balabkins speaks of the economist's need for the official and semiofficial documents of developing countries, the "grey literature" that is not distributed through the usual book-trade channels and is not found in libraries.[7] Corporations, too, require international data. An executive commented that "the data in some countries may be inconsistent internally or aggregated so as to render [them] incomparable with data from other nations."[8]

At the same time, the North-South transfer of data and information relevant to development goals must be considered. In recent decades, extensive research on international development assistance has demonstrated that international professional cooperation has to be based on two-way communications.[9] Although the merging of computers and telecommunications has brought relevant and timely information closer to people in some countries, at the same time it increased the gap between the industrialized and the economically less developed societies. Therefore, it seems that an awareness of the current information imbalance may be an appropriate philosophical framework for our thinking on how to obtain information resources from the developing parts of the world.

This paper addresses a threefold challenge faced by the reference librarian: (a) expanding information requirements in international studies, business and professional work; (b) the consideration of information counseling as an approach to in-depth assistance to the user; and (c) policies that affect client-practitioner relationships. We will confine ourselves to a few selected examples and citations that may lead to further readings. The term "developing countries" is used with the understanding that a wide range of economic, social and cultural differences exist among nations as well as among regions within the same country.

THE ENVIRONMENT OF INTERNATIONAL INFORMATION USE

As the news media, travel, and expanding educational, business and cultural activities brought far-flung parts of the world closer, the need for international information intensified. Several recent volumes of the *Annual Review of Information Science and Technology* offered state-of-the-art discussions of information resources and uses in different countries and areas. Observations have pointed to a few generalizations which can serve as the basis of the following assumptions. Accordingly, information requirements may be grouped in several categories:

— Primary data from and about other countries needed by specialized users in their field of work;
— Analyzed, aggregated and interpreted data for users external to the field of specialization where the data had been collected;
— Texts of laws, regulations, judicial decisions, treaties and agreements, standards, proceedings of meetings, official statements, etc.;
— The views of writers, social critics, philosophers, historians, politicians, artists, educators and others in the United States and elsewhere concerning their interpretation of international developments;
— Non-technical information including news and current awareness sources for general dissemination.

Such information resides in a vast collection of forms including print, microform, machine-readable record, tape, cassette, disc/disk, integrated network, etc. In an oversimplified scheme, international information resources encompass (a) numeric sources such as statistics, indicators, scientific measures and assessments, models, computer software, etc.; (b) primary documents, reports, files, archives, official records, conference papers, theses, graphs, etc.; (c) interpreted information in books, journals, compilations and other documented sources; (d) the opinion literature of commentaries, editorials, policy statements, etc.; and (e) information access tools such as the bibliographic apparatus at the secondary and tertiary levels.

It would be helpful to identify the main categories of potential information end-users of international information. Such an exercise was attempted many times in the past. For example, a ten year study by UNESCO's Science and Technology Policies Information Exchange System (SPINES) has found that potential users were hard to locate because they were only vaguely aware of what could be offered to them.[10] Research on three related areas: "user studies," "knowledge utilization" and the "diffusion of innovations" suggests that information requirements are so interdisciplinary as to defy categorization of user groups.[11,12,13] The following notes simply want to convey the sense of immense diversity reference librarians and online searchers encounter in international information work.

Public libraries are familiar with people who are interested in international relations, current events, travel and its hazards, communications with other countries and specialized topics. Businessmen, planners, writers, historians, club programmers, speakers, professional practitioners and students check out facts and figures. Many users have roots in foreign lands and some of them are active in organizations. There is a resurgent interest in ethnography, cultural studies, comparative religion, linguistics, folklore and self-help practices in other countries. In the midst of changing community trends and diverse user expectations, the reference librarian needs both communication and decision making skills.[14]

Academic libraries search for sources of international data for researchers in well defined disciplines and in newer interdisciplinary areas in environment, health, energy, population studies. Many educational programs, especially area studies, focus on contemporary international topics.[15] Also, the rise of policy sciences created a number of foreign policy research and teaching centers. Courses with an intensive need for international sources include, among others, subjects in telecommunication networks, transborder data flows, communication planning, technology transfer, trade relations, management techniques, business practices, and information studies. Academic libraries are also called upon to supply information to international development assistance projects involving faculty.

Corporate libraries and information centers support strategic decisions, market research resource acquisition, plant siting and design, research and development, production and materials purchasing and other activities often requiring international data and information for the corporation.[16] Corporate librarians are accountable for the timeliness, accuracy, credibility, clarity and cost effectiveness of the information they supply and thus the monitoring and evaluation of reference services are desirable.

Other special libraries and information centers assist a very heterogeneous group of organizations from medical colleges through newspapers to professional associations. In every case, international information is an integral part of the reference service. For example, organizations are responsible to their membership for the dissemination of current awareness information, often involving international affairs and foreign legislation. Citizen movements as well as lobby groups aim at the building of consensus about international issues in the American public, and this process now requires the intensive use of supportive data.[17]

School libraries and media centers cannot remain outside of the controversy surrounding the long-range, unintended effects of innovations in instructional technology. While many educators and parents praise the classroom use of microcomputers, others worry about the influence of these devices on the student's analytic thinking. The National Research Council warned that if schools want to improve performance in mathematics and science, they must increase learning time and enhance the abstract reasoning of students. Other debates focus on bilingual education and on the quality of learning about foreign affairs. School librarians can integrate these diverse strains of concern by counseling teachers not only on online searching and software, but also on international information sources. This enables the librarian to span a bridge between computer literacy and information literacy.

International Information Resources

The reference librarian's choices are complex and elusive. Information originates from United States domestic publications, foreign countries, intergovernmental organizations and international nongovernmental organizations (NGOs). Requirements for information from developing countries present acute problems and call for new approaches. In the following, our special attention to them is no indication that the other needs and resources are less important.

The characteristics of information resources and their availability vary from country to country. For example, in an industrializing society, government funds may flow to the generation of scientific and technical information at the expense of the collection of data on social conditions. Other countries may be in the process of creating domestic social accounting systems or may conduct research on quality of life indicators. These examples suggest that in the United States, acquisition of and referral to information resources produced within developing countries depend on the international information specialist's awareness of indigenous social infrastructures. Readings about the development goals and data generation priorities of at least some countries can build a useful background. Recognizing that there are many variations in information availability depending on a country's cultural tradition, political style and socioeconomic status, one may still identify a few institutions common to many developing countries:

— Scientific and technical information (STI) center
— National library and bibliographic network
— Technology transfer center
— Development planning agency
— Industrial documentation center
— Social science data center
— Sectoral information systems (agriculture, energy, health, forestry, etc.)
— Information dissemination and extension services.

Following independence, many developing countries struggled with the problems of creating modern institutions or infusing old ones with new national roles. Today, some segments of the social infrastructures are emerging as information producing entities.

Ministries of national governments carry out surveys, studies and administrative programs which generate official reports. It has been observed that such locally produced materials reflect conditions not described anywhere else, and are most important for understanding the planning process in a developing country.[18] Documents range from typescript to computer printout, with only a few in printed form. Few countries have an effective central distributing agency. Nevertheless, the official gazette of many governments carry announcements of documents which then may be requested from their source. The growth of national planning agencies and of the professional associations of public administrators can be expected to improve overall access to official publications.

Institutions and organizations usually take active part in local development processes either through data collection for a specific project or through voluntary participation in group activities. Since the early 1970s, many internationally-sponsored technical assistance projects have been mandated to involve local organizations, such as professional and religious associations and farmers' and women's clubs in project planning and development. Organizations represent indigenous patterns of self-help and service, and their work is often described in local reports or in the studies of international donor agencies.[19]

Universities and research institutes are relatively prolific in generating reports, papers and studies. These reflect the rise of indigenous expertise and are frequently deemed unique sources by researchers. Because proceedings of international conferences held in developing areas sometimes take several years to get published, direct acquisition of papers from or referral to the authors or academic departments is the only timely solution. The publication exchange programs American university libraries used to have with foreign institutions may be worth a second look.

Extension services in agriculture, industry and education produce informational materials which are now perceived as useful beyond the original target group. For example, some countries with remote geographical areas have been accumulating valuable experience in distance education.[20] Community development projects and literacy programs result in local or international reports reflecting the social and psychological profiles of local people. Communication and information dissemination programs which play a considerable role in rural development, produce mimeographed newsletters on village-level activities and methods.

Traditional cultures and the arts, known for a long time as vehicles of information dissemination in developing countries, are generally overlooked as information resources for libraries. Yet expressions of culture in popular drama, poetry and tales can provide social commentary on how people see themselves and their governments.[21] The newsletter *Development Communications Report* is rich in insights as well as references to publications on the topic. Social psychological research is a relatively new field that explores the interdependence of culture, education, communications and development. Not only academic but also public librarians will find its results relevant to their work.

Many users would cherish the opportunity to obtain original information sources from developing countries. In reference work, referral to indigenous institutions might become a service of significance. But reference librarians would have to decide when to use this particular path and when to turn to international organizations. Development assistance agencies maintain publication programs, bibliographic information systems, map collections and, in some cases, socioeconomic databanks. Sector policy papers, country reports, research studies and case histories reflect the entire process of development. Almost all agencies may be approached for current awareness service through mailing lists, query answering and referrals.

Information Counseling

Currently, few reference librarians have the opportunity to specialize in international information and to refer clients to indigenous sources of knowledge. The practice of referral requires not only familiarity with information resources abroad, but also understanding of the user's requirements, behavioral patterns and modes of information use. There are many decision situations in the client-librarian interaction which call for a more in-depth assistance than currently possible with reference service and online searching. Only a few examples can be given here:[22,23,24,25]

- ethical quandaries which require an open discussion with the user, based on mutual trust;
- searching in complex interdisciplinary areas where users need to reveal more than the usual information about their search objectives;
- language barriers that may be surmounted only by referral to other librarians, specialists, translated sources or technological solutions;
- facing a lack of good indexing and abstracting services, timelags of inclusion and poor or no document delivery of international sources;
- needing more familiarity with the users' cognitive styles and communication patterns in order to expand the reference or search interview;

— deciding whether or not informal networks and personal expertise should be tapped;
— recognizing the appropriate extent and method of information counseling in any particular situation.

It has been suggested that a new information counseling role with appropriate insights and skills, based on specialized courses, research and experience, would expand the intermediary's professional influence on advisement results.[26,27,28] There is nothing revolutionary about this. As our social institutions become more structured and impersonal, many professions respond by seeking new forms of interaction.[29] In numerous settings, one sees a trend toward information learning and problem solving in groups with the help of facilitators. In corporations, the use of quality circles gave rise to a new kind of intermediary who guides groups to participative decisions.[31] Hall identified the information analyst and evaluator in industry who can bridge the gap between the technical expert and the usual information specialist.[32] Adams contributed an important role to the advanced information utility consultant for linking nontechnical office workers with automated office tools.[33] Nielsen proposed to bring together the information mediation and teaching functions into a new model.[34] In librarianship, probably the best known practice of information consultation is carried out in clinical medical settings.[35]

Information counseling is the interactive process by which an information intermediary (a) assesses the needs and constraints of an individual through in-depth interviewing; (b) determines the optimal ways available to meet such needs; (c) actively assists the client in finding, using and, if needed, applying information; (d) assures systematic follow-up to ascertain that the assistance enabled clients to achieve their goals; and (e) develops systematic quality control and evaluation processes.[36] Shaver et al., have warned that

> the searcher needs to be acutely aware of the line which divides negotiation and problem clarification from information counseling. While information counseling may often be

the highest professional service a searcher can provide, it must be done with searcher awareness and client consent.[37]

Information counseling, where properly used, may enhance current reference advisement methods by accessing not only formal systems and library collections but also informal information sharing networks. This is an especially significant step in view of the complexity of international information resources. Today many researchers and decision makers are becoming used to electronic conferencing and consultation across continents. Is it a fair assumption that currently not many reference librarians participate in the informal communication networks of subject specialists although they might network with other librarians? It seems that in order to become an equal partner in information transactions, at least subject-specialized reference librarians should engage in information sharing networks in which end-users also participate.

There is another trend that necessitates the consideration of information counseling. More and more end-users access data and information without the help of intermediaries. In industry where management information systems brought disappointments, some users turn to performing their own computing.[38] With new gateway systems, online searching of data bases can be conducted by users with growing ease. Much research effort is devoted to expert systems that embody reasoning capacity derived from the analysis of an individual's domain of knowledge and a set of heuristics the expert used in formulating alternative approaches to problems.[39,40] However, speculation about the declining importance of human intermediaries could be dismissed if the intermediary role would expand to include information counseling. It is likely that the more options will be available for acquiring information, the greater will be the need for assistance.

Firstly, people without the means or ability to take advantage of these options must not be left out where the benefits of information are concerned. Secondly, users who perform their own searches will need specialized assistance in assessing, costing, selecting and planning strategies. The information counselor should be prepared also for the analysis, evaluation and organization of retrieved information for ready use.

Information Policies

Information counseling is a form of intervention. It attempts to introduce changes in the user's habits of seeking and selecting sources. It reverses the traditional relationship between the librarian and the "patron" in which usually the patron leads. The information counselor needs the knowledge, the professional ethical foundation, and the technique to decide how best to assist the information seeker and how to build rapport between two people. The acceptance of information as something that can be trusted to be valid and credible, is the basis of its use and eventual application to thought, process and action. This is not the place to discuss the psychological and legal implications of the practitioner-client relationship.[41] But the information policies that affect the strategy of advisement should be considered from the outset. Professionals frequently view policies in one of two extreme ways: either as inconsequential or as all-decisive. Much philosophical reflection is needed to view policy in the right context.

Information policies are plans and strategies for the development of information resources and their optimal use. Fragmented and uncoordinated as they are, policies attempt to guide the work of all types of information workers. Policy instruments may be informal and formal, ranging from beliefs and norms to standards, laws, regulations and international agreements. Often in conflict with each other and always debated, they deal with the freedom and ownership of information; the equity and economic diversification of access; compatibility of form and the marketplace of ideas; the privacy of the individual and the right to obtain information; the promotion of competition and the promotion of cooperation. Most of these issues fall into three broad categories according to the public, private and commercial value of information.[42] But with all of our efforts to reach consensus and express it by standards or legislation, occasionally our public policies, professional codes of conduct and personal beliefs will clash. In such a quandary, we will come to think of Bronowski's words:

> The world is not a fixed, solid array of objects, for it cannot be fully separated from our perception of it. It shifts under

our gaze, it interacts with us, and the knowledge that it yields has to be interpreted by us. There is no way of exchanging information that does not demand an act of judgment.[43]

The international exchange of information is dependent not only on the resource knowledge and individual contacts of American information professionals with colleagues and subject specialists abroad, but also on the general climate of global communications. Differences between the industrialized and economically less developed countries have already created regrettable tensions in North-South relations. The political tenor of the literature of technology transfer and transborder data flow attests to this. As they gradually take shape, policies may provide better guidance to international information work. However, they can never become substitutes for the individual's responsibility to foster professional cooperation at the person-to-person level.

REFERENCES

1. Teague, S. J. (1985). *Microform, video and electronic media librarianship.* Stoneham, MA: Butterworth.
2. Kissman, H. M. & Wexler, Philip. (1983). Toxicological information in *Annual review of information science and technology,* v. 18, White Plains, N.Y.: Knowledge Industry Publications, Inc., pp. 185-230.
3. Talbert, L., Bikson, T. K. & Shapiro, N. Z. (1984). *Interactive information environments: A Plan for enabling interdisciplinary research.* Santa Monica, CA: The Rand Corporation (Rand report N-2115).
4. Rodgers, J. L. (1977). *Citizen committees: A guide to their use in local governments.* Cambridge: Ballinger.
5. American Library Association. (1984). *Online catalogs, online reference: Converging trends.* Chicago: ALA.
6. Neufeld, M. L. & Cornog, Martha. (1983). Secondary information systems and services, in *Annual review of information science and technology,* v. 18. White Plains, N.Y.: Knowledge Industry Publications, Inc., pp. 152-183.
7. Balabkins, N. W. (1984). Collecting information in a developing country. Harvard library bulletin, 32:1, pp. 54-72.
8. Train, R. E. (1984). *Corporate use of information regarding natural resources and environmental quality.* Washington, D.C.: World Wildlife Fund.
9. United Nations University. (1979). *Basic human needs: Methodology and mobilization.* Tokyo: UNU (Human and social development programme research papers).
10. United Nations Educational, Scientific and Cultural Organization. (1979). *Sci-*

ence and technology policies information exchange system (SPINES) feasibility study. Paris: UNESCO (Science policy studies and documents 33).

11. Martyn, John & Cronin, Blaise. (1983). Assessing the impact and benefits of information and library research. *Journal of documentation* 39:3, September, pp. 171-191.

12. Paisley, W. J. and Matilda Butler. (1983). *Knowledge utilization systems in education*. Hollywood, CA: SAGE.

13. Rogers, E. M. (1983). *Diffusion of innovations*, 3d ed. The Free Press.

14. Shuman, B. A. (1981). *The river bend casebook: Problems in public library service*. Phoenix, Oryx Press.

15. Samore, Theodore (ed.). (1982). *Acquisition of foreign materials for U.S. libraries*, 2nd ed. Metuchen, N.J.: Scarecrow.

16. Train, R. E. op. cit.

17. Langton, S. (1984). Consensus building—new roles for citizens. *National civic review*, 73:3, pp. 132-135.

18. Woodward, A. M. (1980). Future information requirements of the Third World. *Journal of information science*, 1, pp. 259-265.

19. Smith, W. E., Lethem, F. J., & Thoden, B. A. (1980). *The Design of organizations for rural development projects: A Progress report*. Washington, D.C.: The World Bank.

20. Stewart, David et al. (eds.). (1983). *Distance education: International perspectives*. London: Croom Helm.

21. Kidd, Ross & Coletta, Nat (eds.). (1980). *Tradition for development, indigenous structures and folk media in non-formal education*. Bonn: German Foundation for International Development.

22. Shaver, D. B., Hewison, N. S. & Wykoff, Leslie. (1985). Ethics for online intermediaries. *Special libraries*, 76:4, pp. 238-245.

23. Guha, Bimalendu. (1985). *Study on the language barrier in the production, dissemination and use of scientific and technical information with special reference to the problems of developing countries*. Paris: UNESCO/PGI and UNISIST.

24. Sager, J. C. (1981). New developments in information technology for interlingual communication. *Aslib Proceedings*, 33, pp. 320-323.

25. Cronin, Blaise. (1982). Invisible colleges and information transfer, a review and commentary with particular reference to the social sciences. *Journal of documentation*, 38:3, pp. 212-236.

26. Debons, Anthony. (1975). An Educational program for the information counselor, in *Proceedings of the 38th ASIS Annual Meeting, 1975* v. 12. Washington, D.C.: American Society for Information Science.

27. Penland, P. R. (1971). Counselor librarianship in *Encyclopedia of library and information service*, v. 6. New York: Marcel Dekker, pp. 240-254.

28. Horton, F. W. Jr. (1982). The emerging information counselor, a new career in need of a champion. *ASIS Bulletin*, 8, pp. 16-19.

29. Ferguson, Marilyn. (1980). The Aquarian conspiracy: Personal and social transformation in the 1980's. Los Angeles: J. P. Tarcher.

30. Boulding, Kenneth & Senesh, Lawrence (eds.). (1983). *The Optimum utilization of knowledge*. Boulder, CO: Westview Press.

31. Swanson, G. C. & Scherer, John. (1982). Participative problem solving techniques. *Quality circles journal*, 3, pp. 34-42.

32. Hall, H. J. (1982). *Services for the analysis and evaluation of information*. New Brunswick, N.J.: Rutgers University, School of Communication, Information, and Library Studies.

33. Adams, M. Q. (1983). The Role of the advanced information utility consultant in achieving office productivity. *Proceedings of the 46th ASIS Annual Meeting 1983*, v. 20. White Plains, N.Y.: Knowledge Industry Publications, Inc., pp. 86-87.

34. Nielsen, Brian. (1982). Teacher or intermediary: Alternative professional models in the information age. *College and research libraries*, 43, pp. 183-191.

35. Tobia, R. C. et al. (1983). Clinical information consultation service at a teaching hospital. *Medical Library Association Bulletin*, 71, pp. 396-399.

36. Dosa, M. L. (1978). Information counseling. *Information reports and bibliographies*, 7:3, pp. 3-41.

37. Shaver, op. cit., p. 241.

38. Guimaraes, Tor. (1984). The Benefits and problems of user computing, 1:4, pp. 3-9.

39. Pollitt, A. S. (1984). A 'front-end' system: An Expert system as an online search intermediary. *Aslib Proceedings*, 36, pp. 229-234.

40. Buchanan, B. G. and Duda, R. O. (1983). Principles of rule-based expert systems. *Advances in computers*. Academic Press, pp. 164-217.

41. Mintz, A. P. (1984). Information practice and malpractice — do we need malpractice insurance? *Online*, 8:4, pp. 20-26.

42. U.S. Office of Technology Assessment. (1981). *Computer-based national information systems: Technology and public policy issues*. Washington, D.C.: OTA.

43. Bronovski, Jacob. (1973). The Principle of tolerance. *The Atlantic monthly*, 232:6, pp. 60-66.

International Comparison and Problems in the Application of Information Technology to Information Services

Esther E. Horne

The intent of this paper is to examine both currently and globally the varying degrees of application of information technology to information services in the various countries and regions around the world. These specific instances are not intended to be inclusive. Primarily the focus is on the use of international services; prevalence of user interface software; development of national and regional networks; and the role of libraries or information agencies. The status and condition of reference librarians, intermediaries, and libraries themselves will naturally arise throughout the whole of this paper. While assessing the present, trends and counter-trends are certain to surface. Insofar as possible these will be stressed in the context of identified indicators and actual instances.

Furthermore no attempt is being made to assess or evaluate any information service. What is wanted is to uncover, when possible, the extent of any application of information technology. Generally speaking, the underlying assumption is that networking, application of interfaces, and more successful document delivery capability should increase the efficiency and effectiveness of services by granting to the user a greater degree of access to the world's literature and a more rapid delivery time of source materials. A natural doubt arises as to which is of more

---

Dr. Horne is on the faculty of the School of Library and Information Science, Catholic University of America, Washington, DC 20064. Dr. Horne would like to acknowledge the generous assistance of Linda Knowles, Master's student at C.U.A., for the time and work spent on this paper.

importance: to access one's own literature or the world's literature. For the developed countries, having both options, the underlying assumption is probably true.

Schiller (1981) sets the tone for what is to follow. He believes that for all the change that seems to be pervading the world of information and communication, a synthesis is emerging.

> . . . a breathtaking and overarching synthesis seems to be, if not already emergent, at least present in some dim recognizable form. It takes the shape of networks — national and international systems linking powerful computational units, data bases, and transmission circuits.[1]
>
> Third World recognition of what has been occurring in electronic information generation and transmission is still at an early stage. This in no way, however, minimizes the level of awareness and the intensity of feeling among many segments of the population in a good part of the world against information dependency and cultural domination in general.[2]

Lundu (1984) echoes this third world concern. He claims that training abroad does not fit one for employment at home. The fear of dependency on the developed countries and concern about the unmet needs of his own society are expressed by him when speaking about "cultural traditions" and "psychological orientations" special to Zambia.[3]

A decision was made on whether to examine the situation in the developed or in the developing countries by choosing the former. It seems easier to understand what could be possible; why it often isn't; and what is not possible at all, by studying instances of the actual and possible.

Thus our attention is directed to Western Europe.

WESTERN EUROPE

It is now possible to make on-line data base searches in practically any part of Europe. All that is needed is a terminal, usually a microcomputer, and an acoustic coupler. The user thus switches into relatively cheap communication channels like EURONET. For the *untrained* user a software interface is provided from a Swedish firm that allows storage of automatic log on and log off with passwords for up to fifty hosts. In addition the interface permits the user to work in a preferred search language. Up to twenty-four search questions predefined off-line can be included as well as a complete search strategy. This is not only reduced effort but a cost reduction as well.[4] European users want on-line friendliness. They prefer a data base supermarket with one stop information shopping. This involves using a software interface. A common command language (CCL) would also increase usage.[5]

It is of interest to identify this user population. After a survey of 261 organizations in the UK, France, Germany, Italy and others, it was found that 54% of the scientists/engineers polled were users as were 43% of the libraries, 32% of the information specialists and 21% of the managers. (No breakdown was given for libraries as to type.)[6]

From the 1984-1985 issues of DIANE NEWS (Direct Information Access Network for Europe) can be derived the ongoing and planned activities for Western Europe. (There are other sources of course.) For instance EURODOCEL (European Document Delivery) involves networking several countries through *user service centers* which if successful will provide information services via satellite distribution. Presently it is possible to publish journals electronically and to provide on-line delivery of patents. One step beyond is electronic publishing and delivery. To make all this possible involves the utilization of full text storage, bibliographic files, electronic mail and decentralized document storage either by optical disc or microfiche.[7]

UNITED STATES

In the United States the specific cases examined give an insight into applications other than commercial on-line services. The following case involves the automation of reference services in the Salt Lake County Library System (1985). A patron can conduct searches via a computer terminal, review the citations on the screen, select a citation then receive by high speed printer a facsimile of the periodical pages from the periodicals center at the main county library. The service is offered to each of its fourteen branches. Patrons are provided with up to fifty citations on a topic at no cost. This does not imply free facsimile copies. Librarians offer assistance when needed or requested. Needless to say, the users have become very skilled. They have available all the time needed to set up their search. It doesn't cost until the software, SEARCH HELPER, is activated to dial the commercial search service. There is no charge for any of the reference services because of the savings realized in staff time.

All of the foregoing is possible because of SEARCH HELPER which Salt Lake County subscribed to in 1982. There are presently seven data bases available, the most popular being the MAGAZINE INDEX. SEARCH HELPER is self-coaching, allowing the patron to set up a search strategy off-line. Having the new periodicals center relieves the system of duplicating all the periodicals in the magazine collection at each of its fourteen branches, plus binding and providing shelf space for the retrospective issues.[8]

The University of Illinois Library of Urbana-Champaign provides interface software for the benefit of the user. This software is on an IBM PC. The data base searched is the on-line catalogue comprised of brief titles and authors from the circulation system and the full bibliographic system. The system search commands are formulated internally by the interface.[9]

Much effort is now afoot to sell interface software or gateway software to home and office microcomputer users. For example, if successful, IN-SEARCH, a Menlo Corporation product, will be the first to use the graphic search form as the interface. This could conceivably, dramatically change the future form of all gateway software.[10]

In providing information services the still difficult or problem areas are in document delivery and the use of full-text storage. Nevertheless DOCEL intends to use user service centers and satellite distribution while the Salt Lake County library system sets up a periodicals center and utilizes facsimile transmission.

Turning to the corporate world, the Cable Repair Administrative System of Bell Systems Co. has provided in-house users with what they term the *electronic* library. This library is a computer acting as a repository of documents, training materials or planning information organized and formatted for its users who have on-line access via dial-up terminals in their normal work environment. One of the goals of this library is to minimize the need for maintaining paper documents. The most reliable and current information is in the computer. The users, however, do both, use the paper documents and the computer versions. On-line documents are printed and then replaced with their new electronic versions.[11]

Another approach to providing information services is that of Battelle's. This is an international information network by way of its BASIS system.

> BASIS is now installed on over 100 computers worldwide supporting 1,000 user organizations. Key features of the system include multiple keyword searching, ANSI-standard thesaurus capabilities, an on-line report writer, and on-line computational capabilities. Also, multilingual term searching and command language capabilities are supported through the thesaurus features.[12]

BASIS in 1982 supported bibliographic, full text, and numeric data bases for library litigation, publishing, scientific and other applications.[13] By merging the BASIS system with Informart's TELIDON viewdata system in 1981 the hybrid system provides keyword and full text searching with videotex display and picture graphics.[14] Future direction of this hybrid information retrieval/videotex system is toward the general home information system marketplace.[15]

MEXICO

Mexico has for some time seen information as a resource to be applied to its continuing efforts toward economics and social development. Therefore in 1974 INFOTEC was created to provide technical assistance for the production of goods and services. Its information services are quite sophisticated and incorporate some information analysis center activities. These are *Consulting* (toward solution of problems in industry, etc.), *Research Surveys* (for decision making and usually containing statistical materials relating to new products, importing and exporting, etc.), and *Training* directed at the user community in order to market the idea of the usefulness of INFOTEC).

Among its resources are a very highly trained staff recruited from industry and a collection of very specialized document titles. Many of the periodicals are on microfiche. In addition, standards and patents from Mexico, Europe, U.S., and Canada are made available. INFOTEC has access to the commercial on-line services of U.S. and Europe. On-line searching is a very busy service, 50% being done of foreign data bases.

There are two current awareness services. One is published each month by subject specialists who select from the in-house periodicals collection; the other is published bimonthly in Spanish and English. Selection for the latter is made from NTIS (National Technical Information Services) U.S.A. to match the needs and interests of those developing countries where it is distributed. Other than NTIS, INFOTEC draws from publications such as ASIAN Productivity Organization, World Bank, etc. There is a branch in Monterrey, Mexico's second largest industrial city. An industrial information network is being promoted to encourage collaboration between the technical research institutions of the country.[16]

ASIA

Turning our attention to Asia it is obvious that *Japan* recognizes information to be a resource necessary to its national welfare and the need to promote its transfer and utilization. There are thousands of specialized information centers as well as specialized information systems and services. Needless to say, a very strong information infrastructure exists.

Although smaller by far than Japan, the *Republic of China* also has a strong infrastructure for information. There has been a 119% growth in special libraries. On-line service from U.S. is available; networking is strong; much interlibrary cooperation exists as well as many information systems and services. It is clearly stated that librarians are the foundation of these available services.

On the other hand, the *Peoples Republic of China* is struggling to rebuild its information infrastructure, principally its schools for Library and Information, its public libraries, its National Library Association and along with these, information centers and interlibrary loan procedures. There is just a lot of hard work ahead but it is underway and going strong.[17]

DEVELOPING COUNTRIES

In order to understand more fully the information service situation for developing countries, representative cases are examined in some detail. These are the Southeast Asia Region, the Muslim countries in general, Trinidad/Tobago—the Caribbean region, and then Pakistan.

Southeast Asia

The region of Southeast Asia and the nations within it have a common problem of increasing access to information in the language of the people. The periodicals of this region are published in a multiplicity of languages and in small quantities. The libraries exchange catalogs with one another but they also need to compile lists of their serials holdings for themselves for their own reference services and then for each other. "To date, a comprehensive union list of serials covering either an individual country or all the countries as a whole is still not available in Southeast Asia."[18] What does exist are MARC-COM data bases at the university and national libraries in Southeast Asia from which union lists of serials on COM fiche could be produced at regular intervals. These MARC-COM are INDOMARC in Indonesia, MALMARC in Malaysia, PHILMARC in the Philippines,

SINGMARC in the Republic of Singapore, and THEIMARC in Thailand.

Indexes and abstracts to national periodical literature are available. Abstracting is done in Thailand, Indonesia and the Philippines, but mostly on specific subjects and disciplines resulting in numerous gaps in the literature. Thus many journals compile and publish their own indexes thereby giving quick access to their own material. The frustration of the researchers is great because of the absence of an abstracting/indexing service to cover the region as a whole. For example, imagine the difficulty posed by the lack of access in local reference tools to any periodical literature published in another country. (Indexes as reference tools are not used by the average library patron but are used by reference librarians.) Without regional access to the periodical literature much information is lost to the researcher/reference librarian.

The problem of access is somewhat alleviated in that a journal may be indexed or abstracted internationally if it is written in English. Acquisitions of these journals is easier as well. By way of contrast, periodicals of the region are often not acquired because many publishers do not announce and libraries then cannot know, except through indirect means, how to go about acquiring them. Even having the order information does not assure success, because the desired publication may not be available any longer. The point of this is that primary journal literature is not often available to reference librarians. It is only through their personal contacts, association with library groups and acting as *mediators* on reformulating requests that they are able to compensate for the resource lacking in their library. Thus often a patron is given a referral in lieu of the needed article, but even this capability is of limited usefulness since the available directories of information centers in the region are seldom comprehensive or up-to-date.

Clearly then it is time for an effective national library network for resource-sharing from which a regional network could be developed and through which international networking could take place. Numerous consortia have been formed but due to the low priority given to librarians, projects are needed that produce immediate, visible results to attract more libraries to join.[19]

Muslim Countries

"No comprehensive bibliographic service is available in the Muslin World."[20] Sixty-six % of the literature produced in the Muslim Countries is not covered by any of the major indexing services of the West. Index Islamicus which concentrates exclusively on Islamic literature has an inadequate coverage of 33.8% of the references sought. Clearly the Muslim countries, specifically Nigeria, Pakistan, Malaysia, and Turkey should start indexing services in each of the individual countries, and work toward a broad base information infrastructure.[21]

Caribbean Region

Here is a viable example of the beginnings of networking and access sharing. Librarians in the Caribbean through cooperation and coordination have developed CARDINDEX, an index to the serials publications of the region in the area of the social sciences and humanities. CARISPLAN abstracts the socioeconomic information of the region and CAGRINDEX abstracts the region's agricultural information. However there are no printed indexes and abstracts in the area of science and technology. Access to these sources is through commercial on-line services. The Caribbean Industrial Research Institute (CARIRI) and the University of the West Indies at St. Augustine have on-line access to international data bases. Both use TYMNET in Miami to access Dialog. This service is available to all in the region. Free text searching capability enables the librarian to deal with the semantic barrier. (A professional librarian acts as the search intermediary.) Searching on several data bases is made quick and easy through the use of interface indexes DIALINDEX (Dialog), DATABASE INDEX (SDC) and CROSS (BRS).

The University of the West Indies library has access also via DATANETT to Dialog and SDC. DATANETT is the Trinidad and Tobago Public Data Network which utilizes packet switching. The Trinidad and Tobago Telephone Company (TELCO) provides the telecommunication facilities and services to data networks in other countries. Despite all of this, Trinidad and Tobago have no organized interlibrary system. Both the British Library and the U.S. National Library of Agriculture are heavily used. Most users, however, cannot accept the response time of three weeks for the photocopy to arrive. This response time could be shortened by doing on-line ordering and having the data base vendors do the document delivery, but for most, the price is too high, and foreign exchange resource is scarce.

Furthermore, in order to truly realize a Regional Information System there must exist a directory of librarians, union catalogs of serials and report collections, and the building of national data bases. Each country should provide a national inter-lending or resource sharing system.[22] Therefore,

> librarians in Trinidad and Tobago and indeed the Caribbean have an important part to play in document delivery. Comprehensive listing of serial publications in all subject areas is a critical need if we are to provide the maximum impact and benefits from on-line searching. If individual countries in the Caribbean would record their serial holdings according to a predetermined standard, these records could easily be merged to form a union listing of serials in the Caribbean.[23]

Pakistan

Pakistan is placed here in order to compare its Agricultural Information System and Canada's which is to follow. ". . . Pakistan, like any other country whose economy is primarily based on agriculture, needs a library-based national agriculture information system in order to support the country's programme of agriculture research and extension work, aimed towards increasing productivity."[24]

Part of the problem in Pakistan is that the working librarians of Pakistan are not agricultural specialists. As in Southeast Asia, they provide the usual traditional services of lending books, making available reading room services, and in some rare cases bibliographic references. Equally scarce are announcements of new books or acquisitions, inter-library loan and any indexing. PARC (Pakistan Agricultural Research Council) created the Directorate of Scientific Information in order to supply their scientists with information being generated within the country and abroad. This directorate includes the Documentation Center, the Library, the Publication Section, and the Audio-Visual Section. The Document Center has been the National liaison office for AGRIS (the U.S. Agricultural Information System) since 1978. As such it supplies bibliographic data on all the literature published in Pakistan in agriculture and its allied subjects. In exchange the Center receives the printed AGRINDEX. The procurement of documents requested by scientists in or outside the PARC, appearing in AGRINDEX, is the responsibility of the Center.

There is a need to develop a bibliographic service for accessing the AGRIs data base, the Pakistan Bibliography of Agriculture, and the SDI service. There are a number of other problems that need attention, for instance lack of manpower training, resource sharing among libraries, union lists of agricultural serials, the need for increasing the amount of available periodical literature in agriculture, and strong leadership from PARC.[25]

This matter of self-sufficiency in agriculture is a very serious matter for the developing countries. The guiding principle of AGRIS is international cooperation. The goal is to achieve universal bibliographic control in the field of agriculture. AGRINDEX by 1977 became one of the world's biggest abstracting and indexing services. Its selection policy includes publications of the developing nations.[26]

CANADA

"Canada is a major producer and exporter of agricultural products. Its national bibliographic and information systems are adequate and its agricultural research extensive. It has now been approximately ten years since Canada joined the AGRIS network."[27]

CAB (Commonwealth Agricultural Bureau) indexes and abstracts 36% of the periodical output in agriculture and is almost the only Canadian input to AGRINDEX. This literature is scientific/research oriented; literature directly concerning farmers is missing. Therefore the Canadian farmer must access information through Agriculture Canada and the provincial governments. The

Canadian farmer is able via his micro to access crop, weather and market information if such information were available. The University of Western Ontario has a project underway to offer this type of information as well as offer the AGRINDEX tapes to the networks for accessing by the farmers or their community information centers.

AGRINDEX as a research tool should promote interaction among scientists. Title and abstracts in English facilitate the transfer of information written in Japanese, Russian or German. Sharing of knowledge is very important since agriculture is or should be a priority in most countries.[28] This news item makes the point. In Greece (1984) Video Greece is launching a pilot program to provide an information service for Greek farmers that will require little or no expertise in information systems. This project will run parallel to that of VIDEO PILOT, a similar service for Irish and Italian farmers.[29]

SOME TRENDS IN INFORMATION TECHNOLOGY

In all the foregoing examples reviewed, access becomes the central issue. It appears that it is a matter of degree as one progresses from the developed to developing countries, the developed countries being better off in resources and the organization of them.

An additional problem for the developing countries is the lack of a mass market. This may be alleviated in the future with the introduction of end-user software for native language use. It is encouraging to note that India and Kuwait have been adapting U.S. self-instructional software to local situations by rewriting it in native languages. Networking will also strengthen the information infrastructure now that portable operating systems are available. The preferred model for information dissemination services leans to decentralized services and distributed operations. A true solution lies in a national information system which by definition is the result of Information Technology and a National Information Policy. Such a system would ensure compatibility, standardization and the development of markets.

If access is a primary issue, once having achieved it, the delivery issue takes precedence. Videotext should be important for information delivery. The television set is an accepted medium as is the telephone and both are involved in this form of information technology. However this is difficult to effect since television and telecommunications in most countries are run by separate agencies. Laser optical disks allow for the economical distribution of large masses of digital data for local, in-house and personal use. Thus it is possible for university libraries to operate licensed data bases in-house at a lower per search cost. In spite of all the information technology available, it would appear that the developing countries must address the economic problem before the great leap into the post-industrial age can be made.[30]

Appropriate Technology

What then is appropriate for the developing countries if the following is true?

> Developing countries share many concerns regarding the introduction of information technologies. There is fear of a loss of cultural identity. They do not wish to be dependent on a foreign power. There is the desire to meet the basic needs of their people and to decrease the gap between the developed and developing nations.[31]

The utilization of information technologies in each developing country is at a different stage of development. They need mass education and basic technical training more than printed materials. Many of the developing countries have areas without electrical power. Along with a poor information infrastructure, telephone services are poor or unavailable because of no or poor transmission. Postal systems are slow and unreliable. Libraries are not well supported and have a low status. There is, therefore, little or no bibliographic control.

Regardless of the seriousness of the situation, developing countries must have information for the process of development.[32] "The ability to improve local resources of information and to have control of these, is an essential step in meeting the basic needs of developing countries."[33] The microprocessor may very well provide the necessary breakthrough. Lest it be overlooked, the *rural areas* of North American and Europe still lack easy access to information resources. *Economically depressed areas* of the developed countries have problems similar to those in developing countries. Generally all of these people wherever they are feel a loss of privacy and inability to cope with change.[34]

Some Solutions for Developing Countries

The situation is not totally lost because information systems can be built using microcomputers. The telecommunication system can be bypassed and stand-alone micros can exchange disks via the mail (even though the mail may be unreliable) or by some manual means. Downloading from remote data bases is possible in some cases as is the acquisition of SDIs or floppies from data base producers. All these make accessing and acquiring of information possible from many sources. In addition the new user friendly interfaces facilitate use by librarians not trained as search experts.

To overcome the lack of trained personnel requests can be sent to an information center set up to give services on a national basis. Sharing of a bibliographic data center on a regional basis would allow several countries to enjoy the benefits each cannot afford. We have seen that some of this is happening already in some situations. An outside donor may be essential in order to provide funding to accelerate the development of regional cooperation since no one country will have to part with a great deal of money.

Again it is the socioeconomic system that determines whether or not the information technology will be used. A need for information must be present as well as an awareness of its value. Then the information system will gain real support.[35]

NEWER TECHNOLOGIES

There are three prominent newer technologies available which will increase the use of on-line searching by end-users. The first is *gateway software*. Throughout this paper the use of interface (gateway) software was mentioned in connection with on-line searching. The most sophisticated packages do a number of things for the end-user.

> Gateway software packages are designed for the end-user market. They claim to eliminate the mystery of searching bibliographic and numerical data bases on-line. They have some or all of the following characteristics: auto-dial and automatic login capabilities; down loading features; user friendly communications mode; link-up facilities to other micro-computer software systems, such as word processors, graphics and so on, thus providing report formatting, report writing, and similar facilities.[36]

The most popular of these is the In-Search package which is used as a training device in information/library schools but is also targeted for business and industry.

The second is *full text data bases* which end-users will find useful for fact retrieval or current awareness. In all probability they will still go to the information specialist or reference librarian for lengthier and more in-depth literature searching. Most systems contain both full-text and bibliographic data bases. At present full-text usually means title and abstract, and handbooks or directories.[37] Full-text data bases are critical to electronic publishing and necessary in order to solve the problems of document delivery and access. However there are mass storage devices available to handle full-text data bases. But the speed that is gained with gateway software is lost because at the moment full-text data bases have a slower response time.[38] Today electronic transmission of text and videodisk for graphics is a reality.

The third is the *expert system*, the objective of which is to perform like an information specialist. Two trends have pushed the need for such a system: the increased use of on-line searching and the decentralization of systems and their users. The knowledge base for such a system is the thesaurus and whatever else in the way of additional terms, meanings and associations. The computer program is made up of the procedures and decision rules derived from the human expert. These expert systems will either do the search and yield the final findings or allow the end-user to intervene by judging the results and directing the search. (The system will be informing the end-user of the direction of the search.)[39]

Impact of Information Technology on Libraries and Librarians

Many have tried to discern where technology may be pushing the profession. Lancaster has always thought that librarians will perform their work outside the library. He sees the information specialists/reference librarians as information consultants, as facilitators of access, as guides to resources, and interpreters of search results. In addition this new breed of librarians will be teachers, training people on how to select sources, how to access them, and exploit them. These librarians of the near future will have detailed knowledge of information resources. He doesn't see any competition from the 'expert' system.[40]

> In future integrated information-transfer networks, librarians will be the most valuable human resources of the network. Their detailed knowledge of the contents of the networks and their ability to employ retrieval techniques that will extract the maximum amount of information from it will create intense demand for their expert services.[41]

Intermediaries will not become obsolete but will be employed to deal with difficult and complex problems.[42] (A sometimes overlooked function of the reference librarian is that of supplementing formal library records with their own informal reference procedures. If this were to be formalize and computerize more would be known about how to access the collection and develop it.)[43]

De Gennaro believes that the new technology will multiply the reference librarians capabilities, raise the level of expectations of staff and users, and create demand for on-line searching and on-line interlibrary loan. If RLG (Research Library Group) is able to electronically combine collections into a coordinate library system, the end-users will see this as a single large collection which they can access on-line and receive delivery of items electronically.[44]

Surprenant[45] sums up the whole outlook for reference librarians by stating that:

1. Reference librarians as a helping profession are well suited to going out to the public.
2. Since information and access to it is a critical issue, the reference librarian can be seen as becoming a vital component in the new concept of the library as an "information switching mechanism."
3. Reference librarians will be outside the library at service points within the user community and electronically connected to the library.
4. They will become 'personal librarians' or consultants.
5. They will have subject expertise.
6. Assist in the organization of information.
7. Train others and be guides.

CONCLUSION

Many of these aforementioned points have been stated by others as well, so the conclusion to be drawn is that reference librarians, information specialists, and libraries themselves will remain and become even more important factors in society; become partners in the cooperative venture to propel the developing countries into the self-sufficiency they yearn for; and continue to influence with their humanistic values the development of the post-industrial age. BUT—the profession must embrace the new technologies and make them do *their* bidding. Leadership and vision are as necessary and powerful as ever.

NOTES

1. Schiller, H. I. (1981) *Who knows: Information in the age of the Fortune 500*. Norwood, NJ: Ablex, pp. 40-41.
2. Ibid., p. 164-165.

3. Lundu, Maurice C. (1984) Adapting to change in library and information science and training: The overseas experience. *SIG Newsletter, III* (9), p. 2.
4. Softening the ache out of online searching. *Euronet DIANE News*, No. 35, March/May 1984, p. 12.
5. European users want online friendliness. *Euronet DIANE News*, No. 34, Jan./Feb. 1984, p. 5.
6. Who uses online? Study finds it's still mainly scientists. *Information Market*, No. 38, Jan./March 1985, p. 10.
7. Softening the ache out of online searching. *Euronet DIANE News*, No. 35, March/May 1984, p. 5.
8. Ellefsen, David. (1985) Automated periodical reference service. *Information Technology and Libraries*, 4(4), 353-355.
9. Cheng, Chin-Chuan. (1985) Microcomputer-based user interface. *Information Technology and Libraries*, 4(4), 346-351.
10. Levy, L. R. (1984) Gateway software: Is it for you? *Online*, 8(8), 67-79.
11. Glushko, R. Jo. and Bianchi, M. H. (1982) Online documentation: Mechanizing development delivery and use. *The Bell System Technical Journal*, 61(6), 1313-1323.
12. Griffith, William G. (1982) Advances in merging full text and videotex features for information retrieval. *National Online Meeting: Proceedings*, 1982. Martha E. Williams and Thomas H. Hogan, compilers, Medford, N.H.: Learned Information Inc., p. 159.
13. Ibid., p. 160.
14. Ibid., p. 159.
15. Ibid., p. 161.
16. Carrion-Rodriguez, G. (1985) Information Activities in INFOTEC. *SIG Newsletter*, February, Issue No. 11-12, p. 4.
17. Black, Donald V. and Fung, Margaret, C. (1983) Information systems and services in China and Japan. *Annual Review of Information Science and Technology (ARIST)*, Vol. 18, 1983. Martha E. Williams (ed.). White Plains, NY: Knowledge Industry Publications, Inc., pp. 307-354.
18. Ming, Ding Choo (1985) Access to serials in Southeast Asia. *Libri*, 35(4), 302.
19. Ibid., p. 317.
20. Sattar, A. and Rehman, S. (1985) Coverage of Islamic literature in selected indexing services. *International Library Review*, 17: p. 365.
21. Ibid., p. 370.
22. Salisbury, L. (1985) Online access to international databases and its role in information provision in Trinidad and Tobago. *International Library Review*, 17: p. 433.
23. Ibid., p. 432.
24. Haider, Syed Jalaluddin (1985) Some aspects of agriculture information in Pakistan. *Libri*, 35(1), p. 49.
25. Ibid., p. 60.
26. Cano, V. (1985) International bibliographic network participation: AGRIS in Canada. *Libri*, 35(4)a: p. 342.
27. Ibid., p. 343.
28. Ibid., p. 347.
29. CIDST recommends video projects. *Euronet DIANE News*. No. 35, March/May 1984, p. 6.
30. Davies, D. M. (1985) Appropriate information technology. *International Library Review*, 17: p. 248.
31. Ibid., p. 248.
32. Ibid., p. 251.

33. Ibid., p. 251.
34. Ibid., p. 257.
35. Thorpe, Peter (1984) The impact of new information technology in the developing countries. *Journal of Information Science*, 8: p. 219.
36. Wagner, G. (1984) Online information retrieval instruction in schools of librarianship: The problems and some solutions. *LASIE*, 15(3), p. 12.
37. Tenopir, Carol (1985) Full-text and bibliographic databases. *Library Journal*, 110(9), pp. 62-63.
38. Tenopir, Carol (1984) Full-text databases. *Annual Review of Information Science and Technology (ARIST)*, Vol. 19. Martha E. Williams, editor. White Plains, NY: Knowledge Industry Publications Inc., pp. 235-237.
39. Shoval, Peretz (1985) Principles, procedures and rules in an expert system for information retrieval. *Information Processing and Management*, 21(6), p. 278.
40. Lancaster, F. W. (1984) Implications for library and information science education. *Library Trends*, 32, pp. 342-343.
41. Ibid., p. 344.
42. Neufeld, M. Lynne and Cornog, Martha (1983) Secondary information systems and services. *Annual Review of Information Science and Technology (ARIST)*, Vol. 18. Martha E. Williams, (ed.). White Plains, NY: Knowledge Industry Publications, Inc., p. 162.
43. Kriz, Harry M. and Kok, Victoria T. (1985) The computerized reference department: Buying the future. *RQ*, 25(2), p. 199.
44. DeGennaro, Richard (1981) Libraries and networks in transition: Problems and prospects for the 1980's. *Library Journal*, 106(10), p. 1048.
45. Suprenant, Thomas T. and Perry-Holmes, Claudia (1985) The reference librarian of the future: A scenario. *RQ*, 25(2), pp. 234-238.

BIBLIOGRAPHY

And now . . . your documents delivered electronically. *Euronet DIANE News*, Issue no. 35, March/May, 1984, p. 7.
Black, Donald V. and Fung, Margaret C. (1983). Information systems and services in China and Japan. *Annual Review of Information Science and Technology (ARIST)*. Vol. 18. Martha E. Williams (ed.). White Plains, NY: Knowledge Industry Publications, Inc., pp. 307-354.
Bring electronic information to the public. Call by E.C. Director. *Euronet DIANE News*, Issue no. 35, March/May 1984, p. 1.
Cano, V. (1985). International bibliographic network participation: AGRIS in Canada. *Libri*, 35(4), pp. 341-348.
Carrion-Rodriguez, G. (1985). Information activities in INFOTEC. *SIG Newsletter*, February, Issue no. 11-12, p. 3-5.
Cheng, Chin-Chuan (1985). Microcomputer-based user interface. *Information Technology and Libraries*, 4(4), pp. 346-351.
CIDST recommends video projects. *Euronet DIANE News*, Issue no. 35, March/May 1984, p. 6.
Daries, D. M. (1985). Appropriate information technology. *International Library Review*, 17, 345-358.
DeGennaro, Richard (1981). Libraries and networks in transition: Problems and prospects for the 1980's. *Library Journal*, 106(10), pp. 1045-1049.

Dowlin, Kenneth E. (1985). The 'Integrated Library System.' *Electronic Library*, 3(5), pp. 340-345.

Eason K. D. (1982). The process of introducing information technology. *Behavior and Information Technology*, 1(2), pp. 197-213.

Economic commission for Latin America and the Caribbean. *Report of the Meeting of the Experts on Design of a Regional Information System on Information Activities.* Santiago, Chile, 10-14 June, 1985.

Electronic document and delivery . . . and satellites too. *Euronet DIANE News*, Issue no. 35, March/May 1984, p. 9.

Ellefsen, David (1985). Automated periodical reference service. *Information Technology and Libraries*, 4(4), pp. 353-355.

European users want online friendliness. *Euronet DIANE News* Issue no. 34 Jan/Feb 1984, p. 5.

Euronet DIANE News, Issue no. 37, Oct/Dec 1984.

Euronet DIANE News, Issue no. 39, April/June 1985.

Free guide to online information systems. *Information Market*, Issue no. 38, Jan/March 1985, p. 5.

Glushko, R. J. and Bianchi, M. H. (1982). Online documentation: Mechanizing development, delivery, and use. *The Bell System Technical Journal*, 61(6), pp. 1313-1323.

Griffith, William G. (1982). Advances in merging full text and videotex features for information retrieval. *National Online Meeting, Proceedings—1982*. Martha E. Williams and Thomas H. Hogan, compilers. Medford, NJ: Learned Information, Inc., pp. 159-161.

Haider, Syed Jalaluddin (1985). Some aspects of agriculture in Pakistan. *Libri*, 35(1), pp. 43-61.

Hayes, P., Ball, E., and Reddy, R. (1981). Breaking the man-machine communication barrier. *Computer*, 1981 March 19-30.

Hoover, R. E. (1980). The potential impact and problems of online retrieval services in developing countries. *4th International On-line Information Meeting*. London, 9-11 December 1980. Learned Information, Oxford, 1980, pp. 345-353.

Horton, F. W., Jr. (1984). Software's next dimension. *Computerworld*, 18(26), pp. 7-11.

Hubbard, Abigail and Wilson, Barbara (1986). An integrated information management education program . . . Defining a new role for librarians in helping end-users. *Online*, 10(2), pp. 15-23.

Information Market, Issue no. 40, July-Sept. 1985.

Institute for International Information Programs Newsletter, Vol. 1(2), Winter, 1986.

Kesselman, M. (1985). Front-end/Gateway software: Availability and usefulness. *Library Software Review* 4(2), pp. 67-70.

Kriz, Harry M. and Kok, Victoria T. (1985). The computerized reference department: Buying the future. *RQ* 25(2), pp. 198-203.

Kupferberg, Natalie (1986). End-users: How are they doing? A librarian interviews six 'do-it-yourself' searchers. *Online* 10(2), pp. 24-28.

Lancaster, F. W. (1984). Implications for library and information science education. *Library Trends*, 32, pp. 337-348.

Levy, L. R. (1984). Gateway software: Is it for you? *Online* 8(6), pp. 67-79.

Lundu, Maurice C. (1984). Adopting to change in library and information science and training: The overseas experience. *SIG Newsletter, III* (9), pp. 1-2.

Meadows, A. J., Singleton, A., and Van der Lem, M. (1983). New technology and r and d information: An international comparison of trends. *Information Management Research in Europe*. P. J. Taylor and B. Cronin (eds.). London: ASLIB, pp. 93-97.

Mehlmann, M. (1981). *When people use computers: An approach to developing an interface*. Englewood Cliffs, NJ: Prentice Hall.

Ming, Ding Choo (1985). Access to serials in Southeast Asia. *Libri,* 35(4), pp. 298-319.

National Telecommunication and Information Administration, Washington, D.C. *Long-range goals in international telecommunications and information: An outline for United States policy*. February 1983.

Neufeld, M. Lynne and Cornog, Martha (1983). Secondary information systems and services. *Annual Review of Information Science and Technology (ARIST)*, vol. 18. Martha E. Williams, (ed.). White Plains, NY: Knowledge Industry Publications, Inc., pp. 151-183.

Palme, J. (1979). A human-computer interface for non-computer specialists. *Software-Practice and Experience,* 9, pp. 741-747.

Pisciotta, H., Evans, N. and Albright, M. (1984). Search helper: Sancho Panza or Mephistopheles? *Library Hi-Tech,* 2(3), pp. 25-32.

Publishing of electronic journals. *Euronet DIANE News,* Issue no. 35, March/May 1984, p. 8.

Rada, J. F. (1984). Trends and effects of information technology. *Communication Regulation and International Business*. J. F. Rada, and G. R. Pipe (eds.). Amsterdam: North Holland, pp. 5-21.

Rankine, L. J. (1981). The socio-economic consequences and limits of the information revolution. *Information Services and Use,* 1(2), pp. 65-73.

Salisbury, L. (1985). Online access to international databases and its role in information provision in Trinidad and Tobago. *International Library Review,* 17, pp. 425-433.

Sattar, A. and Rehman, S. ur (1985). Coverage of Islamic literature in selected indexing services. *International Library Review,* 17, pp. 357-370.

Schiller, H. 1. (1981). *Who knows information in the age of the fortune 500*. Norwood, NJ: Ablex.

Scholfield, D., Hillman, A. L. and Rodgers, J. L. (1980). MM/1, a man-machine interface. *Software-Practice and Experience,* 10, pp. 751-763.

Shoval, Peretz (1985). Principles, procedures and rules in an expert system for information retrieval. *Information Processing and Management,* 21(6), pp. 475-487.

Slamecka, Vladimir (1985). Information technology and the third world. *Journal of the American Society for Information Science,* 36(3), pp. 178-183.

Smith, S. L. (1980). Man-machine interface requirements definition: Task demands and functional capabilities. *Proceedings of the Human Factors Society*. 24th Meeting, 1980. Santa Monica, CA: Human Factors Society, pp. 93-97.

Softening the ache out of online searching. *Euronet DIANE News*, Issue no. 35, March/May 1984, p. 12.

Surprenant, Thomas T. and Perry-Holmes, Claudia (1985). The reference librarian of the future: A scenario. *RQ,* 25(2), pp. 234-238.

Stonier, T. (1983). The Microelectronic Revolution, Soviet Political Structure, and the Future of East/West Relations. *Political Quarterly* 54(2), pp. 137-151.

Tenopir, Carol (1985). Full-text and Bibliographic Databases. *Library Journal* 110(19), pp. 62-63.

Tenopir, Carol (1984). Full-text Databases. *Annual Review of Information Science and Technology (ARIST)* Vol. 19. Martha E. Williams, editor. White Plains, NY: Knowledge Industry Publications, Inc., pp. 215-246.

Thorpe, Peter (1984). The Impact of New Information Technology in the Developing Countries. *Journal of Information Science* 8, pp. 213-220.

Turning Paper into Electrons — The Commission's DOCDEL Projects Dissected. *Euronet DIANE News*. Issue no. 35, March/May 1984, p. 7.

van Brakel, P. A. (1985). Gateway Software For Microcomputers: An Overview. *South African Journal of Librarianship and Information Science* 53(2), pp. 72-82.

Wagner G. (1984). Online Information Retrieval Instruction in Schools of Librarianship: The Problems and Some Solutions. *LASIE* 15(3), pp. 10-17.

Who Uses On-line? Study Finds It's Still Mainly Scientists. *Information Market* Issue no. 38, Jan./March 1985, p. 10.

Reference Services and Global Awareness

Mohammed A. Aman
Mary Jo Aman

During the past forty years, the world has changed dramatically. World War II, the nuclear age, nationalism, revolution, energy dependence and communications technology have inexorably drawn the United States into a global environment, with tremendous potentials as well as awesome risks. As a world power, the United States bears special responsibilities to promote international order and understanding.

Our national inadequacy in foreign language skills is a serious liability to effective international participation. The inability of most Americans to communicate in a foreign setting in any language but English is a handicap that our institutions have not done enough to overcome. In addition to language barriers, Americans lack significant intercultural knowledge or experience to enable comprehension of other cultures.

Many authorities in higher education today, recognizing that economic, diplomatic and technological changes have created an irreversible world interdependence, have voiced the critical need to reinforce the commitment of universities to international education.

DECLINE OF FOREIGN LIBRARY ACQUISITIONS

As the study of foreign languages and cultures declines, so do our foreign library acquisitions. Recent studies of the last ves-

---

Professor Aman is Dean of the School of Library and Information Science, The University of Wisconsin-Milwaukee, P.O. Box 413, Milwaukee, WI 53201. Ms. Aman is Reference Librarian at the same University.

tiges of national programs for foreign acquisitions predict that Public Law (PL) 480 is now threatened. According to Sanchez, "libraries will be forced to contribute to the full cost of materials ordered, and university participation in the customary blanket orders is likely to shrink." He also predicts that the "number of items available through the program may decrease, and the format may be less acceptable due to a microfilming trend."[1]

The decrease in the quantity and quality of foreign acquisitions (whether from PL 480 or other internally or externally funded programs) brings with it a decrease in the quantity and quality of reference materials acquired by U.S. libraries. Thus, primary sources of information being generated from foreign countries will not be easily available to America's library users. The alternative will be for these users to rely upon secondary or tertiary sources in the form of reference books printed in English and published in the U.S. or Western Europe.

In the absence of reference materials from foreign countries, like Third World countries, the reference librarian may have to rely on reference books published in Western Europe or the U.S. There are advantages and disadvantages to this method. The advantages are: (1) reference books published in Europe or the U.S. are of good quality, both in content and format; (2) there is a tendency to keep these reference books up-to-date, through revisions and/or supplements; (3) most of these reference books are published in the English language.

There are also advantages for reference books that have joint editorial board or co-sponsorship in the U.S. or Europe. This cooperation may be in the form of distributorship on behalf of the indigenous publisher, or joint production and editorship. *Who's Who in Saudi Arabia* is an example of a reference book written in English, published by an Arab publisher in Saudi Arabia (Tihami Publisher), and distributed by an American publisher (Gale Research Co.).

Other tools published in foreign countries use the English language to ensure wider distribution in the East and West by bridging the language gap. Examples are *Who's Who in the Arab World* (Beirut: Publitec Editions); *The APS Who's Who in Middle East Banking & Trade* (Nicosia, Cyprus: APS Press & Enterprises, Ltd.), *Major Companies of the Arab World* (London: Graham & Trotman). Other foreign tools have been adapted and translated in the English language. An example is *Larousse Encyclopedia of Music* which is based on *La Musique: les hommes: les instruments; les oeuvrages*, edited by Norbert Dufourcq.

The disadvantages are: (1) unless the reference book has an editorial board or some form of representation from the foreign country or countries being treated, there are the risks that the item will suffer from inaccuracies of information or lack of objectivity and/or balance; (2) the information is often out-of-date and un-verified.

WEAK BIBLIOGRAPHIC CONTROL

Another problem facing reference librarians is the weak and sometimes nonexistant bibliographic control of non-European reference books. While attempts have been made to identify reference books published in non-Western countries, the majority of the bibliographies or reviewing guides give special preference to reference books printed in the English language.

Both *Choice* and *ARBA* limit their reviews to English reference books—for reasons of marketing and intended readership. *Choice* limits itself primarily to the four-year college market, while *ARBA* has a wider market. Furthermore, most review sources rely upon information provided by publishers without attempting to identify and seek out review copies of non-English reference books.

The question often raised by editors of reference review publications and some reference librarians alike is why should they review French, Italian, Japanese, Chinese, Arabic or Hebrew reference books when the library market is not demanding such tools? The argument does not take into consideration other factors such as lack of substitutes to foreign sources of information such as demographic data, atlases and gazetteers, historical documents and many other examples of primary sources of information.

FOREIGN REFERENCE TOOLS
IN LIBRARY SCHOOL CURRICULUM

The study of international/comparative librarianship, foreign bibliographies and foreign languages for librarians has declined significantly after the 1960s. The reasons for such a decline can be identified as following: First, declining interest in foreign languages, which were taken out of the general education requirements for undergraduate students, thus limiting the library schools' intake to foreign language illiterates. Second, instructors of reference courses are to a large extent familiar with languages other than English. In those instances where instructors have introduced foreign reference titles, the instructors are usually foreign born with knowledge of one or more European languages. Third, courses which were introduced in the curriculum in the '60s, such as Foreign National Bibliographies, Area Studies or International Librarianship, were dropped to make room for new courses in information science, media and automation. Fourth, American publishers began to produce reference tools in certain fields which were the primary domain of European publishers, such as Art reference books from Italian publishers, and scientific reference books from the Germans, etc. The result was that foreign reference tools lost their primacy in the reference class as well as the reference room. Fifth, many reference instructors argue that there are not enough hours left in the core course or advanced reference courses to cover English tools and search strategies, interview techniques and on-line information retrieval, in addition to foreign reference tools.

While on the surface these arguments seem convincing, they run diametrically opposite to the argument that librarianship is an international field. Few, if any, of our graduates could negotiate a search in foreign (non-English) reference tools. While these graduates are familiar with such on-line data bases as DIALOG, BRS, or SDC, they ignore other data bases such as the German DIMDI, INKA, or the French QUESTEL.

The emphasis placed by a growing number of reference course instructors on teaching types of tools, rather than specific tools is a good one if it includes direction to the foreign review tools from which foreign reference books could be selected. Otherwise, the emphasis will remain on the English tools which librarians and instructors can identify from the available reviews and publishers' announcements.

International library/information science education must become a fundamental part of the MLS or MLIS education. The question of integrating international aspects of library and information science was raised by a number of library educators. According to Martha Boaz, most internationalists would recommend the inclusion of a course or two in comparative and international library science as well as impregnating the entire curriculum with internationalism.[2] Internationalizing the curriculum can be accomplished only through the commitment of faculty members and with the financial support and encouragement of the administration.

International preparation should be added as a requirement for graduation in all library and information science programs. These programs should build into the curriculum opportunities for students to study or work in major foreign libraries for credit.

The presence of foreign students in our library and information science programs provides diversity in the student body and enhances the cultural dimension of the educational experience for other students and faculty. Many of our schools neglect to capitalize on the experiences or intellect of these students. In a reference course, these students could present for discussion and evaluation reference tools commonly used in their native tongue. Special effort should be made to make these tools available in the university library which services the library and information science program.

International enrichment of library and information science programs depends, to a great extent, on the international orientation of the faculty. Like other faculty, library and information science faculty are enriched through opportunities to study, teach and engage in research in foreign libraries and library schools. The exchange of information that results from such involvement constitutes a valuable contribution to the host school as well as its American counterpart.

By closing the gap between developed and developing countries, our libraries should be able to provide reference tools in any language to satisfy a user's request for information. Without the development of a global perspective in the instruction of librarians, no international thrust in the library/information profession can reach full potential.

NOTES

1. Sanchez, James J. Public Law 480: Declining Prospects for the Continued Support of Area Studies, Nov. 1983, 12p. ERIC Document (ED 245550)
2. Boaz, Martha. The comparative and international library science course in American library schools, in John F. Harvey, (ed.). *Comparative & international library science*, Metuchen, N.J.: Scarecrow Press, 1977. p.175.

Information Service: Supporting the Educational Program Around the World

Jean E. Lowrie

The purpose of the social library/media center is to aid the fulfillment of the instructional goals and objectives of the school and to promote this through a planned program of acquisition and organization of appropriate media and technology and through instruction in the exploitation of information technology and dissemination of materials to expand the learning environment of all students.[1]

Thus the school library must be a center for reliable information with rapid access for retrieval and transfer of information and a planned program to aid teachers and students in the utilization of information now and for the future. Information service then is the raison d'être for school libraries.

Information service in school libraries/media centers anywhere in the world must be defined in the broadest of terms. It may mean helping a student to find answers to an assignment in the classroom; it may mean helping a youngster to answer questions which he/she alone has in relation to a special interest; it may mean introducing the microcomputer as a tool for searching. It regularly includes locating and/or creating material which the teacher may use to enrich classroom experiences. Such reference service requires an enriched program of joint instruction in teach-

---

Professor Lowrie is Professor Emeritus, Western Michigan University. Correspondence should be directed to her at 1006 Westmorland, Kalamazoo, Michigan 49007.

ing youngsters how to use all types of media to find their answers, to find support for their personal wants, to promote creative thinking and activities. This in turn implies that the media specialist, teacher-librarian, whatever his or her title may be, understands what is being presented in the classroom and, conversely, that the classroom teacher has some knowledge about and skill in utilization of the library/media center. Teachers must develop a concept to information and the sources to which they can turn, be able to retrieve and interpret information, evaluate its usefulness and utilize actively in the classroom.[2]

A recent and still unpublished international study suggests a series of questions which serve as a good basis both for the teacher to use in presenting a new approach within the curriculum and for the librarian to use when guiding students in their search for information.

> What do I need to do? (formulation and analysis of need)
> Where could I go? (identification and appraisal of likely sources)
> How do I get to the information? (tracing and locating individual resources)
> What resources shall I use? (examining, selecting, and reflecting individual resources)
> How shall I use the resources? (interrogating resources)
> What should I make a record of? (recording and storing information)
> Have I got the information I need? (interpretation, analysis, synthesis, evaluation)
> How should I present it? (presentation, communication, shape)
> What have I achieved? (evaluation)[3]

Whether one is describing a center in the western world where countries such as Australia, United Kingdom, Scandinavia have developed extensive programs of service and support and comparatively rich collections of matter; have explored the use of new technology; or, since such conditions do not exist equally, globally, one is examining schools which offer the barest of assistance and minimum of materials, the above concept of a school library/media center and the work of the teacher and librarian is the premise for planning. The breadth of the actual program is related only to the economic, educational, cultural capacity of the specific country.

TWO INTERNATIONAL PROGRAMS

There are two aspects of the word international to which this paper applies: (1) developing sensitivity to the mores and customs, similarities and differences among countries, and (2) the specific efforts and techniques which are used in schools around the world to further information service in their particular locales. A brief comment on the first rather obvious aspect will suffice—important though it is in today's society.

An analysis of the role of the school library/media center easily demonstrates that the richer the collection is as it pertains to past and present developments in many countries, the more the students become aware of similarities and differences. With the daily exposure to TV which most children in developed countries have today, there is an absolute need for the library/media center to secure and make accessible information which is on the level of the child's understanding, which expands the "highlights" of the six o'clock news, which presents as unbiased a picture as possible and most of all, which helps him/her to see the roles which any country plays in promoting understanding and cooperation. Even the youngsters in primary grades are aware of the famines, the riotings, the different cultures depicted, the similarities as well as the differences in as peer activities. Obviously the level of sophistication increases as the grade level rises—but the learning experiences are the same. Youth in the United States are fortunate that for the most part boys and girls read and speak English, that there is one official language and therefore publications, audio-visual aids, TV programs are accessible in quantity—if not in quality—and are distributed widely and fairly inexpensively. Thus access to media which helps build understanding is not a difficulty in the U.S. Similar conditions prevail in other countries of the western world. School libraries profit from these and can give strong support to classroom activities in this effort.

DEVELOPMENT OF INFORMATION SERVICE

To further the development of information services to all countries, school or teacher librarians should work with teachers for a common understanding of the society in which they find themselves. Both must have an understanding of how children learn and the strategies that help them learn; employ skills for teaching the use of information through the curriculum; know the role of the school librarian in accessing, evaluating and producing learning resources; be willing and able to do cooperative planning-teaching.[4] Despite this obvious set of needs objectives, schools, that is the teachers and librarians, in many countries have not yet perceived the library's role in the educational process. The librarian presumes to be the giver of information service but the teacher (let alone the student) has not been truly educated to receive or accept. Thus the full use of library media and information service is still in the process of being understood and employed in most countries. Even the constant changes in curricula and course content have not promoted a better awareness of the need to develop within both groups a better use of the resource and skills available in and through a media center.

This is intensified as a problem when seen from the point of view of a developing country. More often than not the ratio of teacher to student is very high and that of librarian to student almost impossible to reckon. This is due to the number of primary school age children, the infinitesimal number of teachers and the almost complete lack of anything resembling a school library. Secondary schools fare somewhat better but on the other hand the number of students has diminished for many have gone into the work force such as it is. On top of that the material available is quite likely not to be in the indigenous language of the student but in their second language. The use of the second language may be mandated by law or result simply from the lack of publishing or producing materials in the native tongue. In some instances the use of several official languages within the country will make publication almost an economic impossibility. Whatever the case, the opportunity for students or teachers to be exposed to a broad resource center, to learn research or information skills is not great. Some of this difficulty is because of strength of oral tradition in the culture. Again the adult literacy rate may not be high and the existence or non on the amount of support being given to develop resource centers. In many instances basic needs—food, clothing, shelter—must take priority over the desirability of an education program enriched by a library/media center.

ANECDOTAL ILLUSTRATIONS

Some examples from various countries may further illustrate the various levels of utilization. In Vancouver, Canada, the "aim of the school library is to assist students to develop a commitment to informed decision making and the skills of life long learning." Their policy statement supports planning and cooperative teaching to extend research skills as well as language improvement and the promotion of voluntary reading. The emphasis is on communication "between the two groups of teachers—classroom and library in order to provide and utilize full information services."[5]

The Banco del Libro, Venezuela, is an experiment which was originally designed to renovate education and develop information skills in that country. A "book bank" was established in Ciudad Guyana under the auspices of the Ministry of Education and the Venezuelan Guayana Corporation. One of the major objectives was to update teachers' knowledge and stimulate full use of educational materials. They also wished to stimulate student curiosity, to produce better and more varied materials and to create a regional system. Moving from a private subsidized group to a national program, the book bank is now stimulating reading and research skill oriented programs throughout the country, the major collection now being located in Caracas. Recent research studies show an increased use of materials by both students and teacher wherever a school library/media center has been developed and a teacher-librarians trained to promote the program.[6]

A report on the use of school libraries in several English schools in Surrey indicated that students who had had some introduction to library tools often did not use them but rather used more general aids (even asking the librarian!), exhibits, home materials, television programs, etc. Here communications in the broadest sense was an important part of research skills and the interaction among the students themselves as well as with the teacher and librarian was a revealing learning experience.

Despite the lack of reading materials in one small rural school in Malaysia the need for a "school library" was still recognized. Books made out of brown paper with pictures pasted in them and the information printed by hand in Tamil were made available in a tiny all purpose room. A supplement to the basic curriculum and the simplest of introductions to information service for the primary children, but nevertheless an introduction upon which hopes were built for the future. Over the last two decades, however, Malaysia has developed a program of school library expansion. There is a School Libraries Union Director within the Ministry of Education and expansion in urban and semirural communities has been evident. Commitment to this information service concepts underlies the national standards.[7]

The Abidina Resource Center connected with the University of Ibadan, Nigeria, is an outstanding example of a program where indigenous materials are limited but good use has been made of overseas media while actively attempting to overcome the handicap of language. Indigenous authors are encouraged through workshops while the students in the surrounding area have regular library programs and service. Furthermore efforts have been made to develop a network among contiguous states. This is a slow process for there is a great lack of information about each other's collections, but with the strong center in Lagos, for example, as well as Abidina, it is possible that this will develop. Support from the state libraries and the institutions developing teacher-librarians will encourage publications, production and sharing. The Nigeria National Policy on Education states that educational resource centers are to be established in each school. That will be sometime in coming but the understanding of the value and need for information service exists and as the economy changes it is hoped that such an expansion of libraries will happen.[8]

In Tanzania there is a Libraries Coordinator for school library development in the ministry of National Education who promotes secondary school services. The National Central Library also maintains a program for library work for schools and children in public libraries. The two institutions work closely together in planning for facilities, staff training, standards, etc. Again a slow process but the acknowledgement of the need is visible.

The most recent revision of the curriculum for library skills from the Ministry of Education in Japan (1983) particularly emphasizes that subject and classroom teachers and teacher-librarians have the joint responsibility of helping students understand the use of library materials and the meaning of information service. Each school must develop its own program and the emphasis is on "classroom guidance" in order that all students are not only introduced to tools through formal instruction, but also they will see how the material can be used for formal study and in extracurricular activities.[9]

In analyzing the efforts in Kenya to provide information service through schools, one must first realize that there is an almost total absence of school libraries outside of the urban area. Therefore much of the service comes from the Kenya National Library Service on a payment of fees by the school. Such a fee has definitely limited this service. Since there are not too many libraries, a negative effect on publishing has been felt. Whether foreign or indigenous or government supported, the emphasis is on prescribed textbooks. With the introduction of universal primary education, it is expected that the literary market will expand and with it the possibility of school library services. In Nairobi there are some school libraries where the parents have been supportive, i.e., built library rooms, helped acquire books and furniture, promoted reading through competitions. Though this is obviously not a consistent effort in the country, the understanding of the need for information service is not absent and should grow if supported by the Ministry.[10]

The use of library materials to develop understanding among students of many cultures in the world today and the need for sharing attitudes, feelings, responses which will help to transcend cultural barriers and social realities is found in schools around the world. Although it is a given that indoctrination can also be achieved by selection of material, teacher librarians try as far as possible to search for the best and most honest presentations of life whether it be Africa, Canada, Australia or India. An expansion of information services to enhance the curriculum, to enrich the individual and to promote lifelong learning is certainly the major aim of every teacher-librarian, school library/media specialist, in every country from China to Zambia. It is the acceptance of the philosophy which is important and is worldwide; the service will come as each country sees the benefit and finds the means.

NOTES

1. Policy statement on school libraries. Adopted by World Confederation of the Organizations of the Teaching Profession and the International Association of School Librarianship, 1984.

2. Hall, Noelene. Teachers, information and school libraries. Prepared for International Federation of Library Associations and Institutions Section on School Libraries Working Group, 1985. (unpublished final draft, p. 19)

3. *Ibid.* p. 35.

5. Haycock, Ken. Resource sharing: Vancouver's developmental approach. In *Sharing: A challenge for all.* Proceedings of the Eleventh Annual Conference, International Association of School Librarianship, Red Deer, Alberta, Canada, August 1-6, 1982. Compiled and edited by John G. Wright. pp. 328-336.

6. From oral presentation by Nelson Rodriquez-Trujillo at the IASL conference in Kingston, Jamaica, 1985.

7. Author's personal observations.

8. Elatoruti, David. Resource sharing among school libraries in Nigeria. In *Sharing: A challenge, op. cit.*, pp. 317-327.

9. Nagakura, Mieko. School library research and information sharing in Japan. In *Sharing: A Challenge, op. cit.*, pp. 281-289.

10. Mwathi, Peter. School Libraries in Kenya . . . in *School libraries/Media centers: Partners in Education.* Proceedings of the Thirteenth Annual Conference, International Association of School Librarianship, Honolulu, Hawaii. July 30-August 3, 1984. Compiled and edited by Ira W. Harris, pp. 345-56.

Integrating a Central Reference Service in an International Studies Program

W. Daviess Menefee

International studies' programs have existed in this nation's universities since the 1930s, but their significance was not fully appreciated until the end of the second World War.[1] Realizing the need for a greater understanding of the world we inhabit, foundations and the federal government infused money to initiate area studies in the country's centers of higher education. But along with these area studies programs, as Frederick Wagman has noted, come organizational questions concerning where they belonged in the library hierarchy.[2] Unable to find a suitable home in any of the traditional library departments (public and technical services), these collections together with their staff come to be considered semi-autonomous. separate units within the organizational structure. The unique characteristics of these units, e.g., special language skills, cataloging and acquisition procedures, and a highly specialized clientele within the university community have been the major contributors to creating this separate status within the library structure.[3]

The trend towards decentralization of public services within libraries over the last several decades, moreover, has served to reinforce the isolation of international programs from the mainstream of library services.[4] Recently, however, the International Studies' program at The Ohio State University Libraries had the opportunity to consolidate their public service functions and to

---

The author will be found at The Ohio State University Libraries, 1858 Neil Ave., Columbus, OH 43210

create a single information desk representing six different geographical and subject areas. This article proposes to describe the methodology and procedures employed to achieve this centralization of library service.

The decision to consolidate the public service functions in the Main Library began with a report by a group of librarians and staff selected to investigate public services within the building and to produce a report of their findings. The task force completed their assignment in 1983, and after an Assistant Director for Main Library Public Services was appointed to the staff, planning commenced on combining the six separate service points representing the areas of Eastern Europe, Latin America, Middle East, East Asia, Jewish Studies, and Classics into one individually staffed information desk.

FIRST TASK

The first task was, of course, planning all the required changes. The subject specialists from these areas scheduled meetings to determine what physical changes were required (i.e., removing furniture and establishing a central desk) and also to write the policy statements that would be in effect at the service desk. Heated discussion and revision were not uncommon during these sessions. Besides physical rearrangement, on-line terminals had to be moved, the configuration of the Information Desk itself had to be determined and an overall policy for its operation required decision. Accommodating everyone's desires and needs was not possible, and the decision of the group was final. The success of this reorganization rested upon the willingness of all areas to participate in the change and to lend their energy and creativity to it. It was agreed from the start that each person would report their recommendations to the group who would then have ultimate approval.

At the initial planning stage, diagrams for all the physical changes were drawn up and a flexible timetable adopted since virtually every step was dependent upon the completion of the previous by workers outside the group's control. Unused service points were emptied and scheduled for dismantling; pieces, though, were saved for the later construction of student work areas near the offices of the librarians. Noise in the Reading Rooms was anticipated so signs were placed at entrances indicating where quiet study areas could be found. The central service point was constructed from pieces of the former desks and installed during the demolition. The group decided to bunch the on-line catalog terminals near the Information Desk in order to provide assistance to users from the central point and to equip it with both a terminal and a printer. A modular unit capable of holding three terminals was moved from another department into the Reading Room, and coaxial cable was laid to form the connection.

The question of staffing and service hours was probably the most difficult decision encountered during the planning stage. The Assistant Director for Main Library Public Services devised an optimal model for the group to follow. This provided 68 hours of service a week during the normal academic calendar and 40 hours during the breaks between quarters. Bibliographers would spend two hours per week at the Information Desk and maintain regularly scheduled office hours while the remainder of the schedule would be staffed by both the full-time and part-time classified staff. Twenty of the twenty-eight hours of weekend and evening coverage would be allotted to a graduate assistant and, by group decision, the remaining eight hours per week would be shared equably by all personnel.

TRAINING STAFF

The question of training staff in the area of general reference service and in the collections of the Reading Rooms arose at an early point of discussion since no one unit was completely familiar with the physical arrangement of the others, it quickly became apparent that orientation sessions within the Reading Rooms were required as well as printed guides describing the different collections and how they are organized (the international collections of the Reading Rooms had, over a number of years, independently grown to reflect the needs of their respective academic departments). Each subject specialist produced a brief guide describing his or her collection and listing the important works with their respective call numbers. With that information, orientation sessions were scheduled over a week's time so that each librarian could devote at least thirty minutes to the more salient aspects of their collections. During the course of these sessions, more information was exchanged about the unique nature of these Reading Rooms than had ever before been known to the entire staff. A number of questions were generated, the answers to which provided an explanation for many of the varied procedures each Reading Room employed.

Since the Reading Rooms are in essence a specialized reference collection, it was agreed that any in-depth service should be performed by that particular subject specialist. The service desk was designed to be the entry point to the bibliographers and to the general aspects of each collection (e.g., dictionaries, card catalog for non-Roman languages, indexes, etc.).[5] The training for reference service, therefore, focused on the directional questions associated with an information desk. A ready-reference collection of some forty titles was also acquired to assist users with common questions. This collection rests directly behind the service desk and is easily accessible from all Reading Rooms. The training for this service is a continuous process, and special workshops are scheduled when the need is perceived. (Subject searching in the on-line catalog was a recent topic presented by catalogers from two of the units.)

To summarize, establishing a central service point where one had not previously existed requires the cooperation and assistance of all affected by the change. This kind of positive approach begins at the initial planning stage and continues through implementation and even into the review of the process. It is of major importance that the planning be participatory at the outset so that any resistance can be managed at this time. The concept to bear in mind throughout is the final result of everyone's effort, namely the benefits to the patron. While not all personnel at the information desk are able or qualified to answer every question about each collection, the user receives general assistance and a referral, if necessary, to a specialist. Advantages to the specialists include spending more time with specific questions about their areas and also direct contact with those users who need their help and guidance. An ancillary benefit to the bibliographer is an increased awareness of their users' needs and problems, a definite asset when making collection decisions. In short, it has shown to be advantageous to all concerned to consolidate the services of these units into a single organized and accessible information service.

NOTES

1. Stueart, Robert D. *The Area Bibliographer: An Inquiry into his role*. Metuchen, N. J.: Scarecrow, 1972, pp. 17-28, and Chauncy D. Harris, Area Studies and Library Resources. *Library Quarterly*, 35, no. 4 (Oct 1965), pp. 205-217, p. 207.

2. Wagman, Frederick H. The general research library and the area studies programs. *Library Quarterly*, 35, no. 4 (Oct 1965), pp. 343-355.

3. Stueart, pp. 91-11, notes the role confusion of area specialists in their job performance. Harris, p. 215, also discusses this organizational quandary.

4. Moore, Everett T. Reference service in academic and research libraries. *Library Trends*, v. 12, no. 3 (Jan 1964), pp. 362-373. Mr. Moore comments that the nature of these foreign materials demands "the utmost resourcefulness of reference librarians in making them useful to students" (p. 363).

5. Wagman, p. 348, describes the difficulty patrons encounter when trying to find the bibliographer's desk. One of our goals was to lessen this frustration.

UNITED STATES

Hospitable Harvard:
Five International Libraries
and Their Services
to International Readers

Barbara Mitchell

Archibald Cary Coolidge Hall, a modest brick building a few blocks from Harvard Yard, houses eight separate centers and institutes focusing on international studies. It is entirely fitting that the university chose to name this building for Coolidge, since as a faculty member he worked with singular zeal to establish the study of Russian, East European and East Asian history here in the early part of this century. And, as director of the Harvard University Library from 1910 through 1928, Coolidge developed an extraordinary acquisitions program, providing the foundation

---

Ms. Mitchell is Librarian, Center for International Affairs, Center for Middle Eastern Studies, Harvard Institute for International Development, Harvard University, 1737 Cambridge St., Cambridge, MA 02138.

© 1987 by The Haworth Press, Inc. All rights reserved.

for Harvard's present preeminence as the largest academic library in the world.

Like the university itself, Harvard's library system is wildly decentralized. There are over ninety Harvard libraries and five of them occupy the lower level of Coolidge Hall. Each is funded by organizations located throughout the rest of the building: the Center for International Affairs, the Center for Middle Eastern Studies, the Harvard Institute for International Development, the Fairbank Center for East Asian Research and the Russian Research Center. All of Coolidge Hall's centers are autonomous components of Harvard's Faculty of Arts and Sciences. They receive no direct subsidies from the university, relying on private and public funding—endowments, grants and the like. The Coolidge libraries are considered part of the Harvard University Library and not the Harvard College Library, the twelve units that make up the bulk of the system supported by the Faculty of Arts and Sciences.

Coolidge Hall Library, as it is collectively known, may be viewed as a microcosm of the Harvard library system as a whole. The Russian and East Asian collections, with their own librarians, catalogs and separate stacks, sit in Sino-Soviet proximity on one side of the library level. On the opposite side are the three other libraries, mercifully merged in one catalog and one stack area and overseen by one librarian—myself. However, my salary is broken down into a 39-39-22 percentage, I work with three separate budgets and I report to the executive directors of the three centers which fund the libraries.

The five libraries' budgets do not provide much in the way of support staff. We three librarians rely mostly on student help and three emigrant women who work part-time. As a result, we serve not only as reference librarians, but we are also in charge of acquisitions, oversee circulation, pay the bills and deal with the Harvard maintenance crew vis à vis backed-up toilets and other facility problems that occur in a basement library setting. Reference and acquisitions are easily the most enjoyable aspects of our work. And, because we do the selection, we maintain an intimacy with the collections that enables us to provide fairly comprehensive reference service.

PRAVDA, LE MONDE AND THE CIA

The libraries' collections comprise approximately 50,000 monographs and 550 serial titles. Despite the interdisciplinary nature of area studies, the libraries reflect the chief interests of the Coolidge Hall centers, politics and economics. The Fairbank Center for East Asian Research (FCEAR) Library concentrates on post-1949 China, with a much smaller collection on Japan. The Russian Research Center (RRC) Library focuses on the Soviet Union, with less emphasis on other East European countries. About half the materials in both libraries is in English, the rest in Chinese, Russian and so forth. The RRC Library has a heavily-used collection of foreign newspapers, including full runs of *Pravda* and *Izvestia* on microfilm. Like the RRC collection, the Center for Middle Eastern Studies (CMES) Library concerns itself somewhat with history as well as current affairs. A 1960s gift to the center of seventeenth- through nineteenth-century books on travel in the Middle East adorns my office shelves and I continue to purchase a number of monographs each year on the history of the region. The CMES collection is almost entirely in English. Widener Library, the flagship of the Harvard College Library, has the finest Middle Eastern language collection in the country, so we leave foreign publications to it.

The three Coolidge Hall area libraries subscribe to a series published by the CIA under the aegis of the U.S. Department of Commerce which is uniquely valuable to the current research of center affiliates. The Foreign Broadcast Information Service (FBIS) *Daily Report* appears in six regional reports five times a week and includes translations of foreign radio and television broadcasts, approximately ten to fourteen days after the original transmissions. We subscribe to the reports for the Middle East and North Africa, China, East Asia, Eastern Europe and the Soviet Union. Although Widener Library receives all the reports on microfiche, we have hard copy — a great boon to readers.

A similar service, *Current Digest of the Soviet Press* (CDSP, Columbus, Ohio), is subscribed to by the RRC Library. They have as well the highly-regarded research reports published by Radio Free Europe/Radio Liberty. The FCEAR Library receives the *Survey of World Broadcasts* (from the BBC, London) for the

Far East and the *Joint Publications Research Service* (JPRS) translations of print media on China, which is yet another CIA series. In this library there is also a complete set of *Survey of China Mainland Press and Magazines*, translations that were published by the U.S. consulate in Hong Kong from 1950 to 1977. Both the RRC and CFEAR libraries offer their readers newspaper clippings relating to their particular regions from *The New York Times*, *The Washington Post*, *The Christian Science Monitor* and *The Asian Wall Street Journal*. The twenty-two percent of me that CMES owns does not allow me the time to provide a clipping service for the Middle East.

In addition to books and serials, the library of the Harvard Institute for International Development (HIID) contains about 16,000 reports, working papers and government documents relating to economic development in the Third World. Unlike the other Coolidge Hall centers which are concerned primarily with research, HIID operates as a project consulting firm and maintains field offices in Africa and Southeast Asia. The collection, most of it in English, reflects these regional biases. In addition, there is a separate group of materials on women in development, used extensively by students and scholars from the Boston area.

Finally, there is the overarching collection of the Center for International Affairs (CFIA). The granddaddy of the libraries within my charge (HIID grew out of the CFIA's Development Advisory Service in the 1960s), this is a strong collection of basic literature in international relations, chiefly English-language. The center supports several regional programs and one on nonviolent sanctions and is concerned with U.S. involvement with Canada, Japan and Europe. But its major interests are U.S. foreign policy, national security, comparative politics and international economics and organizations. To keep tabs on all this, we subscribe to eight daily newspapers, including *Le Monde*, and *The Times* and *Financial Times* from London.

COLOR TV IN CHINA

"Were Marx and Engels homosexuals?" "What is Gorbachev's address?" (Just The Kremlin, but people don't believe it.)

"How many color TV sets are there in China?" Coolidge Hall Library gets its share of simple, nutty reference questions. The reference collections, although somewhat constrained in size due to limited budgets, abound in directories and other works which provide answers to the frequent requests for names, addresses and phone numbers. Two Lambert publications, *Worldwide Government Directory* and *World of Trade, Finance and Economic Development*, are useful in this regard, as are the *Yearbook of International Organizations* (Saur); *U.S. Non-Profit Organizations in Development Assistance Abroad* (Technical Assistance Information Clearing House); *Directory Guide of European Security and Defense Research* (Pergamon); *Who's Who in European Institutions, Organizations and Enterprises* (Sutter's); and, of course, *International Who's Who* (Europa).

All the libraries share in a subscription to yet another group of CIA publications, which includes directories of officials in the individual communist-bloc countries. This series provides us with the handy *Chiefs of State and Cabinet Members of Foreign Governments*, published six times a year, as well as various country and regional maps issued monthly. We have telephone directories for New York City, Washington, Chicago and the U.S. departments of state and defense. The Moscow phone book is in Russian, but the *China Phone Book and Address Directory* (China Phone Book Co., Hong Kong), an enormously convenient item, is in English.

Biographical works in the RRC Library include *Who's Who in the Soviet Union* (Saur), *Who's Who in the Socialist Countries* (Saur), *Who's Who in Poland* (Professional Translators and Publishers) and *Who Was Who in the USSR* (Scarecrow), which lists the dead and the purged. The FCEAR Library has *Who's Who in the People's Republic of China* (Sharpe) and the *China Directory* (Radiopress, Tokyo). This is one of the few research libraries in the United States which maintains the Biographical Appearances File. Issued in card form by Universities Service Centre in Hong Kong since the 1950s and arranged by name, it indicates any mention of Chinese leaders in the print news media and cites the source.

The RRC and FCEAR reference collections include the *Facts and Figures Annual* for the USSR and China, published by Academic International Press. These librarians are often asked for travel information and they have numerous tourist guides, among them *A Motorist's Guide to the Soviet Union* (Pergamon) and an English translation of the *China Railway Timetable* (China Railway Publishing House, Beijing). There are, of course, many atlases, gazetteers, encyclopedias and dictionaries, in English as well as in Russian and Chinese. The RRC Library receives the *Yearbook on Communist Affairs*, published by the Hoover Institution Press. The FCEAR Library places greater emphasis on business and economic affairs, so it has on hand the *China Investment Guide* (Longman), the *Almanac of China's Economy* (Economic Management Company, Beijing), the *Statistical Yearbook of China* (State Statistical Bureau, Beijing) and the *Tabulation on the 1982 Population Census of the People's Republic of China* (Beijing), all in English.

The CFIA/HIID/CMES libraries maintain a small, fairly standard reference collection that is reasonably adequate for answering factual questions. Scholars' searching for basic population figures and world leaders' terms of office are often surprised to learn how useful the *World Almanac & Book of Facts* can be. Each year we receive *The World Factbook* and the *Handbook of Economic Statistics* (both from the CIA), *The Statesman's Year-Book* (Macmillan) and the statistical and demographic yearbooks published by the United Nations. The *World Development Report*, issued annually by the World Bank, is exceedingly useful for information on Third World countries, as is their *World Tables*, which has social as well as economic data and is now in its third edition.

When readers ask for the signatories of the Helsinki Accords or the treaty establishing the European Economic Communities, for example, I direct them to the *European Yearbook* (Martinus Nijhoff), which has an excellent documents section. If, to use another instance, a reader needs the famous text of Paul Nitzes' NSC 68 (the National Security memorandum on the containment of the spread of communism), or other U.S. foreign affairs documents, I refer him to *Foreign Relations of the United States* (U.S. GPO). Between the five Coolidge Hall libraries, we have all the volumes of this massive, on-going series which were published after 1940. Since Widener is a depository library for U.S.

as well as U.N. documents, I subscribe to only a select number of these, including annual reports for the Department of Defense and the Arms Control and Disarmament Agency; *Weekly Compilation of Presidential Documents* and the handier *Public Papers of the Presidents*; and the *Current Policy* memoranda series of the Department of State.

Publications issued regularly by the International Monetary Fund, although somewhat difficult to use because of their density, provide a wealth of statistical information. These are *World Economic Outlook, International Financial Statistics, Balance of Payments Yearbook, Direction of Trade Statistics* and *Government Finance Statistics*. Given the strong security interests of center affiliates, there is much demand for the following annuals, which we keep on reserve: *World Military Expenditures and Arms Transfers* (U.S. Arms Control and Disarmament Agency), *World Armaments and Disarmament Yearbook* (Stockholm International Peace Research Institute), *Military Balance* and *Strategic Strategy* (both published by the International Institute for Strategic Studies, London) and *Middle East Military Balance* (Westview). Because they offer solid analysis as well as information, the regional reference works of greatest value are *Middle East Contemporary Survey* and *Africa Contemporary Record*, both published annually by Holmes & Meier.

Naturally there are reference queries that are not answerable through sources at Coolidge Hall. I frequently refer readers to other Harvard libraries whose collections are more appropriate for their needs. During my first year here I made a number of field trips to those other libraries so I would make fewer blind or "good guess" referrals. Because the Harvard University is so dispersed, every reference librarian must have a fair grasp of all the units within the system.

Glaring omissions in the CFIA/HIID/CMES collections are indexes to serial literature and bibliographies. In addition, there is no complete subject catalog for these libraries. As a result, this is not a good place to start cold on a research topic. The reference staffs of Widener and the two undergraduate libraries are much better able to help people who are just beginning to pursue research. The collections at Coolidge Hall were intended to be resources for readers who were already knowledgeable in these fields. And this determines the nature of reference services, to some extent. Most readers arrive here armed with specific citations and much of what we do is point them to the sources.

MOM AND POP LIBRARY

To the hundreds of affiliates of the Coolidge Hall centers, the library has a "mom and pop convenience store" aura. Our readership is made up largely of regulars—undergraduate and graduate students whose academic work is in area studies; junior and senior faculty in the government, economic and history departments whose offices are in the building; and various center members who are visiting for the year. For the latter, especially, the library serves as home base, the Harvard library of first resort.

Although all of the centers sponsor year-long visiting fellows, most of them are academics of one sort or another, well accustomed to conducting research in large university libraries. Within CFIA, however, there is one group that is rather different each year. Known simply as the CFIA Fellows Program, it brings together men and women from all over the world who are considered "practitioners." These are senior and mid-level government officials, diplomats, military personnel, business leaders, international organization staff members, lawyers and journalists. In recent years the fellows included two distinguished world leaders: Kim Dae Jung, opposition leader from Korea, and the late Benigno Aquino of the Philippines.

In a sense the fellows spend a "summer camp for adults" sabbatical year at Harvard, attending seminars, classes and sherry hours, meeting new colleagues and sharing ideas (free from official restraint), away from piled-high desks, busy agenda and ringing telephones. But although the atmosphere is relaxed, each of the fellows conducts research to produce a paper on a topic of his or her choice. The papers are presented in seminars toward the end of the academic year and in some cases they are published as articles or become the basis for a book.

During the fellows' orientation week at Harvard, they are given formal tours of Coolidge Hall and Widener libraries, the two units they are almost certain to use. At that time I emphasize the collections in other Harvard libraries that deal in some measure with current international relations. The Littauer Library, housed in an august building down the street, is the principal economics collection at Harvard. Across the Charles River via shuttle bus is the Baker Library of the Harvard Business School. The library of the John F. Kennedy School of Government near Harvard Square has an excellent, comprehensive reference collection; in the same building is a small collection belonging to the Center for Science and International Affairs, which contains a good deal of material on military hardware and defense technology. The International Legal Studies Library at the Law School is a depository for European Communities' documents. A few blocks away from us are the small library at the Center for European Studies and the considerable collections (all in Asian languages) of the Harvard-Yenching Institute. In addition to the Middle Eastern Department, Widener Library the most imposing building in Harvard Yard, has a Judaica Department and a separate government documents and microforms area.

Coping with this sprawling system is made much easier by the Distributable Union Catalog (DUC), a microfiche record of books received and ordered by all Harvard libraries since 1978 (the year Harvard began using LC classification). Updated monthly and accumulated twice a year, the DUC provides access by author, title and subject. There are two DUC readers at Coolidge Hall and I urge the fellows to use them in order to get a bibliographic handle on the topics of interest to them and, when our copy of a book is in circulation or lost, to determine other locations for that title. I also tell them at the outset about database searches, which can be run at Widener and the Kennedy School libraries. Many of the fellows were not aware of database searching; some had never used microfiche before.

But the fellows do have impressive college degrees, they read and speak English fluently, and they have considerable backgrounds in the field of international relations. One problem I have encountered on a few occasions is that, having left their administrative assistants behind, they hope that the librarian will do part of their research for them. There is a distinct emphasis on personal service here; the Coolidge Hall atmosphere is informal and everyone is on a first-name basis. Like other members of the

CFIA staff, I am responsible for making the fellows feel welcome and at home. In September I generally discuss with each of them how they may best pursue their research amidst the myriad Harvard libraries.

Predictably, most fellows choose to work on topics that have an American angle. Many complain that libraries in their countries receive very little current American literature on international affairs, other than newspapers and a few of the leading journals. Ferdinando Nelli-Feroci, Deputy Head of the European Economic Community Desk at the Foreign Ministry in Rome, notes that the ministry library has few U.S. government documents and ordering them is time-consuming. Barbara Emerson, a British author of three biographies of world figures and the wife of a CFIA Fellow, says that the collections of U.S. embassy libraries are "not serious," consisting of *Time* magazine and the like. She has done research in the Bibliotheque Royale in Belgium, the British Museum and the Bibliotheque Nationale in Paris and finds they receive a sparse number of recent books published in the United States; moreover, she deplores the scarcity of seats in these national libraries.

Overall, the fellows are most appreciative of the richness of the Harvard collections and the accessibility provided by open stacks, which is not the policy in many foreign libraries. A number of fellows are quite grateful for the privilege of checking out books and journals; others wish the main collection at Widener were non-circulating, to ease the frustration of having to recall materials from borrowers.

Some fellows quickly get the hang of maneuvering among the various Harvard libraries, and some don't. All admit that, initially, Widener Library, with its three million plus books and two classification systems, is dauntingly complex. "It's a problem at first, then it becomes easy and fascinating, really," comments Farouk Jabre, a Lebanese political adviser and businessman. "It looks huge, but it's so splendid," says Ukeru Magosaki, who agrees with Jabre that browsing in the Widener stacks is an adventure. Magosaki is with the Japanese Ministry of Foreign Affairs in Tokyo and previously served in the Japanese embassies in London and Moscow. In researching the changes in the strategic importance of the Far East from 1945 to the present, he has made use of all five Coolidge Hall libraries (he is fluent in Russian), and those of Widener, Kennedy School, Harvard-Yenching and even the M.I.T. Library. Gonzalo Biggs, a Chilean lawyer and senior counsel for the Inter-American Development Bank headquartered in Washington, is studying the legal, political and economic aspects of Latin American debt. Although he has relied most on the International Legal Studies Library, he has been to Littauer, Widener, and Baker. "I'm delighted, I love libraries and I'm having a ball every day."

But Widener has more detractors than fans. "It takes you a hell of a long time walking along the stacks trying to find things," notes Barbara Emerson. "Too big" and "too vast" are common descriptions of Widener, although most fellows have to resort to it occasionally. Nai Su Kim, a Korean diplomat who served at the U.N. for many years, made his research easier by bringing with him to Cambridge the Korean and U.N. documents he needed; anything else he required was either here or at Harvard-Yenching. Many fellows find they can limit their trips to Widener to the fairly manageable Government Documents and Microforms Division. Randa Mukhar, a researcher in the office of Jordan's Prince Nassar used *The New York Times Index* there in her event data analysis of recent U.S.-Syrian relations. For his study of the Strategic Defense Initiative, Roger Jackling, Assistant Secretary in the Ministry of Defence in London, has relied on congressional hearings and other U.S. government documents.

Dieter Ziesler and De Zhao Chen were very happy to find the RRC Library here when they arrived at CFIA. Ziesler, a secretary at the Foreign Office in Bonn and former consul in Leningrad, is researching the ongoing arms reduction negotiations and laments that there are no German translations of the Soviet media comparable to the FBIS series and the CDSP in English. Chen is a member of the Academy of Social Sciences in Beijing. He has been comparing Soviet journals' reporting of Western sources on U.S.-European economic relations with those original sources and, not surprisingly, finds countless discrepancies.

Afif Safieh, a Palestinian scholar with European training who is fluent in three languages, is working on the Arab-Israeli conflict from 1973 to 1982, focusing on the U.S.-European Communities-Middle East triangle. He has had little use for the other

Harvard libraries. "I'm lazy," he says. Indeed, his only post-tour visit to Widener was made in conjunction with an errand I had there, so that I steered him to the book he needed. But his use of the CMES and CFIA libraries has been indefatigable. Like many other fellows, Safieh is especially attracted to the current journals, daily newspapers and new books. In the case of the latter, I try to receive books as hot-off-the-press as possible and make them available immediately as uncataloged "new books," far more quickly than the other libraries can do.

The fellows do find a great many of the current books and journals they need here. Roger Jackling remarks that the papers they write "are excused the highest standards of academic rigor," hence it is possible to rely heavily on our collections without tracking down every last source elsewhere. The point of Coolidge Hall Library is to provide a comfortable, convenient, personal setting in which much research may be accomplished. Apparently, for the visiting CFIA Fellows, this small haven amidst the vast Harvard holdings is just what is needed for a year of study in Cambridge.

Overseas Publications of the Library of Congress: Their History and Use as Reference Resources

Jack C. Wells

The Library of Congress Offices in New Delhi, Jakarta, Cairo, Nairobi, and Rio de Janeiro have for some years been publishing accessions lists of materials acquired for the Library of Congress and also, in the case of the first four offices mentioned, for a number of research librarians in the United States. Although the accessions lists are heavily used by area specialists they do not appear to be widely known to non-specialist reference librarians in those libraries which do not participate in the L.C. acquisition programs. In most libraries, requests for information about many of the countries covered by these accessions lists are probably not too common but reference specialists should be aware of these lists and the information they can provide. This discussion is intended to provide a brief overview of those accessions lists currently being published, their history, and the kinds of information they are able to provide.

AREAS OF COVERAGE

Accessions list: Middle East – (Cairo)
  Algeria, Bahrain, Egypt, Iran, Jordan, Lebanon, Libya,

Mr. Wells is South and Southeast Asian Bibliographer, Memorial Library, University of Wisconsin, Madison, WI 53706.

© 1987 by The Haworth Press, Inc. All rights reserved.

Morocco, Qatar, Saudi Arabia, Syria, Tunisia, Yeman (North).

Accessions list: Eastern Africa—(Nairobi)

Burundi, Comoros, Djibouti, Ethiopia, Kenya, Madagascar, Malwi, Maritius, Mayotte, Reunion, Rwanda, Seychelles, Somalia, Sudan, Tanzania, Uganda, Zambia.

Accessions list: South Asia—(New Delhi)

Afghanistan,[1] Bangladesh, Bhutan, Maldives,[1] Nepal, Pakistan, Sri Lanka.

Accessions list: Southeast Asia—(Jakarta)

Brunei, Indonesia, Malaysia, Singapore, Thailand,[1] Burma.[1]

Accessions list: Brazil.

Brazil.[1]

1. Collected for the Library of Congress only.
2. Collected for the Library of Congress, New York Public Library, and Yale Law School Library.

The national distribution of the materials acquired and sent by the Library of Congress overseas offices includes those libraries which have major responsibilities for supporting research and teaching in one or more of the areas covered by the various acquisition programs. The Cairo office, covering the Middle East and North Africa, sends materials to twenty-six U.S. libraries, including the Library of Congress. No library in this program receives the full range of materials that the program provides; each institution tailoring its receipts to match local needs and budgets. The South Asian program supplies materials to thirty-three libraries but at least six of these institutions have narrow collection interests, either in subject coverage or in the number of countries from which they receive materials.

The Southeast Asian program sends materials to twelve libraries; each having somewhat different collection interests and levels of receipts. The programs for Eastern Africa and Brazil provide materials primarily to the Library of Congress; with selected materials being sent to the New York Public Library and law titles going to the Yale University Law School Library. The Center for Research Libraries, Chicago, receives almost all serial titles, except in medicine and agriculture, from the South Asian and Southeast Asian programs. The quantity of material sent annually by all the overseas offices is formidable. In FY 1984, a total of more than 840,000 pieces was sent to the libraries, including the Library of Congress, participating in the five programs.[1]

THE PL-480 PROGRAM

In the late 1950s efforts were made by librarians and scholars to seek appropriations for library acquisitions from American-owned foreign currency accounts generated by the sale of surplus agricultural commodities to foreign countries by the United States government. It was anticipated that these funds could be used to provide printed materials to the Library of Congress and to other research libraries which would wish to receive them. World War II and the subsequent "cold war" had brought home to many the fact that the United States lacked the information resources to adequately deal with the world that had emerged from the chaos of the war and the changes accompanying decolonization. It was intended to use the sought after funding to acquire printed materials from countries where the routine acquisition of these materials was difficult because local book trades were not well established or other impediments to the free exchange of information existed.

After some legislative disappointments, a bill was enacted in 1958, amending the *Agricultural Trade and Assistance Act* (PL 83-480) of 1954, which permitted the Library of Congress to obtain annual appropriations from the surplus currency accounts. Enactment of the new legislation, however, did not mean automatic appropriations by the Congress and it was only after several annual efforts that funds for the purpose were finally appropriated in 1961. By 1962, teams from the Library of Congress had visited New Delhi, Karachi, and Cairo, offices were open in those cities, and materials were starting to flow to libraries.

The acquisition policy to be followed in these programs was to collect in the categories listed below.[2]

1. Comprehensive sets of government publications at national and state levels.

2. Wide selections of commercially published serials.
3. Every currently published monograph of research value.
    EXCLUSIONS
    a. Juvenile
    b. translations of western languages into the vernaculars.
       titles
    d. Textbooks below college level.
4. Institutional publications

NATIONAL PROGRAM FOR ACQUISITIONS AND CATALOGING

Since 1901, the Library of Congress has been providing cataloging information to U.S. libraries through the sale of its catalog cards but, in 1964, it was estimated that this service was providing cataloging for only fifty percent of the total number of titles acquired by all U.S. libraries.[3] Those titles not covered by the Library of Congress card service had to be cataloged by the libraries acquiring copies; an expensive duplication of effort. Clearly, with world-wide, annual publication steadily increasing, great savings could be obtained with a system that would centralize the production and distribution of cataloging information.

Because the Library of Congress was already providing cataloging for fifty percent of the national book intake, a convincing argument was made that the Library should increase its acquisitions and cataloging efforts. The Congress was persuaded to expand Title II of the *Higher Education Act of 1965*; adding Part C "Strengthening College and Research Library Resources." Among the provisions of this amendment was the stipulation that the Commissioner of Education would transfer funds to the Librarian of Congress to:

> Acquire, so far as possible, all library materials currently published throughout the world which are of value to scholarship . . . Provide catalog information for these materials promptly after receipt and distribute bibliographic information by printing catalog cards and by other means, and enable the Library of Congress to use for exchange and other

purposes any of these materials not needed for its own collection.[4]

Of interest for the purposes of this discussion is a section of the plan of operation developed by the Library which stated: "In areas where the book trade is not well organized and where there is no national bibliography LC will accelerate and expand its purchasing arrangements by establishing acquisitions centers."[5] By 1966/67, NPAC acquisitions centers had been opened in Nairobi and Rio de Janeiro.

By the end of the 1960s, two acquisitions mechanisms were operating under LC's Office of the Coordinator of Overseas Programs. PL-480 programs operated in Israel, the Middle East, Yugoslavia, Poland, Nepal, Ceylon, Pakistan, and India; funded with excess currencies from U.S. accounts. The NPAC offices for Brazil and Eastern Africa were funded by annual dollar appropriations for Title II-C. expenditures. Over the next fifteen years, as the excess currency funds were expended or became unavailable for library purposes, some of the PL-480 programs ceased (Israel, Yugoslavia, and Poland) and the others, over time, became cooperative acquisitions programs funded jointly by Congressional appropriations for the Library of Congress and by contributions from the participating research libraries to cover the costs of the materials received by them and a portion of the program overheads. No acquisitions lists were published for the Yugoslavia and Poland programs and *Accessions list: Israel* ceased with that program and will not be discussed here.

CURRENT ACCESSIONS LISTS

It seems to have been recognized from the very beginning of these acquisitions efforts that libraries receiving the materials would require considerable, and regular, bibliographic support. Few, if any, research libraries in the United States were adequately staffed to deal with the wide variety of materials in exotic languages and the anticipated volume of the items to be received would have exacerbated the problem to the point where routine processing of the incoming books and serials would be difficult, if not impossible. It was obviously more practicable to use local field office staff to provide preliminary cataloging information and to make this information available to the recipient libraries by means of accessions lists.

Examination of the several accessions lists discussed here shows a general evolution from rather modest beginnings to, in several cases, highly elaborate bibliographic efforts. The lists, over time, reflect both the expansion of collection activity by the Library of Congress offices and increasing sophistication in providing cataloging and bibliographic information.

Program Developments

Middle East

During the first years of the Middle East program acquisitions were largely limited to imprints from Cairo and Alexandria with considerably fewer titles from other publishing centers in the Arabic-speaking world; Bagdad, Beirut, and Kuwait being other principal sources.[6] By the mid-1970s, the Cairo Field Office was making strenuous efforts to expand coverage to include the remaining Middle Eastern countries, including Iran. By 1984, a network of local agents and representatives working for the Cairo office was acquiring academic, non-commercial, and government publications from thirteen Middle Eastern and North African countries for the Library of Congress and the research libraries participating in the Middle East Cooperative Acquisitions Program [MECAP].

Southeast Asia

In 1963, an American Libraries Book Procurement Center was opened in Jakarta to acquire books and other printed materials for the Library of Congress as well as for other research libraries which had elected to participate in the acquisitions program. Excess currency funds were used for this purpose until 1969 when the funds were declared no longer surplus and unavailable to the Library of Congress program. Since that time, the office has been operating as a part of the National Program for Acquisitions and Cataloging using both dollar appropriations and the contributions from a dozen research libraries to pay for the materials each receives as well as sharing program overhead costs. In 1971, this program was expanded to include Malaysia, Singapore, and Brunei. Since 1979, *Acquisitions list: Southeast Asia* also includes materials acquired only for the Library of Congress from Thailand and Burma.

South Asia

The South Asia program began with the creation of the American Libraries Book Procurement offices in New Delhi and Karachi; the latter office having a branch in Dacca, East Pakistan. Within five years the New Delhi office was collecting materials in Nepal and Ceylon and, with the creation of Bangladesh in 1972, the collection responsibility for that country was assumed by the New Delhi office. Through the 1970s, as excess currency accounts were expended or became unavailable for library purposes in Ceylon and Nepal these programs also were converted to cooperative dollar funded efforts. The Bangladesh program began as a cooperative program since no surplus currency funds existed in the new nation. By 1985, special foreign currency funds were no longer available in India so that this program, too, has become a cooperative effort. By 1986, the book procurement program in Pakistan will have undergone a similar transformation.

These changes from special foreign currency funding to cooperative dollar collection efforts have, and will continue to have, serious consequences for the national South Asia collection in the U.S. As the demand for dollar-support from the participating libraries has increased, many research libraries have been forced to reduce their collection levels by dropping languages and limiting subject coverages. These changes mean that materials will not be as readily available as they were when they were paid purchased with surplus foreign currencies. It is expected, however, that with careful planning, one or more copies of every title of research interest will be somewhere available in this country.

From the beginnings of the country programs mentioned above, India, Pakistan, Bangladesh, Sri Lanka, Nepal, and Afghanistan, a separate accessions list was issued for each nation through 1980. From 1981, *Accessions list: South Asia* covers monographs and serial titles acquired from all these countries; providing preliminary catalog information for books, serials, and materials acquired in microform for the Library of Congress, as well as monthly announcements of new serials, changes and cessations.

Eastern Africa

In 1966, the Library of Congress established a regional acquisitions center in Nairobi to acquire books and other printed materials for the Library under the provisions of Title II-C of the *Higher Education Act of 1965* that funded the NPAC program. In addition to providing materials for the Library of Congress the Nairobi center, since 1977, has been sending selected materials to the New York Public Library and legal publications to the Yale University Law School Library.

Coverage provided by *Accessions list: Eastern Africa* has altered over time as new countries have been added to the program. Material from ten countries was included in the early lists and, by 1985, this number had increased to eighteen. The lists also include publications of the United Nations issued in the region, materials published outside the normal area of coverage but acquired by the office, and non-book materials, particularly sound recordings.

Latin America

Although a regional acquisitions center was established in Rio de Janeiro in 1967, it was not until 1975 that the office began to issue *Accessions list: Brazil*. The list is unique among the currently published lists discussed here in that it covers only one country. The material included reflects Library of Congress collection policy and includes commercial, institutional, and government publications. Reprints, translations into Portuguese, textbooks, popular fiction, etc. are not normally acquired. Bimonthly issues appear with a section for monographs and a serials sections citing new titles and changes. Special materials, including sound recordings, are listed in a separate section.

INFORMATION PROVIDED BY THE ACCESSIONS LISTS

Of the five accessions lists described here, only *Accessions list: South Asia* is published monthly, the others are currently issued bimonthly. The accessions lists have certain features in common. Titles are listed under country of publication, and in some of the lists, these groupings are subdivided by language as well. Each list has a separate section for new serial titles, changes and cessations, as well as separate sections covering special materials. The preliminary cataloging prepared by each of the Library of Congress offices conforms to the second edition of the *Anglo-American Cataloging Rules* but the lists may also include entries prepared before the adoption of these rules. Each new monograph or new serial title is also assigned a card number from the series 9xxxxx prefaced by the year when the cataloging was prepared. Some titles may have card numbers prefaced by "shadow numbers" (e.g., X9-xxxxx or Y1-9xxxxx) with the "X" indicating 1970s preliminary cataloging and "Y" indicating titles cataloged in the 1980s. The "shadow numbers" are assigned to those titles normally outside L.C.s collecting interest but which may eventually be included in that library's collection. If the title is cataloged by the Library of Congress the "X" is changed to "7" and the "Y" is changed to "8." The presence of a title in these lists does not indicate that the Library of Congress will automatically retain the title for its permanent collection.

Author/Title Indexes

Indexes to the materials cited in the accessions lists vary from program to program and these differences are worth noting. The bi-monthly issues of the lists covering accessions from Eastern Africa and Brazil have main/added entry indexes which are cumulated in the last issue of each year. The bimonthly lists for Southeast Asia and the Middle East programs have no author/main entry indexes but annual author/title indexes appear in the last issues of the year. The monthly lists covering South Asian accessions have author/title indexes which are cumulated in a Part 2 of the last issue of the year.

Subject Indexes

Only *Accessions list: South Asia* is subject indexed. Each monthly issue has a subject index for that issue and the last number for each year has two parts with the second part containing both the annual author/title and the subject cumulations. Subject entries in the accessions list conform to Library of Congress practice and indicate the page listing the full citation, the language of the work cited, and the location of the citation on a page.

Serials Lists

New serial titles, changes and cessations are listed in separate sections in the monthly or bimonthly lists. An annual cumulation of the July/August issue of *Accessions list: Middle East* and a separate annual serial supplement to *Accessions list: Eastern Africa* appears within a few months of the end of the year covered. Cumulated serials lists are published periodically to describe serial acquisitions for South Asia, Southeast Asia, and Brazil. Coverage of Southeast Asian serial titles has been provided by serial supplements dealing with varying time periods which have been separated into two publications, *Cumulative list of Indonesian serials . . .* and *Cumulated list of Malaysia, Singapore, and Brunei serials . . .* A third serial cumulation is planned; providing coverage of serials acquired from Burma, Laos, and Thailand. The sheer volume of serial titles acquired by the Library of Congress Office, New Delhi has forced that office to shift from publishing an annual cumulated serials list to quenquenial lists with additional supplements covering one or two years. The most recent volume, *Serials supplement, 1981-1983* appeared in two parts; part two having both title/main entry and subject indexes.

Additional Information

Other useful features of the accessions lists are the names of the research libraries participating in the Middle East, South Asia, and Southeast Asia programs. The lists for the Middle East and South Asia programs also indicate the countries from which materials are being acquired by each participating library and, for the Middle East, indicate these institutions' general subject and language coverages. A separate list of non-trade publishers in Eastern Africa is published as a supplement to the list covering that area and a similar list for Brazil is expected in 1985. A brief description of the subject content of each title appears with monographic entries in the lists for South Asia, Southeast Asia, and the Middle East. The South Asia and the Southeast Asia lists also cite current and retrospective titles acquired in microform for the Library of Congress. A list of microform materials acquired by the South Asia program was published as part of *Accessions list: South Asia* (v.1, no.12, pt3).

ACCESSIONS LISTS AS REFERENCE TOOLS

For the reference and interlibrary loan librarians who are not area specialists the several accessions lists can provide varieties of information not readily gained elsewhere. It should first be understood that the lists are not efforts at bibliographic control but are intended to provide a record of titles likely to be available at one or more libraries in the United States.

As mentioned earlier, the lists provide AACR II catalog information, announcements of new serial titles, and for some areas, provide indexes for authors, titles, and subjects. Current and retrospective microform acquisitions held by the Library of Congress as well as new sound recordings are also described. Acronyms for public and private agencies as well as government organizations are also defined. The example below is from *Accessions list: South Asia* (v. 6, no.1. Jan. 1986).

Author/Title Index: ATDO *search under* Appropriate Technology Development Organization (Pakistan)
Appropriate Technology Development Organization (Pakistan) 76d
USAID (Pakistan) *search under* United States. Agency for International Development. Mission to Pakistan.
Pakistan Council of Scientific and Industrial Research 76d

Village Level Food Processing Program 76
United States, Agency for International Development. Mission to Pakistan 76d
Village Level Food Processing Project in Pakistan 76

Subject Index:
Village Level Food Processing Programme 76d(E)
Food Processing Plants—Pakistan 76d(E)

Citation:
Microfiche 85/58103
P-E-84-931613
Village-level Food Processing Programme.
Village-level Food Processing Project in Pakistan. —Karachi: Pakistan Council of Scientific & Industrial Research; [Denver] d Colorado, U.S.A., Denver Research Institute, [1982?]
5 v.:ill., charts, maps: 27 cm.
Vols. 2-5 rec'd this month; v. 1 acquired earlier.
Project sponsored by ATDO and USAID
(Pakistan)
Includes bibliographies.
Includes tables.
Contents: v.1. Executive summary—v.2. sugar—v.3. Sugar appendices—v.4. oilseeds—v.5. Manuals.

For a large number of titles the kinds of information listed above will be sufficient to locate a copy of the title using MARC records in one of the cataloging utilities if the work has been cataloged. However, if the Library of Congress has not selected the title for its collection there will be no MARC record or any record at all unless another library has cataloged the work. The reader should also be aware that, in some cases, the Library of

Congress cataloging units will alter a temporary record main entry to conform to L.C. practice so that an accessions list main entry will not be part of the MARC record. The obvious alternative search strategy is to also try the L.C. card number or title approaches. Recently, it has been noted that L.C. cataloging for English-language titles from some of the areas covered by the accessions lists is quite current; frequently appearing even before the books have been received by the program participants. Cataloging for non-English language titles, in most cases, takes somewhat longer. Unfortunately, this happy situation may not survive those funding reductions for L.C. which have already been announced or which have been projected for the next several years. A "stretch out" of cataloging time seems almost inevitable and this means that a greater number and variety of titles will likely be held by research libraries in controlled backlogs for longer periods of time.

Under these conditions, the accessions lists will continue to be of major importance in describing titles which are available, even though uncataloged, in several research libraries and will suggest where they are likely to be found. Titles described in the accessions lists covering South Asia, Southeast Asia, and the Middle East are likely to be in those libraries listed in issues of the accessions lists covering those areas but the intake of South Asian materials by those libraries still participating in the new, dollar-funded program is likely to be much more specialized and limited than heretofore. The new Indian acquisitions program permits each library to use a complex collection profile statement that allows a great number of selection choices and combinations based on language, subject, geographic region, and depth of collection interest. It is expected that a similar mechanism will be in operation by November 1986 to supply books and serials from Pakistan. It is obvious that these changes will make it more difficult to predict from where a specific title might be borrowed if cataloging is delayed. Many research libraries will loan an uncataloged title but an interlibrary-loan request should provide the main entry citation from one of the accessions lists and, to be safe, the assigned L.C. card number.

The five accession lists discussed here should be available in those reference collections which have to deal with a significant number of questions about the regions covered. At present, current subscriptions to these publications are free from the addresses listed below.

Library of Congress. Library of Congress Office, New Delhi. *Accessions list: South Asia*	Field Director New Delhi-LC Department of State
Library of Congress. Library of Congress Office. Brazil. *Accessions list: Brazil/*	Library of Congress Office American Consulate General APO Miami 34030
Library of Congress. Library of Congress Office, Jakarta. *Accessions list: Southeast Asia/*	Field Director Karachi-LC Department of State Washington, D.C. 20520
Library of Congress. Library of Congress Office, Nairobi. *Accessions list: Eastern Africa*	Field Director Karachi-LC Department of State Washington, D.C. 20520
Library of Congress. Library of Congress Office, Cairo *Accessions list: Middle East*	Field Director Karachi-LC Department of State Washington, D.C. 20520

Copies of completed volumes of some of these lists are available on microfiche from the Photoduplication Service, Library of Congress, Washington, D.C. 20540.

The accession lists described here have obvious limitations as reference sources but they do provide the most current bibliographic information available for the forty-five countries covered by the five programs. Some of the field offices have carried on operations through civil unrest, coups, counter-coups, and regional military conflicts. The American Field Directors and their local staffs deserve the highest praise for their unstinting efforts in the face of, at times, great adversity. It would be most unfortunate if these remarkable acquisition programs and their publications were to become the victims of shortsighted budget reductions.

NOTES

1. Library of Congress. Annual report of the Librarian of Congress, 1984. p. 63-64. (Acquisition figures for the Eastern Africa program were not included)

2. *Library of Congress PL-480 newsletter*. no.3 (March 1962)

3. William S. Dix. Testimony to the Special Sub-Committee on Education. U.S. House of Representatives. May 10, 1965. *Cited in:* Library of Congress. Annual report of the Librarian of Congress, 1966. p. 25.

4. Library of Congress. Annual report of the Librarian of Congress, 1966. p. 27.

5. Library of Congress. Annual report of the Librarian of Congress, 1966. p. 29.

6. Mortimer Graves. *The Library of Congress PL-480 foreign acquisitions program: user's eye-view. ACLS newsletter*. Special supplement. September 1969. p. 9.

International Information Activities of the U.S. Geological Survey

Gary W. North
Nancy B. Faries

The U.S. Geological Survey has conducted an extensive program of internationally oriented earth science information activities since the 1940s. In addition, the Survey maintains a comprehensive earth science reference library that was founded in 1879, and it also actively participates in the International Federation of Library Associations, the International Geophysical Union, the International Cartographic Association, and a number of other international associations. The Geological Survey is one of the principal distributors of manned spacecraft photographs and images and Landsat satellite images of the world. The Survey maintains several information offices that assist researchers in obtaining international and national earth science information and products.

INTERNATIONAL EARTH SCIENCE TECHNICAL ASSISTANCE AND COOPERATIVE SCIENTIFIC PROGRAMS

The Geological Survey meets several objectives through international activities. The Survey finds that it can perform national research best through comparative studies of scientific phenomena in both the United States and overseas. The Geological Survey also uses its international activities program to exchange in-

---

The authors are at the U.S. Department of the Interior, Geological Survey, Information and Data Services, 12201 Sunrise Valley Dr., Reston, VA 22092.

© 1987 by The Haworth Press, Inc. All rights reserved.

formation about existing and potential earth science resources worldwide as well as to develop and maintain relations with other international institutions and programs.

The Geological Survey's activities outside the United States support the international programs of other Federal agencies, such as the State Department's Agency for International Development, the Office of Foreign Disaster Assistance, and the Scientific Committee on Antarctic Research.

The international activities that the Geological Survey supports are usually of two types, either technical assistance to other countries and international organizations, or cooperative scientific projects to achieve common objectives. Cooperative programs generate a number of information products, such as international geological and mineral resource reports, coal-resource assessments, satellite image maps, geoscience and topographic maps, marine geological and geophysical surveys/reports, volcano studies, and marine seismic studies of continental margins. This information is usually published in either microfilm or lithograph form by the Geological Survey and is available for purchase or reference by the general public.

In 1985, one of the major international activities in which the Geological Survey participated was a Central American workshop held in Guatemala to plan an initial assessment of the earth and water resources in Central America and to identify potential geologic hazards in the region and opportunities for resource development and hazards mitigation. Countries represented at the workshop include Belize, Guatemala, Honduras, El Salvador, Costa Rica, and Panama.

A second major international activity by the Geological Survey was the continuation of the World Energy Resource Program, which involves the compilation and exchange of geologic and mineral economic information on the world's major mineral deposits for inclusion in the International Strategic Mineral Inventory. Other activities during 1985 included the completion of studies of the petroleum geology of South Asia (including Pakistan, India, Sri Lanka, Bangladesh, and Burma), Indonesia, Eastern Siberia, Western China, and the Barents Sea and surrounding lands.

The Survey has provided technical assistance or conducted cooperative scientific projects in over 52 countries and 9 regional areas (see side box). Information on 1985 and previous years' international projects may be obtained from Office of International Geology, U.S. Geological Survey, 917 National Center, Reston, Virginia 22092, telephone 703-860-6551 (after June 1, 703-648-6070).

U.S. GEOLOGICAL SURVEY LIBRARY

The Geological Survey maintains a comprehensive library in the areas of geology, paleontology, mineralogy, petrology, mineral resources, water resources, surveying and cartography, chemistry, physics, oceanography, soil science, zoology, natural history, remote sensing, environmental science, and geothermal energy. The library was founded in 1879 with the passage of the legislation establishing the Geological Survey. In the same legislation, the library was authorized to start the extensive international and national exchange program, which forms the basis of today's comprehensive collection. Its first major acquisition was the collection of more than 1,000 earth science volumes belonging to Ferdinand V. Hayden, Superintendent of the U.S. Geological and Geographical Survey of the Territories.

In 1882, the collection of Robert Clarke comprising nearly 2,000 early geologic reports was purchased by the Geological Survey. To the two original collections over the years were added nearly complete sets of State geological survey publications and earth science literature from all over the world. Today the library maintains a complete collection of all official publications on geology issued by any country in the world as well as a worldwide collection of professional society, university, and institutional geological publications. About 75 percent of the collection consists of magazines and periodicals, almost 10,000 of which are kept current.

The library now has more than 1 million books, periodicals, bound and unbound monographs, and government publications; more than 350,000 maps; approximately 4,000 Environmental Impact Statements; and many field notebooks, prints, doctoral dissertations, and technical reports. In 1980, the library circulated nearly 105,000 books, periodicals, maps, slides, photographs, and microforms; made 17,700 interlibrary loans; and answered some 27,000 requests for information.[1]

The main holdings of the library are housed in Reston, Virginia, at the national headquarters of the Geological Survey. Branch libraries are also maintained in Denver, Colorado; Menlo Park, California; and Flagstaff, Arizona. More detailed information about the library may be obtained from the Reference Desk, U.S. Geological Survey Library, 950 National Center, Reston, Virginia 22092, telephone 703-860-6671 (after June 1, 703-648-4302).

GEOLOGICAL SURVEY PARTICIPATION IN INTERNATIONAL ORGANIZATIONS

The Geological Survey has been active in a number of international organizations almost since its inception. Among these international groups are the Pan American Institute of Geography and History, the International Society of Photogrammetry and Remote Sensing, the International Geophysical Union, the International Association of Hydrological Sciences, the International Cartographic Association, and the International Federation of Surveyors. A group that agency personnel have worked closely with over the past several years is the International Federation of Library Associations' Section of Geography and Map Libraries. The principal goals of the section are improving international communication in the geographic and cartographic disciplines; compiling and publishing bibliographic directories, glossaries, and technical monographs; and holding workshops and other training sessions for map librarians from all over the world. Reference librarians who are interested in obtaining more information on the Section of Geography and Map Libraries may contact the International Federation of Library Associations.

International Earth Science Products Produced by the Geological Survey

Principal among the international information products produced by the Geological Survey are the series of space photographs taken during the 1973-1974 Skylab satellite program. These photographs provide coverage of the Earth between the latitudes of 50° North and South. During the three Skylab manned flights, more than 35,000 photographs were taken. This coverage includes most of the United States, a large part of South America, and parts of Africa, Europe, and the Middle East. The photographs are useful for planning purposes and for agricultural, geographic, and other scientific studies. The standard print size for Skylab images is 4.5 inches square.

A second international product is the Earth resources satellite (Landsat) images taken from an altitude of 570 and 425 miles. Each image covers approximately 115 square miles and is used by students, engineers, scientists, and others interested in investigating landforms, land use, geology, shallow seas, environment, and vegetation. Images in black-and-white, as well as other spectral bands, are available for most of the Earth's surface. The images are useful for conveying information about large features such as mountain ranges or the outlines of major cities.

Another international product is a series of 1:80,000-scale color-infrared aerial photographs of the U.S./Mexico border procured under a joint project between the two countries. The final published products will be a series of 203 border-centered, simulated natural color, 1:25,000-scale photoimage maps. The primary use of the photoimage maps will be by the International Boundary and Water Commission and the U.S. Customs Service, but the maps will also be available for sale to the general public.

Research Information for U.S. Geological Survey International Activities and Products

Because of its widespread earth science activities, the Geological Survey produces a number of publications describing its information activities. The Geological Survey publishes a Yearbook that includes descriptions of the agency's mission, goals, and on-going programs and selected articles written by the agency's scientists describing research activities. The Yearbook can be purchased through the Superintendent of Documents, U.S.

Government Printing Office, Washington, D.C. 20402. The 1985 Yearbook will be released within the next several months.

The Geological Survey also publishes a number of free information aids. Chief among them is U.S. Geological Survey Circular 900, "Guide to Obtaining USGS Information." This useful reference aid describes the wide variety of earth science products and services available from the Geological Survey, and provides addresses and telephone numbers on where these products and services may be obtained. Another useful reference publication, particularly for those interested in international earth science activities, is U.S. Geological Survey Circular 934, "Worldwide Directory of National Earth-Science Agencies and Related International Organizations." This circular was recently updated and lists the national earth science agencies of 160 countries and 87 international organizations that are active in one or more of the earth sciences. The entries are coded to indicate whether an agency's major function is geologic, hydrologic, cartographic, or regulatory. The publication lists the address of more than 900 major governmental earth science agencies.

These two reference publications may be ordered free from the U.S. Geological Survey, Books and Open-File Reports, Federal Center, Bldg. 41, Box 25425, Denver, Colorado 80225.

The Survey also prepares a monthly list of "New Publications of the Geological Survey," a compilation and description of the studies, investigations, reports, books, and maps produced by the Geological Survey. To place your name or organization on the mailing list for this free publication, send a request to the U.S. Geological Survey, 582 National Center, Reston, Virginia 22092.

U.S. GEOLOGICAL SURVEY INFORMATION OFFICES

The Geological Survey maintains a number of offices that provide earth science information and, in some cases, sell materials produced by the Geological Survey.

The Public Inquiries Offices (PIOs) are the mainstay of the Geological Survey's public information services. The Survey opened the first PIOs more than 34 years ago in the downtown areas of Denver, Colorado; Salt Lake City, Utah; and Los Angeles, California. Within a few years, the Survey had established additional PIOs in San Francisco, California; Dallas, Texas; Spokane, Washington; and Anchorage, Alaska, where the interest in mineral exploration, geologic formations, monitoring water resources, and topography was the keenest. In recent years, to further improve the availability of information regionally, the Geological Survey has opened PIOs in Reston, Virginia, and Menlo Park, California. A PIO also has been established in downtown Washington, D.C., to serve the Federal Government and the metropolitan area. In addition, a branch Public Inquiries Office was recently opened in Anchorage.

The specialists in the PIOs provide information on the various programs of the Geological Survey, especially projects underway in their respective regions, and have in-depth knowledge of the Survey's maps and reports.

In recent years the PIOs have been strengthened by the introduction of an Earth Science Information Network (ESIN). Through the use of microcomputers, the Geological Survey has linked the 11 PIOs across the country electronically and provided them the capability to search major bibliographic and geographic data bases maintained on major computer systems by the Geological Survey.

Through the ESIN network, the PIOs update the information available to the public by accessing the news released daily by the Geological Survey. Among the most useful computer data bases are those listing publications of the Survey from 1879 to the present and those listing sources of water resources information. Also there is access to a dictionary of earth science information systems, sources of cartographic information, and the status of digital mapping.

The addresses and telephone numbers of regional PIOs can be found in local telephone books. The PIO at the Geological Survey's National Center can be reached by writing Public Inquiries Office, U.S. Geological Survey, 503 National Center, Reston, Virginia 22092 or telephoning 703-860-6167.

In addition to the PIOs, which handle sales of all of the Geological Survey's products, the National Mapping and Geologic Divisions operate their own information and research offices. The National Cartographic Information Centers (NCIC) of the National Mapping Division concentrate on helping researchers find maps made by Federal agencies, as well as much of the data and materials used to make the maps. The NCIC's are located in Reston, Virginia; Rolla, Missouri; Denver, Colorado; Menlo Park, California; Anchorage, Alaska; and Bay St. Louis, Mississippi. These offices provide cartographic information and sell custom cartographic products, such as aerial photographs and digital map data produced by the Geological Survey. Regional NCIC office addresses are listed in local telephone books. The headquarters NCIC office can be reached by writing the National Cartographic Information Center, U.S. Geological Survey, 507 National Center, Reston, Virginia 22092, or by telephoning 703-860-6045.

The Geologic Inquiries Group (GIG) is the principal information group for geologic inquiries. The Group can research questions about the geology of a specific area, volcano hazards, earthquake information, energy and mineral resources, and branches of science related to geology such as geophysics and geochemistry. The Group also prepares geologic map indexes that are available to the public, as well as packets of teaching materials. They can be contacted by writing the Geologic Inquiries Group, U.S. Geological Survey, 907 National Center, Reston, Virginia 22092, or by telephoning 703-860-6517 (after June 1, 703-648-4383).

The Geological Survey offers a wide range of international earth science information. The research and customer-service offices offer technical expertise for answering a variety of earth science questions and for placing orders for internationally based reports, publications, photographs, and maps. In addition, the Geological Survey library is an internationally recognized source of worldwide earth science information. As part of its services to the public, the Survey gladly makes its information and expertise available to the American people.

REFERENCE

American Geological Institute. *Books, Maps . . . Geotimes Reprint on the Occasion of the Centennial of the U.S. Geological Survey.* Washington, D.C., American Geological Institute, 1979.

APPENDIX

Information is available for the following international technical assistance and scientific cooperative projects conducted by the Geological Survey in fiscal year 1985.

International Activities by Country

Antarctica	Topographic and satellite image mapping; marine geological and geophysical surveys; mineral resources studies.
Australia	Antarctic mapping; tectonics and resources of south Pacific.
Bolivia	Subvolcanic intrusions related to ash-flow tuff terrains and tin resources.
Brazil	Mineral resources studies; river sediment studies; technology transfer in remote sensing.
Canada	Strategic minerals inventory; sea-floor mineral exploration; borehole geophysics; continental deep seismic reflection; cartographic data exchange; techniques for hydrologic data analysis.
Chile	Volcanic and seismic risk investigations; earthquake studies.
Columbia	Streamflow modeling related to dam operations; training in earthquake risk assessment.
Costa Rica	Geothermal energy consultation; magnetic observatory instrumentation; volcanic studies.
Dominican Republic	Offshore geologic studies; phosphate resource assessment.

Egypt	Mapping of subsurface geologic features by remote sensing; training in map preparation and publication.
El Salvador	Earthquake hazards reduction.
Ethiopia	Training in mineral resources study.
Fiji	Study of coastal sediment distribution.
France	Marine hydrothermal mineralogy; mineral deposit modeling.
Germany	Strategic minerals inventory; marine seismic studies of continental margins; radioactive waste; petroleum resource assessment; Antarctic research; multipurpose cadastral information exchange.
Greece	Geochemistry of petroleum; structural geology studies.
Guatemala	Earthquake hazards reduction.
Haiti	Coal resource investigations.
Hungary	Seismic stratigraphy; seismic modeling; electromagnetic, mineralogic, paleomagnetic, and paleoenvironmental studies.
Iceland	Volcanic, geothermal, and glacial studies.
India	Science and technology review for possible cooperative program development.
Indonesia	Volcano research and hazards mitigation.
Italy	Seismic and volcanic monitoring program.
Japan	Joint panels on earthquake prediction, marine geology, and marine mining; ore deposit research; landslide studies; geodetic leveling.
Jordan	Seismic systems; water resources.
Kenya	Regional remote sensing facility; satellite imagery; map publication.
Liberia	Mineral resources project development.
Mauritania	Mineral and energy resources project development.
Mexico	Surface water resources; volcano studies; geochemical and geophysical exploration; mineral and metallogenic map analyses; regional structure and stratigraphic studies;

	tectonostratigraphic terrain studies; base map compilation of U.S. border area.
Morocco	Landsat satellite base-map compilation; mineral deposit assessments; geophysical investigations.
New Zealand	Antarctic mapping.
Oman	Mineral resources studies.
Pakistan	Coal resources assessment; water sediment transport.
Panama	Earthquake hazards reduction; coal geology program development.
Papua New Guinea	Minerals resources data systems and assessment.
Paraguay	Hydrologic hazards related to floods.
Peru	Mineral resources assessment; flood hazards in Cuzco.
People's Republic of China	Surveying, mapping, and geographic information systems; surface water hydrologic studies; China digital seismic network; Beijing digital seismic network computer system; magnetic and deformation observations; crustal stress measurements; intraplate active faults and earthquakes; fault zone xenoliths; landslide and debris-flow studies; rock mechanics; petroleum geology of carbonate rocks; saline lakes and potash deposits; exploration geochemistry; coal-derived gas; isotope geology.
Philippines	Volcano hazards analysis and mitigation; coal resource assessments.
Qatar	Water resources-artificial recharge of ground water.
Saudi Arabia	Geologic mapping and mineral resource assessment; hydrologic studies; Landsat image base maps; seismic studies; and earth science publications.
South Africa	Strategic minerals inventory; seismic studies.

South Korea..........Offshore petroleum resources and geothermal resources assessments.
Spain...................Ground water resources; remote sensing for mineral deposits; earthquake research; marine geology of continental margins.
Sri Lanka..............Ground water resources assessment.
Sudan..................Landsat satellite base map compilation; map publication.
Sweden................Nuclear waste disposal; subsurface water transport.
Turkey.................Karst geophysics consultancy.
United Kingdom.....Marine geology; world coal resources; strategic minerals inventory.
U.S.S.R................Joint committee on earthquake prediction.
Venezuela.............Hydrology and water resources of Orinoco Basin.
Yugoslavia............Crustal structure research; seismology and earthquake hazards; subsidence research; geochemical surveys; remote sensing; engineering geology; geophysics.

International Activities by Region

Caribbean.............Seismic hazards workshop in Puerto Rico.
Central America.....Workshop on development of minerals, energy, and water resources and mitigation of geologic hazards.
Circum-Pacific.......Earthquake and tsunami potential.
East Asia..............Critique multinational coal information system; consultancies on remote sensing program; U.S. Government representation at U.S. Regional meetings.
East-Southeast Asia....................Base map preparation (1:2 million scale); sedimentary basin analysis; tin geology review.

Latin America.........Earthquake disaster mitigation in Andean region.
Pacific Region.........Circum-Pacific mapping program; chromite resource studies.
Southeast Asia........Earthquake engineering and hazards mitigation; engineering seismology.
South Pacific..........Marine cruise for hydrocarbon resources studies; workshop on coastal processes mapping; cobalt crust studies on Marshall Island seamounts; crater studies in Marshalls; mineral reconnaissance in Palau.

Worldwide Activities

Global seismic network; hydrologic training course; remote sensing training workshop; International Strategic Minerals Inventory; World Energy Resources Program; geologic and hydrologic hazards mitigation training.

A Viewpoint for Successful International Marine Data/Information Transfer

Steven J. Tibbitt

The exchange of marine science and technological information is essential for international cooperative research on ocean phenomena and optimal use of global ocean resources. At the present time nations both developed and developing are turning more and more to ocean research and the exploitation of ocean resources as part of their national effort to further their social and economic development, growth and well-being. The consequence of combined international use of this information will be an increase in the "knowledge base" on the world's oceans; and, greater potential for the optimal use of ocean resources. Thus, exchange *mechanisms* are essential to the use of information and data in bridging of technological gaps between countries and strengthening of developing countries' technological capabilities in the fields of marine science and technology.

As in any other scientific and technical effort, the transfer of technology is a multifaceted operation in the marine sciences as it produces and uses data and information. With respect to the transfer process, there is general acceptance by the international community and its intergovernmental and nongovernmental organizations that the mechanisms for technology transfer should be information systems and advisory services. This acceptance and the existence of a large volume of international and national environmental data/information has created the need to develop a way to increase accessibility and availability of these results from

---

The author is at the National Environmental Satellite, Data and Information Service, U.S. Department of Commerce (N.O.A.A.-N.E.S.D.I.S., Assessment & Information Service Center, N.E.D.R.E.S. Program Office (E-AIX3), 1825 Connecticut Avenue, N.W., Universal Building, Washington, DC 20235.

© 1987 by The Haworth Press, Inc. All rights reserved.

scientific and technological activities. The flow of technological information to serve users of science and technology in the marine environment can only be achieved by establishing a means of pooling data/information available in all countries that have a vested interest in the oceans.

Such a way-and-means has been developed by the Intergovernmental Oceanographic Commission (IOC), a semi-autonomous organization attached to the Science sector of the United Nations Educational, Scientific and Cultural Organization (Unesco). The IOC, through its Working Committee on International Oceanographic Data Exchange (WC/IODE) and specialized groups under it, provides a focal point for the exchange of data/information among its 100-plus Member States.

Although science was the primary reason for its creation in 1960, the IOC has from the beginning fostered and encouraged the establishment of national, international and regional centers to serve as focal points to facilitate accessing, analysis, dissemination and exchange of oceanographic data and information. According to technical guidelines for exchange arrangements, data and information system formats and international coordination of national efforts in ocean science management, the IOC/IODE network of national, international and regional data/information centers can make ocean data and information products and services available to the marine community.

AQUATIC SCIENCES AND FISHERIES INFORMATION SYSTEM (ASFIS)

The interest in ocean research and the utilization of living and nonliving ocean resources for the socioeconomic development of nations, both developed and developing, has caused an enormous need for information in this field of man's endeavors to understand his global environment. As the volume of resulting information grows, so does the problem of providing the data/information specific to the needs of the user community of scientists, administrators, technologists and policy makers.

The Aquatic Sciences and Fisheries Information System (ASFIS) is an international information system for the science, technology and management of marine and freshwater environments. It is an integrated system of information exchange sponsored and coordinated by international organizations through a rational approach to meeting user needs/requirements.

The system was originally developed in the early 1960s by the Food and Agriculture Organization of the United Nations (FAO), and was later joined by IOC and the Ocean Economics and Technology Branch (OETB) of the United Nations. In collaboration with national centers, and with support of the United Nations Environment Program (UNEP), the system has expanded in terms of information covered, services and products offered and number of participating countries and organizations. Today, ASFIS centers in Canada, France, Federal Republic of Germany, Mexico, Norway, Peoples Republic of China, Portugal, the UK, the USA, the USSR and South East Asia Fisheries Development Center (SEAFDEC) participate in ASFIS.

The system collects, organizes and disseminates information about literature data services, institutions and scientists. This modular system is comprised of:

- Aquatic Sciences and Fisheries Abstracts (ASFA)
  a monthly abstracting/indexing service, and bibliographic data base containing over 150,000 abstracts and growing at 25-30,000 per year
- Marine Science Contents Tables (MSCT)
  a monthly current-awareness service
- Freshwater and Aquaculture Contents Tables (FSCT)
  a monthly current-awareness service
- World List of Aquatic Sciences and Fisheries Serial Titles
- International Directory of Marine Scientists

To help users take full advantage of ASFIS services and products, various reference and guides materials have been produced to enhance the systems usefulness and benefits to the user.

MARINE ENVIRONMENTAL DATA INFORMATION REFERRAL SYSTEM (MEDI)

MEDI is a resource tool for national and international monitoring and research activities. The objective of the fully operational referral system is to provide the marine community with referrals concerning the availability, location and characteristics of marine environmental data to meet the community's specific needs within the framework of UNEP's international environmental referral system — INFOterra.

Since the mid-1970s development and implementation of the MEDI Referral System has been achieved with the support and participation of the following international organizations and their associated network of data/information centers:

> Food and Agriculture Organization of the UN (FAO)
> Intergovernmental Oceanographic Commission (IOC)
> International Council for the Exploration of the Seas (ICES)
> International Atomic Energy Agency (IAEA)
> International Hydrographic Organization (IHO)
> World Meteorological Organization (WMO)
> United Nations Environment Program (UNEP)

The MEDI Referral System is an automated, systematic method for recording and retrieving information (non-bibliographic) about marine environmental data files that exist in international centers and in national centers associated with an international network. MEDI is designed as an internationally accepted means of cataloguing such data as may be required by agencies, scientists and administrators. It makes possible the systematic identification of what data are available worldwide on a specific topic.

MEDI services and products include a manually searchable MEDI Referral Catalogue, equivalent in content to the MEDI database, with an index showing details of marine data holdings of all participating centers; on-line computer searches of the MEDI database on request; and, specialized indices for broad subject areas and data types.

MARINE DATA/INFORMATION TRANSFER PROGRAM DEVELOPMENT

From the preceding discussion it is obvious that a well established structure exists for marine data and information exchange.

Also, there is a base of long development experience for systems that meet the requirements of those who depend on data and information in the marine sciences.

What is needed now, and in the future, for marine data and information transfer program activities is a development program policy that sets out a program development plan so projects can have a positive and lasting impact on marine science infrastructures of a developing country or countries. Namely, projects with the elements of training, education and appropriate technical assistance to extend and expand those systems products and services for marine data and information transfer *AND* assist those countries in the development of their own systems for marine information and data management.

Development programs in other areas such as energy, health, agriculture are generally planned and designed to strengthen a country's industrial and technological capabilities for continuous growth and improvement of its socioeconomic well-being. In many instances, concerned or involved foreign aid or development organizations have supported programs to try and solve the problem of technology transfer. However, they have often acted independent of each other and/or on a planning basis of short-term results (e.g., "quick-fix" solutions, political expediency, monies-of-opportunity). Others that know and understand the universality of the transfer issues lack sufficient funds for long-term, comprehensive development programs. Often, the end result is that activities started by short duration projects stop when funds are stopped or nothing happens in the first place.

The design of development programs should be to shape, strengthen and condition a nation's capabilities to operate their own data/information systems for them to be able to manage and utilize ocean resources to and for their own benefit. That is to say, a design goal of a development program should be that a knowledge and use of marine science data and information should be an integrated part of a country's marine infrastructure on completion of the program.

Basic to a program development plan is a coherent marine data and information regime that accommodates national interests and needs with those at the international level. Of the possible alternatives, a regional approach or arrangement may be the best regime when bilateral or global approaches are not appropriate. In fact, many developing countries lack the necessary resources of facilities, equipment and infrastructure required to meet their specific data and information interests. Through group effort and participation in development programs on the bases of linguistics or regional arrangements such as marine geographical regions (e.g., Caribbean Sea), institutional/functional regions (e.g., Indo-Pacific Fisheries Commission) the interests of most developing countries could best be served.

CONCLUSION

As the leading intergovernmental organization in the field of international oceanic research, the IOC with its Working Committee on IODE and specialized groups under it have achieved much in establishing systems and standards for data and information exchange to serve IOC Member States and the international marine science community. Now there is a need for the consolidation of efforts on the part of international and national organizations to accelerate developing countries' participation in systems and services of the IOC to a level equal in measure to the importance these countries attach to the development of their capabilities in the marine sciences. Success in meeting this need and the accommodation of national information and transfer needs of developing countries could best be achieved through sound, long-term planning and an approach based on regional arrangements and/or linguistics.

Scientific/Technical Translations in a Research Library

Ted Crump

A translator of scientific-technical material must be a very versatile animal if he is to survive, perhaps today more than ever before, when some technologies are running five to ten years ahead of their lexicographers. Translation is a vital part of the dissemination of information, and translators are finding that they must learn the skills of information scientists, not only to be able to locate information on both the mundane and arcane, but also to find equivalencies on the other side of the language barrier.

Just as no two translation assignments are exactly alike, neither are there to be found identical linguistic Gemini. Translators come to their profession by sundry paths, and the scientific/technical translator may or may not hold a degree in the science or technology that he is translating at a given moment. A graduate student in Russian literature, this writer entered the world of translation as a staff translator/abstractor (T/A) at Biosciences Information Service (BIOSIS). Such was the entree to biomedicine, which spans a number of disciplines from aerospace biology to zoology, including branches of chemistry, mathematics and physics. The translation abstract is a form that challenges one's ability to glean the gist of variously diffuse and rambling papers, while often allowing the translator to avoid considerable research time by writing around any terms he can't solve. Nevertheless, even this is never just a dictionary exercise, and the

The author is at the National Institutes of Health Library, Bethesda, MD 20205.

© 1987 by The Haworth Press, Inc. All rights reserved.

BIOSIS T/A is required to learn or develop research techniques to perform his job.

In this writer's case, BIOSIS was the springboard to an even greater challenge: translating all the words, abbreviations and odd markings in materials of interest to the National Institutes of Health (NIH) in Russian, German, French and Serbo-Croatian. This is also a staff position, in a library setting. The NIH Library directly supports the research of some 3,000 scientists engaged in biomedical research at the Bethesda, Maryland, campus and elsewhere, and the subject matter of the translations varies enormously. The translator must learn to find information quickly and to streamline his search strategies. A translation diary was part of an attempt, largely self-instructed, to develop more efficient techniques, follow higher probabilities of success and avoid pitfalls. Lois Horowitz, in *Knowing Where to Look: The Ultimate Guide to Research*, approaches this concept.[1] The diary was originally divided into three columns: Problem, Answer, Source/ How Solved. A fourth was recently added: Category.[2]

Has the diary succeeded in making its user a more efficient translator, and has anything been learned that is of use to anyone else? It is dismaying to hear those unfamiliar with translation (including novice translators) express the opinion that all that is needed for translation are a couple of dictionaries, a pencil and yellow pad. The diary, now in its sixth year, mostly contains problems not solved by means of one or more of the 500 dictionaries and other references within arm's reach of the author. Solving these problems involved a visit to the main or reference stacks, use of an appropriate on-line data base, consultation (in person or by telephone) with subject experts or translator colleagues, or some other means. In any given NIH translation, seemingly more so with German than with Russian, there will be at least one word, usually three or four, that will defy discovery in any published lexicography, including the six-volume Duden *Das grosse Wörterbuch der deutschen Sprache*. And these are by no means always technical terms. They may be coinages or neologisms introduced by the author, especially in the case of the Germans, who frequently and freely combine smaller words to make bigger words, or they may be a translation on the author's part of a foreign term not yet established in his own lexicography. An example of both is "Durchzugsmanometrie" in German, literally: "pull-through manometry." An example of the latter is "parovaia prilivnaia mashina" in Russian, literally, "stream-driven tidal engine," in an unpublished research paper on a drive for an artificial heart. Neither of these terms was to be found in this author's dictionaries, glossaries or term cards. The chances of supplying accurate American English equivalents without going beyond dictionaries and linguistic principles were not great. Let's examine how these and other types of problems recorded in the diary were solved.

THE LIBRARY AND THE TRANSLATOR

First of all, this author cannot understand how any sci/tech translator can work outside a library. For one thing, one of the most useful tools for this type of work is the *Science Citation Index (SCI)*, whose paper version takes up at least thirty feet of shelf space, and, of course, is a major investment requiring nearby availability of thousands of scientific journals in order to be maximally effective. Another reason is access to a large variety of on-line data bases. (A colleague at the Midwest Research Institute, who is highly proficient in the use of on-line data bases, found something on 50 of 171 problems in a 49-page section of the diary by this means.)

In the case of "Durchzugsmanometrie," access to *Excerpta Medica* (EMBASE) through DIALOG provided the titles to several German articles with this term or versions of it accompanied by the English translation, sometimes labeled as author's translation. *Excerpta Medica* is produced by Elsevier (Amsterdam), which also publishes paper and microform versions. Some sections go back to 1947, and must be searched by individual parts. EMBASE files reach back to 1974 and now include over 3,500 primary journals from over 100 countries. The English translations provided in its recent files were "pull-through manometry," "perfusion manometry" and "continuous-flow manometry." This suggested that a standard usage for the term had not been established. A search of several years of the *SCI* could not find a title in which any of these phrases was used. To the card catalog: there are four entries under "manometric methods." One of these, *Manometric Biochemical Techniques*, mentions "continuous-flow rotors" as part of the apparatus, and the translator settles on "continuous-flow manometry" as an adequate, if somewhat mushy, solution.

The Russian term defied solution by any of the means thus far mentioned, and it was time to take to the telephone. In his detective work the translator knows that usually the client who requests the translation has some inkling of what it is about. If the client is an NIH scientist, chances are he is an expert on the subject matter of the paper. In this particular case, the unpublished Russian research paper was connected to a working visit by Soviet artificial heart specialists to certain U.S. colleagues. By finding out who the hosts were, the translator was able to contact a Massachusetts scientist who knew all about the "tidal regenerator engine" (TRE) which drives the artificial heart in question.

This type of matching-up of proper equivalents accounts for a large share of the diary entries, and here indexes are invaluable as sources of what Horowitz calls "quick-and-dirty research," although she fails to list them along with directories, almanacs, encyclopedias, general reference books and computerized data bases.[3] Indexes are important to keep in mind, because as the translator decides that he doesn't have the answer within arm's reach and must do research, the first thing he has to decide is whether he should categorize the subject. As the diary proves again and again, it is much more time-efficient not to categorize, but to try to find the end term in a subject index with the widest possible sweep. The *Permuterm Subject Index* of *SCI* is a vast net that catches any reference to a person, place or thing in a title appearing in any of more than 3,200 major journals (although not from its inception; this figure gradually increasing from an initial 613 in 1961), plus a number of monograph chapters. Another quick index is the *Subject Index* section of *Biological Abstracts Semi-Annual Cumulative Index (BA)*. Either one of these can be used quickly without stopping to figure out what discipline the problem term falls under. *SCI* is by far the better, thanks largely to the fact that three cumulations have been published—1965-69, 1970-74, 1975-79—and a fourth, 1980-84 is scheduled to appear this year. *SCI* and *BA* are also on-line, from 1974 to 1969, respectively, if one has easy access to their use. Selectivity comes into play to different degrees in the use of other data bases.

On the other hand, if one thinks in categories he will view the world according to the Library of Congress Subject Classification System, the National Library of Medicine's Medical Subject Heading system, or some other method of working his way along a tree structure to find the relevant twig.

Problem: "svechenie po Fal'ku." (Russian. something according to somebody.) Two elements; first, "svechenie" has several meanings—luminescence, fluorescence, luminosity, brightness, glow, phosphorescence; lighting. Second, what is the proper spelling of the person? *BA* lists a number of significant keywords that appear in an author's title, plus some that are added editorially. These words are positioned by computer in order that words preceding and following index terms appear for additional context. Thus, in Vol. 65 (1978) the following entry appears: AST CELL KUPFFER CELL FALKS FLUORESCENCE METHOD ANTI INF. This search was successful practically in a matter of seconds.

Problem: "Lösungscalorimetrie." (German. Do we say "solution calorimetry"?) Here *SCI* was used, first the *Permuterm Subject Index* for 1970-74. Under "calorimetry" there was a subentry "solution," which listed several authors and their years of publication. The second step was to go to the *Source Index* for the same period of time, which lists according to author's names, gives the full title of the article, the citation and even the address at the time of the author. The title of an *American* author (this is important) began "Solution calorimetry of . . . " Search time less than five minutes.

Thus far we have seen the indexes serve as the first and final stop in the search. The third part of *SCI*, the *Citation Index*, can also serve this function. The scientific/technical translator spends a great deal of time solving eponyms, model numbers and abbreviations and confirming spellings. A common feature in research articles is mention of X's method, as modified by Y. A Russian paper, for example, spoke of obtaining an injection preparation of human leukocytic interferon by use of the method developed by "Kantel" as modified by V. P. Kuznetsov. The problem was to determine correct spelling of the first name. Translators of languages with non-Roman alphabets are familiar with the permutations that names undergo and the problem of trying to come up with the correct original version. Here the 1975-79 *SCI Citation Index* showed that a V. P. Kuznetsov had cited a paper by a K. Cantell; he probably also modified the method. Search time less than five minutes.

The indexes, obviously, also refer the researcher to source materials. In another Russian paper where the original eponym from a Western language had been phonetically rendered into Cyrillic: "indeks Ketle" (somebody's index) it was necessary to search by subject area (this writer does not always disdain the mental effort): measurement of body mass. The 1982 *SCI Subject Index* had an entry "body mass" with subentry "adult" referring to an article in the *American Journal of Epidemiology*, which turned out to contain a reference to the Quetelet index.

When Problems Get Really Thorny

Of course, if all problems were solved as easily as these (even granting a certain measure of correct instinct and relatively good resources), the life of the sci/tech translator would seem pretty cozy. The diary also chronicles long hours of blind alleys and sheer frustration.

For example, abbreviations can be the nightmare of translators, and the Russian authors in particular seem to take delight in inserting them without any expansion. A particular paper said that a high titer of HBsAg (hepatitis B surface antigen)—1:8 —was determined by the VIÈF method. This abbreviation was not to be found in the few reference sources available (by the way, somebody, a Russian-English biomedical abbreviations dictionary is desperately needed!). This translator resorted to a slow, but often effective approach: The article appeared in *Voprosy virusologii*. Abbreviations that appear in particular Soviet journals most likely appear elsewhere in the same journal; the editors seem to assume that their readers know what they mean. Indeed, in this case by paging through previous issues of *Voprosy virusologii* the abbreviation turned up, with its expansion: "vstrechnyi immunoèlektroforez," or "counterimmunoelectrophoresis (CIE)." Then this author suddenly realized that the clue had been in the title of the first article to start with. The moral of the story is to look at the title of the present article for a clue to an abbreviation appearing in it before starting off on the search. Unfortunately, Soviet publications don't believe in subject indexes.

This research paid off, however, by alerting this translator to the use of CIE in identification of antigens in blood, as "Überwanderungselektrophorese" also showed up in a German paper on the HBsAg before finding its way into a technical dictionary.

Here is an eponym that has never been solved, even with the help of colleagues: In a Soviet journal on occupational diseases, *Gigiena Truda i Professional'naia Zabolevaniia* (1976;20(8):45-46), N.S. Dorodnova of the Saratov Medical Institute, in checking menstrual irregularities of female workers occupationally exposed to methyl acrylate in the production of nitron, writes that the results of the "Revuar" test were slightly positive. Given the many possibilities of Russian transliteration, what is the proper spelling of this name in Roman letters? The first place to look for possible variations is James F. Shipp's *Russian-English Dictionary of Surnames*, but unfortunately this had no listing for "Revuar." Suspecting everything from "Revier" to "Revoir," this translator in turn consulted *Gradwohl's Clinical Laboratory Methods and Diagnosis*, the Eliseenkov *Russian-English Medical Dictionary*, *Dorland's Illustrated Medical Dictionary*, the subject index to the *Great Soviet Medical Encyclopedia* (in Russian), the Carpovich *Russian-English Biological and Medical Dictionary*, and the *Russian-English-German Dictionary of Names of Organic Reactions*. Finding nothing in these, he searched the *Psychyrembel Klinisches Wörterbuch* and other German medical dictionaries by Zetkin, Lang, Bunjes, etc., then looked in subject indexes in the backs of textbooks on gynecology, reviewed all possible options in *SCI Index*, the card catalogue, books in the stacks on obstetrics and gynecology, and checked out other translation requests to see if there were any on the same subject. He looked for articles by the same author, searched under "nitron—toxicity—gynecologic," "hormone tests" and "menstrual impairment—occupational" (in paper data bases), asked for a computer search which came up empty, looked for an abstract of this article in *BA*, called the requestor, and pursued the publications of Jean Rivier and C. Rivier, to whom there had been a reference in *Cytochemical Assays* — all in vain.

Hopes were raised, only to be dashed, by the discovery in *Chemical Abstracts Service Source Index (CASSI)* that this Russian journal existed in cover-to-cover translation. *CASSI* itself, however, showed the English version, *Labor Hygiene and Occupational Diseases*, to be owned only by the Canada Institute for Scientific and Technical Information in Ottawa. A check of the microfiche of holdings in the National Library of Medicine, on the other hand, showed the journal to be owned by that institution for 1957-1966. This led the present author to suspect that this was one of the many Russian journals translated for a few years in the 1960s and then discontinued. The eponym remained unsolved. Perhaps a reader will come forth with the answer.

Rosetta Pebbles

Translators should be aware, however, that cover-to-cover translations of several journals exist, or have existed for certain volumes in the past. These can sometimes act as Rosetta stones for terminology that has not found its way into a dictionary. Of course, these are no better than the translators and editors responsible for them, and, as translators tend to be a suspicious lot when it comes to trusting someone else, it comes down to establishing credibility on a journal-to-journal basis. Russian may be the language with the most cover-to-cover translations, many of which the NIH Library owns, e.g., *Biochemistry (Biokhimiia)*, *Biophysics (Biofizika)*, *Cytology and Genetics (Tsitologiia i Genetika)*, just to name a few. For German, there is *Angewandte Chemie* to match up page for page with its International Edition published in English. One should also be aware that many authors publish articles in English, often on the same subjects as the articles in their own languages, and will sometimes mention the same techniques in the methods and materials section, for example. Also, sometimes an author will supervise the publication of bilingual editions of his book. This writer was at a loss as to how he was going to translate a long article in German on the anatomy of a mink until he discovered that Trautmann and Fiebiger's *Lehrbuch der Histologie und vergleichenden mikroskopischen Anatomie der Haustiere* existed in an English edition as well. It was possible to place the books side by side and solve the mink anatomy. One of the great mysteries of the universe is why there doesn't seem to be a decent German-English biology dictionary in existence, let alone one on comparative anatomy! There are many other bilingual editions, as well as numerous sources of terminology, which, unfortunately, wait to be exploited. K. Decker's *Klinische Neuroradiologie* (1960) equals Decker & Shehadi, *Clinical Neuroradiology* (1966); Kugler's *Elektroencephalographie in Klinik und Praxis* has an identical version in English, and so on. An on-line search of just eight years in MEDLINE and SCI under the keywords "glossary," "dictionary" and "terminology" produced hundreds of citations of published word lists and definitions just waiting to be transferred to the translator's card file or diskette. But who has the time to do it?

Against Reinventing the Wheel

Finally, as we saw above, there are a number of published translations that appear on a regular basis and are archived. There are various sources which list cover-to-cover translation journals; they can be picked out of *CASSI, Serial Sources for the BIOSIS Data Base*, and the *American Institute of Physics Translation Manual*, but the best source is *Journals in Translation*, published jointly by the British Lending Division and the International Translations Center in The Netherlands. There are also ongoing efforts to archive and index unpublished translations, and the NIH Library Translation Unit takes considerable pains to stay abreast of these collections and to use them whenever practical. First of all, the Unit maintains a card file of all its own translations, copies of which it stores for three years and deposits in the National Translation Center (NTC) of the John Crerar Library in Chicago. The Unit also maintains a collection of *Translation Register Index*, which the NTC publishes. The NTC is a depository and information source for unpublished translations into English from the world literature of the natural, physical, medical and social sciences. NTC files contain information on approximately 1,000,000 translations, 400,000 of which comprise the NTC translation collection. The *Translation Register Index* is indexed annually, and cumulations are occasionally published. The NTC charges varying rates for a copy of its archived translations, depending on the length and age of the article. Another potential source of translation copies is the Consolidated Translation Service of the Foreign Broadcast Information Service (FBIS). Its file dates from World War II and contains more than 1,000,000 entries. FBIS will search for an article free of charge for an outside government agency. Still another potential source of translations is the National Technical Information Service, which published *Translations from the Scientific Literature* from 1960-1979. This bibliography lists translations produced under Public Law 480 and administered by the National Science Foundation and turned over to the NTIS to sell.

NOTES

1. Horowitz, Lois. *Knowing where to look: The ultimate guide to research*. Cincinnati: Writer's Digest Books, 1984, p. 59.
2. See a further discussion of the diary in Cremmins, Edward. Information retrieval diary of an expert technical translator. *Bulletin of the American society for information science*, 1984, Feb. 10(3), pp. 25-26.
3. Horowitz, op. cit., p. 28.

Indexing and Abstracting Services' Coverage of Soviet English Language Periodicals

Gloria Jacobs

INTRODUCTION

The Soviet Union is a country poorly understood by a majority of Americans and one in which they are interested. How are they to find out about the Soviet Union? They can turn to American publications, but culture creates an internal bias that is difficult to overcome. In addition to providing information on a particular subject, periodicals reveal a great deal about the publishers' perspective. An alternative is to read sources generated from the USSR. In this way, the reader gains not only an impression of what conditions are like, but an idea of what the authorities perceive as truth or wish to convey as such. Reality is subjective and even if the average citizen does not accept the official view, its constant, pervasive existence will color their attitudes and perspectives. Periodicals, rather than monographs, were chosen for review because they more accurately reflect the current perceptions of reality.

Periodicals and the index and abstract services (hereafter referred to collectively as index services) can be conveniently divided into two categories: those in English and those in Russian. For the purpose of this study, the concentration is upon English language materials, as they have the greatest potential audience.

The author may be contacted at 580 Madison Avenue, Albany, NY 12208.

© 1987 by The Haworth Press, Inc. All rights reserved.

METHODOLOGY

A list of sources was obtained from Mezhdunarodnaia Kniga's *Newspapers and Magazines of the USSR for 1986*. (See Appendix A.) (*Moscow News* is the only Soviet newspaper available in English. Since it is geared towards tourists and not the average reader of Soviet news it was omitted.)[1] Their annual list includes all items available for foreign purchase in Russian, the languages of the republics and Western European languages. These titles are also available through serials jobbers (i.e., Faxon and Ebsco) and specialized jobbers of Soviet material (i.e., Victor Kamkin, 12224 Parklawn Drive, Rockville, MD 20852), who maintain contact with Mezhdunarodnaia Kniga, and will provide all titles in their export catalog to libraries. Mezhdunarodnaia Kniga requires payment in rubles whereas the jobbers accept payment in American currency.

Being listed in an export catalog in no way reflects the quality of the item, so the master list of twenty-seven English language magazine titles was looked up in Bill Katz's *Magazines for Libraries* (4th ed.). A selective, evaluative source for magazine purchase, *Magazines for Libraries* is widely used in the field by a variety of libraries. *Ulrich's International Periodicals Directory* (1985) was also checked since both sources are used as awareness guides.

Only those index services likely to be found in a school, public or academic library were included. To obtain a definitive list *Introduction to Reference Work, Vol. 1*, by William A. Katz, was consulted. Services which had appeared after the 1982 copywrite or were deemed worthy of inclusion were added. In all, twenty-seven services were identified, eleven of which are publications of the H.W. Wilson Company. A detailed examination was made of the eight services that included Soviet English language periodicals to determine thoroughness and consistency of indexing.

To obtain a cross section of library holdings the list of periodicals was checked against the OCLC system. OCLC has a larger and more diverse member base than RLIN and will, therefore, give a more representative profile of the types of libraries that have subscriptions. Holdings sources fall into six categories: academic, public, special and school libraries, state union lists and cooperative cataloging ventures.

FINDINGS

Of the twenty-seven magazines included in this study thirty percent (eight titles) are not included in either *Ulrich's* or *Magazines for Libraries*. Of those, seven are held by less than twenty OCLC member libraries. (See Appendix C) and only one title, *Soviet Film,* is covered by an index service. Of the remaining titles thirty-seven percent are listed in both services, forty-eight percent are reviewed by *Magazines for Libraries* and fifty-nine percent are included in *Ulrich's*. Yet only twenty-six percent (seven titles) are covered by any index service.

Since such a limited number of titles are covered by index services it is tempting to be grateful for any coverage. This initial joy, however, should be tempered by caution, for if the index's coverage of Soviet periodicals is not adequate, then its usefulness as an index is severely limited. There is disagreement in the literature as to what constitutes a good index. Masse Bloomfield feels that it is an idealized concept:

> Catalogers and indexers perform their work using Cutter's rules as their guide, and do their work without the absolute knowledge of what constitutes a good subject heading or a good index term. Every indexer and cataloger has an intuitive feeling about what a good index or a good catalog should be. No one has ever been able to define that intuitive feeling into a generalization so that quantitative comparisons can be made between two cataloging systems or two indexes.[2]

Others agree with Jean Simpkin who believes that although there is no such thing as an ideal index, there are certain criteria to be included in the evaluation of a service. These include no inaccuracies, sensible terms which are suitable to the readership and are mutually exclusive, and adequate cross-referencing.[3] A title-by-title list of each index service follows:

ARTS & HUMANITIES CITATION INDEX
Indexes: *Soviet Literature* and *Soviet Film*

FILM LITERATURE INDEX
Indexes: *Soviet Film*

HISTORICAL ABSTRACTS
Indexes: *Social Sciences* and *Far Eastern Affairs*

MLA INTERNATIONAL BIBLIOGRAPHY
Indexes: *Soviet Literature*

MAGAZINE INDEX
Indexes: *Soviet Life*

PAIS
Indexes: *International Affairs* and *New Times*

POLITICAL SCIENCE ABSTRACTS
Indexes: *International Affairs* and *Far Eastern Affairs*

SOCIAL SCIENCE CITATION INDEX
Indexes: *International Affairs*

Index services that provide access to Soviet periodicals are to be congratulated for their efforts. The few that do are, with the exception of *Magazine Index*, specialty indexes. They gear their listings to a specific audience. *AHCI* and *SSCI*'s users are those with a particular need. Only in rare instances do they come to the index to do preliminary searching; usually users conduct known author citation searches. The other index services are geared to a narrow subject area and present an international focus.

Unfortunately, few other services appear to be interested in this area of endeavor. The nation's two largest commercial services, the H.W. Wilson Co. and the Institute for Scientific Information (ISI) contained few, if any, titles. According to Kathleen Rais of ISI's Publication Selection department, "[j]ournals must contain research articles with references in order to be considered appropriate for inclusion in [their] citation indexes."[4] The policy of the H.W. Wilson Co. is as follows:

Selection of periodicals for indexing from [a] list is accomplished by subscriber vote. In voting their preferences subscribers are asked to place primary emphasis on the reference value of the periodical under consideration. They are also asked to give particular consideration to subject balance in order to insure that no important field be overlooked in proportion to overall indexing coverage.[5]

While these periodicals are not of primary reference value, some of them would fill a gap in the subject coverage of a particular H.W. Wilson index. Letters were mailed to the editors of each H.W. Wilson index asking for an explanation and suggesting titles for inclusion in future indexes. There has been no response to these inquiries.

CONCLUSION

The larger the library, the more extensive its periodicals collection tends to be and, therefore it is essential that there be means to access holdings. Of the twenty seven titles listed, academic libraries in all but two instances accounted for over fifty percent of the OCLC holdings. (See Appendix D.) Access is needed to these magazines. If traditional services refuse to pick them up, what are the alternatives? In her article on interdisciplinary subject retrieval, Trudy Garder remarks that "disciplines tend to be isolated from each other in method and theory and also in publications"[6] and "the indexes and abstracts have followed along in becoming discipline specific."[7] Soviet studies is not a single discipline, therefore index services which are discipline specific are useless to the patron seeking information on an aspect of Soviet life. An alternative approach is needed.

If the existing subject indexes will not include more esoteric periodicals (esoteric by virtue of being foreign language publications) then either area studies indexes need to expand their coverage or new indexes are needed to fill this gap. The *American Bibliography of Soviet and East European Studies* (ABSEES) and its European counterpart the *European Bibliography of Soviet and East European Studies* (EBSEES) do an excellent job maintaining bibliographic control of publications generated within their geographic specifications. *ABSEES* "seeks to present as complete a record as possible of U.S. and Canadian publications in Slavic and East European studies"[8] and *EBSEES* strives for the same coverage of Western European publications. Inclusion of Soviet periodicals is beyond their stated scope. If coverage is to be gained, short of convincing the major services to change their editorial policy, new indexes must be created. Although there does not appear to be a major untapped market, there are enough libraries subscribing to Soviet periodicals that there is the need for such an index service.

REFERENCES

Bloomfield, Masse. "Evaluation of indexing." *Special Libraries*, 61, pp. 429-32, October 1970.

Gardner, Trudy & Goodyear, Mary Lou. "The inadequacy of interdisciplinary subject retrieval." *Special Libraries*, 68, pp. 193-7, May/June 1977.

Katz, Bill & Katz, Linda Sternberg. *Magazines for libraries*, 4th ed. N.Y.: Bowker, 1982.

Katz, William A. *Introduction to reference work, vol. 1.* N.Y.: McGraw-Hill, 1982.

Simpkin, Jean. "Assessing indexing." *Indexer*, 14(3), pp. 179-80, April 1980.

Ulrich's international periodicals directory. N.Y.: Bowker, 1985.

NOTES

1. As of this writing an American full text English language translation of *Pravda* had just become available but was not indexed in the standard sources.

2. Bloomfield, Masse. "Evaluation of indexing." *Special Libraries*, 61, pp. 429-32, October 1970.

3. Simpkin, Jean. "Assessing indexing." *Indexer*, 14(3), pp. 179-80, April, 1985.

4. Letter from Kathleen Rais of ISI dated April 10, 1986.

5. Preface of the H.W. Wilson Co. indexes.

6. Gardner, Trudy and Goodyear, Mary Lou. "The inadequacy of interdisciplinary subject retrieval." *Special Libraries*, 68, pp. 193-7, May/June 1977.

7. Ibid.

8. Preface of the American Association for the Advancement of Slavic Studies' *American Bibliography of Soviet and East European Studies.*

APPENDIX A

LIST OF JOURNALS CONSULTED

Asia and Africa Today
Books and Art in the USSR
Culture and Life
Far Eastern Affairs
Foreign Trade
International Affairs
Journal of the Moscow Patriarchate
Misha
Muslims of the Soviet East
New Times
Olympic Panorama
Science in the USSR
Social Sciences
Socialism: Principles, Practice, Prospects
Socialism: Theory and Practice
Soviet Film
Soviet Finnougrovedenie
Soviet Life
Soviet Literature
Soviet Military Review
Soviet Theatre
Soviet Union
Soviet Woman
Sport in the USSR
Sputnik
Travel to the USSR
Twentieth Century and Peace

APPENDIX B

Journal Title	In Ulrich's	In Magazines for Libraries
Asia and Africa Today	No	No
Book and Art in the USSR	No	No
Culture and Life	Yes	HS, GA, AC
Far Eastern Affairs	Yes	No
Foreign Trade	Yes	No
International Affairs	No	GA, AC
J. of the Moscow Patriarchate	Yes	No
Misha	No	No
Muslims of the Soviet East	No	No
New Times	Yes	HS, GA, AC
Olympic Panorama	No	No
Science in the USSR	No	No
Social Sciences	Yes	AC
Socialism: Principles . . .	No	No
Socialism: Theory and Practice	Yes	GA, AC
Soviet Film	No	No
Soviet Finnougrovedenie	Yes	No
Soviet Life	Yes	HS, GA
Soviet Literature	Yes	GA, AC
Soviet Military Review	Yes	No
Soviet Theatre	No	GA, AC
Soviet Union	Yes	HS, GA, Ac
Soviet Woman	Yes	GA, AC
Sport in the USSR	Yes	Ejh, HS, GA
Sputnik	Yes	HS, GA, AC
Travel to the USSR	No	HS, GA
Twentieth Century and Peace	Yes	No

AFRICA

Resources for the Study of Africa and the Middle East: An Overview

Julian W. Witherell

Reference librarians, who must often respond to queries relating to foreign countries and civilizations, may sometimes be unaware of the rich library resources available for consultation both locally and nationally. Foreign language and foreign area-related works have been an integral part of library collections from the very beginning, but they have been developed with special intensity during the post-World War II period. It is the purpose of this paper to provide an overview of one specific area of this development—resources collected by American libraries to support the study of Africa and the Middle East. From New England to California, a number of academic libraries, augmented by the Library of Congress and New York Public Library, offer a wide range of

---

The author is Chief, African and Middle Eastern Division, The Library of Congress, Washington, DC 20540.

© 1987 by The Haworth Press, Inc. All rights reserved.

retrospective and current documentation on this vital world area. These institutions have also been at the forefront in compiling bibliographic tools to assist users in identifying and locating sometimes elusive information. The paper will focus briefly on how these resources have come into being, where they are located, and how they are bibliographically controlled, so that they are accessible through the normal reference process.

African and Middle Eastern studies, and the library resources supporting them, encompass a vast area of some 70 countries and regions, from South Africa to Soviet Central Asia and from Morocco to Afghanistan. An area of great cultural and linguistic diversity, it has long been a focal point of research on the roots of civilization and the rise of major world religions—Judaism, Christianity, and Islam. Since World War II, and especially in the past 25 years, it has also attracted attention as a pivotal point in international political and economic relations.

Current American library resources reflect both the historical evolution and the structure of academic research on Africa and the Middle East. Before its emergence as a dynamic force on the world scene during and after World War II, only a handful of libraries had a tradition of acquiring materials from or about this area. American interest in Biblical studies, archaeology, and related disciplines in the 19th and early 20th centuries stimulated the development of significant collections on parts of the Middle East in a few academic and other research libraries. For example, strong holdings of Judaica—materials in Hebrew, Yiddish, and other languages relating to Jews and Judaism—were found in the Jewish Theological Seminary of America, Columbia University, New York Public Library, Harvard University, the Library of Congress, and Hebrew Union College, Cincinnati.[1]

For the African continent and the Middle East in general, library resources were limited primarily to works in European languages relating to anthropology, history, description and travel, and missionary activities. Largely as a result of donations, a few libraries possessed special, sometimes unique collections of specific regions; examples are the Library of Congress' holdings of American Colonization Society records relating to the establishment of Liberia, Africana resources at Harvard University and within the Moorland-Spingarn Collection of Howard University and the Collection of Negro Literature and History (later the Schomburg Center for Research in Black Culture) of the New York Public Library, and documentation on the Ottoman Empire in both the Library of Congress and the Hoover Institution.[2]

With the emergence of the United States as a global power during and after World War II, first the Middle East and later sub-Saharan Africa became focal points of American academic, government, and commercial interest. The growing demand for resource materials on these areas led the Library of Congress and a number of major academic libraries to hire specialists with backgrounds in the languages and cultures of these regions. They were charged with the responsibility of initiating acquisition programs and providing bibliographic controls in order to meet the needs of researchers. As early as 1945, the Library of Congress had both a Hebraic Section and a Near East Section in its Orientalia Division. Fifteen years later, in 1960, it established an African Section in recognition of the emergence of sub-Saharan Africa on the world scene. In this same period, other major research institutions created specialized units or collections within their libraries, such as the Africana centers at Northwestern University (1948) and Boston University (1953) and the Middle East and North African collection in the Hoover Institution (1948). The ranks of major Judaica libraries were considerably augmented by a number of specialized research collections such as those of the YIVO Institute for Jewish Research and the Leo Baeck Institute, both in New York.

AREA COLLECTIONS

The rapid growth of area collections in the 1960s and 1970s brought American libraries to the forefront of research facilities on Africa and the Middle East. Major collections became not only national resources but also attracted scholars from this area who often found these American holdings to have a wider range and a greater depth of coverage than was available in libraries in their homelands. Collection development during these years received a vital stimulus from U.S. Government-sponsored programs aimed at increasing the nation's resources on this emerging area. After 1958, when the National Defense Education Act was passed, the U.S. Office of Education became an important funding sources for the major programs. Title VI of the Act provided for financial support for graduate students to study "uncommonly taught" languages and for the development of area studies centers and relevant library and resource materials.[3] With growth came a rising demand for specialized and often elusive resources. In their efforts to develop the kinds of collections required by researchers, librarians at these centers were forced to overcome a myriad of problems common to many African and Middle Eastern countries—no organized book trade, lack of comprehensive, current national bibliographies, and small press runs as a result of acute shortages of paper.

To alleviate these difficulties, Government-sponsored programs were established in both the Middle East and Eastern Africa under which the Library of Congress assumed responsibility for on-the-spot acquisitions and for bibliographic control of local research materials. Through its Cairo, Egypt field office, in operation since 1962, the Library has provided major American centers of Middle Eastern studies with a wide range of books, periodicals, government documents and pamphlets primarily from the Arab world. A similar program in operation in Tel Aviv, Israel during the period 1964-73 supplied some 25 American research libraries with Israeli imprints. Available documents from Afghanistan and Iran have been acquired through the Library's field offices in Karachi, Pakistan, and New Delhi, India. For the past 20 years, L.C.'s Nairobi, Kenya field office has been the mainstay in its efforts to build comprehensive holdings on Eastern Africa and has also in recent years supplied materials to New York Public Library and Yale University. Accessions lists prepared regularly by these offices are widely distributed to area studies librarians in the United States and abroad and are generally regarded as being the most complete, current bibliographic guides on their respective areas of coverage.

Through a wide variety of channels, African and Middle Eastern specialists in major American libraries have succeeded in the past quarter century in developing the kinds of collections needed to support in-depth, postgraduate-level research. Statistically, these collections may appear small compared to those relating to other world regions. In making comparisons, however, one must consider that only about 2.5% of the world's book production comes from Africa and the Middle East according to the latest available UNESCO estimates (1982).[4]

Accurate, up-to-date statistics on the size of collections are difficult to obtain and must be viewed with caution as the totals given for particular holdings often do not include uncataloged ephemera or non-book materials. Figures for Title VI center libraries for the academic year 1981-82 indicate that the median number of volumes for 10 sub-Saharan collections was 73,000 with a range of 45,000 to 200,000. Only a small fraction of holdings, averaging less than 5%, were titles in the indigenous languages of Africa.[5] Based on recent reports (1983-85), the major academic collections of Africana, all with more than 50,000 volumes, are at Boston, Indiana, Michigan State, Northwestern, and Yale universities, the Hoover Institution, U.C.L.A., and the universities of Illinois and Wisconsin.[6] For 13 Middle Eastern centers funded under Title VI in 1981-82, the figures indicate 162,000 as the median number of volumes, with a range of 67,000 to 300,000. As would be expected for a region in which publishing is primarily in vernaculars (e.g., Arabic, Persian, Turkish), about half to two-thirds of these collections were in non-European languages.[7] Surprisingly, little recent data is available on the size of individual Middle Eastern collections. A report issued in 1974 notes that the largest holdings on the Middle East, all with more than 60,000 volumes excluding material in Hebrew, were at Harvard, Princeton, and Columbia universities, the Hoover Institution, and the universities of Michigan and Utah.[8] The 1974-75 volume of the *American Jewish Year Book* indicates that the largest Judaica collections in academic and research institutions and at rabbinical seminaries, all with more than 75,000 volumes, were those of the Hebrew Union College, Jewish Theological Seminary, YIVO Institute, Harvard and Brandeis universities, and U.C.L.A.; New York Public Library's Jewish Division was listed as including 135,000 items.[9]

As it is an axiom in a university library's collection development that emphasis is placed on fields of research of greatest interest to the institution's faculty, statistics on academic publishing may suggest special strengths in these holdings. During the period 1976-81, scholarly publications on Africa by the staffs of Title VI centers focused on political science, anthropology and sociology, economics, linguistics, and history. For the Middle East in this same period, faculty members in Title VI-funded programs published mainly in the fields of anthropology and sociology, religion and philosophy, linguistics, literature, art, history, and political science.[10]

WIDE COVERAGE

The Library of Congress, as the de facto national library and the nation's preeminent research center for the Federal Government, offers probably the greatest range of materials on Africa and the Middle East of any American institution. Works in its general collections cover fields from anthropology to zoology, and these titles are complemented by a wealth of non-book materials in special holdings—maps, photographs, films, and recordings. As Africana, with special strengths in economics, history, linguistics, and literature, is dispersed by subject throughout the Library's collections, it is impossible to give even an approximate estimate of the total size of holdings. The largest single block of material is the collection of surveys, yearbooks, histories and general descriptive works (DT classification) comprising some 34,000 titles by shelflist count.[11] The major focal points of its rich and varied Middle Eastern holdings are the African and Middle Eastern Division's Hebraic and Near East sections which together have custody of more than a quarter million volumes in the languages of the region, primarily Arabic, Hebrew, Yiddish, Persian, Turkish, and Armenian, with strong holdings in other cognates such as Amharic, Aramaic, and Pushto. An additional 48,000 volumes in both vernacular and western languages are maintained by the Library's Near Eastern and African Law Division. Descriptive accounts of these collections, together with information on other library resources in and around the nation's capital, are found in the African studies and Middle East studies volumes of the "Scholars' Guide" series issued by the Woodrow Wilson International Center for Scholars.[12]

With its national responsibilities for acquisitions and cataloging, the Library of Congress plays a leading role in providing bibliographic controls over materials from the Middle East and Africa. For many years its Hebraic and Near East sections have maintained union catalogs of materials in the major languages of the Middle East to complement the *National Union Catalog* and *Register of Additional Locations* which record titles in western languages or in romanized form. Hebrew and Yiddish author-subject catalogs in the Hebraic Section total more than 750,000 cards representing the holdings of some 50 libraries. A special project in the Near East Section has as its goal the cataloging and inputting into an automated data base of some 164,000 card reports prepared by those American and Canadian libraries which catalog books and periodicals in Arabic, Persian. Pushto, and Turkish. A *Near East National Union List*, a book catalog of the edited citations covering imprints to 1978, is now in preparation. The African Section's unique file of citations to periodical articles has been reproduced in book form as *Africa South of the Sahara: Index to Periodical Literature* with supplements covering titles published through 1977.

For 26 years, the African Section has been recognized by researchers for its comprehensive and selective guides on a wide range of topics, from studies on the official publications of African nations and on U.S. Government documents concerning Africa to works on Islam south of the Sahara. In recent years, its program has been expanded to include topical guides in two series, "Maktaba Afrikana" and "African Directions," covering such subjects as Liberia (1971-80) and Abuja, the new Nigerian federal capital. It has also initiated projects designed to make maximum use of available computer facilities and data bases in order to improve bibliographic access to the Library's collections. Among these is a compilation utilizing L.C.'s MARC (Machine-Readable Cataloging) files to identify recent U.S. imprints on Africa.[13] The Near East Section has expanded its own bibliographic program to include a "Near East" and a"Mideast Directions" series covering such topics as Arab petroleum and U.S.-Iranian relations (1979-81).[14]

OTHER CENTERS

Other major centers have also been active in improving bibliographic coverage of their own resources. Reproductions of card catalogs to their large and often unique collections on Africa and the Middle East have been made available to researchers in book form in most cases through G. K. Hall and Company, Boston. Examples of these compilations are the catalogs of Arabic collections of Harvard University (second edition, 1983) and the University of Utah (1968+), that of the Klau Library of Hebrew Union College—Jewish Institute of Religion (1964), the Jewish collection of New York Public Library (1960; first supplement, 1975) and the Hebrew books of Harvard University (1968; supplement, 1972). For sub-Saharan Africa, there are the catalogs of the Herskovits Library, Northwestern University (1972; first supplement, 1978), Schomburg Collection, New York Public Library (1962, with supplements of 1967, 1972, and 1974), and African government documents of Boston University (third edition, 1976).[15] Since 1962, the bimonthly *Joint Acquisitions List of Africana (JALA)*, issued by Northwestern, has included selected new Africana titles acquired by some 20 libraries.

The *JALA* list is just one example of cooperative efforts among area librarians to develop resources and improve bibliographic coverage on Africa and the Middle East. For almost 30 years, Africana librarians have been at the forefront of interlibrary cooperation as a result of their early recognition that no one American library had the staff or the financial resources to collect comprehensively from all of sub-Saharan Africa. Through the African Studies Association's Archives-Libraries Committee, established in 1957, they have developed highly successful programs relating to acquisitions, bibliographic compilation, cataloging and classification. With the committee's encouragement, a project is under way to share responsibility for acquiring and reporting to *JALA* elusive documents from several small African countries (e.g., Benin, Cape Verde, Togo). Its efforts have also resulted in a joint acquisitions program, the Cooperative Africana Microform Project (CAMP), established in 1963 and administered through the Center for Research Libraries, Chicago. Upon recommendation of its members, CAMP films original materials and purchases commercial microfilm. Selected scarce and often expensive items are thus made available to libraries that might not as individual institutions have access to all of them. A 641-page *CAMP Catalog: 1985 Cumulative Edition* indicates the wealth of material available through this cooperative resource.[16] Librarians in Judaic and Middle Eastern programs also promote exchange of information and encourage cooperative programs through their several organizations, the Association of Jewish Libraries (established in 1965). Council on Archives and Research Libraries in Jewish Studies (1972), and the Middle East Librarians Association (1972).

Collectively, the major research libraries of the United States hold preeminent resources on Africa and the Middle East. Access to these riches by librarians and scholars throughout the country has improved dramatically in recent years in part through the development of two nationwide computerized bibliographic networks—RLIN, the data base of the Research Libraries Group (RLG), and OCLC (Online Computer Library Center). By means of interlibrary loan, photoduplication facilities and microform, materials can be made available to researchers wherever they are located. Title VI centers have the special responsibility of sharing resources with other institutions through "outreach programs" which include preparing bibliographies and curricula guides, holding teacher workshops, and hosting conference and film/slide presentations. "Outreach" may also be extended to nearly small colleges and universities by providing access to library facilities and sharing resources, including slides, films, and classroom speakers.[17]

Through these various channels, the wealth of Africana and Middle Eastern materials in major American libraries has become a true national resource, ready for exploitation in depth, in particular by trained reference librarians and area specialists. Such specialists typically have been exposed to a multidisciplinary approach to the civilization and culture of a country or region, with competence in one or more of the languages used in publishing in the area. They are thus able to interact fully with the scholarly clienteles which they serve, making readily accessible the vast resources accumulated for the study of the world beyond our shores.

NOTES

1. Berlin, Charles. "Library resources for Jewish studies in the United States." *American Jewish Year Book*, v. 75, 1974-75, pp. 3

2. Gray, Beverly. "Africana library resources." *Ethnic collections in libraries*, E. J. Josey and Marva L. DeLoach (eds.). New York, Neal-Schuman Publishers, Inc. [c1983], p. 247; and Jajko, Edward. "The Middle East and North African collections." *The Library of the Hoover Institution on war, revolution and peace*, Peter Duignan (ed.), foreword by W. Glenn Campbell. Stanford, Calif.: Hoover Institution, 1985, p. 92.

3. Schmidt, Nancy J. "African studies in the United States." *African Research & Documentation*, no. 38, 1985, p. 4. In the 1985-86 academic year, Title VI "National Resource Centers" are the following universities—for Africa: Boston, U.C.L.A., Florida, Illinois, Indiana, Michigan State, Northwestern, Stanford (with California-Berkeley), Wisconsin, and Yale; for the Middle East: Arizona, California-Berkeley, U.C.L.A., Chicago, Columbia, Harvard, Michigan, N.Y.U. (with Princeton), Pennsylvania, Texas, Utah, and Washington.

4. United States Educational, Scientific and Cultural Organization. *Statistical Yearbook, 1984*. [Paris] UNESCO, 1984, VI-3. Additional data is available in the Asia (v. 3, 1981) and Africa (v. 4, 1984) volumes of *The book trade of the world*. Munich: K. G. Saur.

5. Lambert, Richard I. *Beyond growth: The next stage in language and area studies*. Washington: Association of American Universities, 1984, p. 238.

6. Gray. "Africana Library Resources," pp. 253-269; and Fung, Karen, "The African collection." *Library of the Hoover Institution*, p. 79.

7. Lambert. *Beyond growth*, p. 238.

8. Partington, David H. *Arabic library collections: A study of the P.L. 480 program by the committee on the Middle East*. Washington: Association of Research Libraries, 1974, p. 7; issued as an offprint of *Foreign Acquisitions Newsletter*, Fall 1974.

9. Berlin. "Library Resources," pp. 29-34.

10. Lambert. *Beyond Growth*, p. 330. For background data on area studies programs and collections, the following guides are of value: *Directory of African and Afro-American studies in the United States*, compiled by Mitsue Frey and Michael Sims. Waltham, Mass: African Studies Association [c1976], 329 pp. Duffy, David and Jacobs, Barbara. *Directory of Third World Studies in the United States*. Waltham, Mass.: Crossroads Press, [c1981] 463 p. Fishman, Samuel Z., and Saypol, Judyth R. *Jewish studies at American and Canadian universities: An academic catalog*. Washington. Published by the B'nai B'rith Hillel Foundation and the Association for Jewish Studies [c1979], 135 p. Gosebrink, Jean M. *African studies information resources directory* (in press); *Graduate and undergraduate programs and courses in Middle East studies in the United States, Canada, and abroad*. Tucson: Middle East Studies Association of North America, 1985, 235 pp. *Research Centers Directory*, 10th ed., 1986. Detroit: Gale Research Co., c1985, 2 v. and *World register of university studies of Jewish civilizations: Inventory of holdings*, Mervin F. Verbit (ed.). New York: Markus Wiener Publishing, Inc., [c1985+], v. 1+.

11. Gray. "Africana Library Resources," p. 258.

12. Bhatt, Purnima M. *Scholars' guide to Washington, D.C. for African studies*. Washington: Smithsonian Institution Press, 1980, 347 p.; and Dorr, Steven R. *Scholars' guide to Washington, D.C. for Middle Eastern studies*. Washington: Smithsonian Institution Press, 1981, 540 p.

13. Zellers, Joanne M. "Directions for the future: The library of congress." *African*

studies: Papers presented at a colloquium at the British library 7-9 January 1985. Ilse Sternberg and Patricia M. Larby (eds.). London: British Library, 1986, pp. 289-298.

14. Recent L.C. publications are cited in a brochure, "The African section in the Library of Congress" and in a list, "Library of Congress Publications on the Middle East, 1978-1985." A limited number of copies of each is available on request from the African and Middle Eastern Division, Library of Congress, Washington, D.C. 20540. "The Hebraic section of the library of congress: Collections, catalogs, services," by Peggy Pearlstein, is scheduled to appear in a forthcoming issue of *Judaica Librarianship.*

15. Full citations to these guides are as follows: Harvard University. *Catalog of the Arabic collection,* Fawzi Abdulrazak (ed.), 3d ed. Boston: G. K. Hall, 1983, 6 v. Utah. University. Middle East Library. *Arabic collection, Aziz S. Atiya library for Middle East studies.* Salt Lake City: University of Utah Press, 1968, 841 p., and supplement (1971+). Hebrew Union College-Jewish Institute of Religion. *Dictionary catalog of the Klau library, Cincinnati.* Boston: G. K. Hall, 1964, 32 v. New York Public Library. *Dictionary catalog of the Jewish collection.* Boston: G. K. Hall, 1960, 14 v. and *First supplement.* Boston: G. K. Hall, 1975. 8 v. Harvard University. Library. *Catalog of Hebrew books.* Cambridge, Mass.: Harvard University Library, 1968, 6 v., and *Supplement 1.* Cambridge, Mass: Harvard University Library, 1972, 3 v. Melville J. Herskovits Library of African Studies. *Catalog of the Melville J. Herskovits library of African studies, Northwestern University library (Evanston, Illinois) and Africana in selected libraries.* Boston: G. K. Hall, 1972, 8 v., and *First supplement.* Boston: G. K. Hall, 1978, 6 v. Schomburg Collection of Negro Literature and History. *Dictionary catalog.* Boston, G. K. Hall, 1962, 8 v.; and supplements of 1967, 1972, and 1974 (1974 supplement cataloged under Schomburg Center for Research in Black Culture). Boston University. Library. *Catalog of African government documents,* 3d ed., rev. and enl. Boston: G. K. Hall, 1976, 679 p.

16. Gray. "Africana Library Resources," p. 252; *CAMP Catalog: 1985 Cumulative Edition.* Chicago, Cooperative Africana Microform Project and Center for Research Libraries 1985?, 641 p. Easterbrook, David L. "International library and archival cooperation: America." *African studies,* pp. 153-160. Boylan, Ray. "Directions for the future: The cooperative Africana microform project." *African Studies,* pp. 299-303. *ASA News,* issued quarterly by the African Studies Association, regularly features lists of recent doctoral dissertations and sometimes has special bibliographical articles; the Jan./Mar. 1986 issue, for example, includes a "Checklist for Updating Holdings on Africa in Community College Libraries," by Nancy J. Schmidt.

17. Schmidt. "African Studies," p. 5.

AUSTRALIA

On-Line Information Services in Australia

Howard Coxon

If we start by looking at library-based information systems it is not because they are considered the most important (I shall return to this) but because they may be the first point of reference for most readers.

Australian Bibliographic Network (ABN) was established in 1981. Based on the Washington Library Network (WLN) system it comprises a large data base of machine-readable cataloguing records supplied in particular by the Library of Congress, British National Bibliography and the National Library of Australia. As a cooperative system it also includes records created by participating libraries. The records essentially cover book materials and some serials with only a very small component of non-book materials. The system has grown rapidly. From the six original full members there are now 95 participants. In addition there are 228

Mr. Coxon is Parliamentary Librarian, South Australia Parliament, Box 572, GPO, Adelaide, South Australia 5001.

dial-up users, mainly small libraries.[1] The system is cataloguer-driven and as result the inquiry features of ABN are weak: subject approaches in particular tend to be reliant on LC subject headings; the system has too low a threshold to achieve adequate retrieval on either subjects or words from titles. ABN has simply automated traditional cataloguing methods rather than using the greater flexibility for searching which computer-based systems provide. The co-operative nature of the system has lead to the delegation of authority work to participants adding a considerable burden to their workload. The result of this has been for some libraries to elect not to add some held material to the national data base. This may be fugitive material which is not otherwise recorded and remains "lost" to inquirers.

A further ground for criticism is the cost of ABN. The more recent annual reports of the National Library have consistently indicated the drain on resources which ABN represents at the expense of other programmes and priorities. The National Library has seen ABN as a flagship and the decision to continue with it despite the failure to obtain any additional funding can be legitimately criticised. The lack of real management of the enterprise has been symptomatic of library-based information systems in Australia and is a topic to which I will return. Whether or not the availability of a pool of cataloguing records has really improved the efficiency of cataloguing departments must remain a moot point when there is so little evidence to go on. The weak information retrieval aspects of the system have certainly not improved accessibility for the user.

On the credit side it must nevertheless be said that ABN has already proved useful for interlibrary loans and certainly has the potential for creating a truly efficient national system in this particular area. An interlibrary loans module is a possible addition in the future.

Many libraries are independently automating their own catalogues which may then become available for on-line access to dial-up users. Again these local developments, whether in-house or turnkey systems, have been dominated by cataloguers with the potential offered by technology lost by simply automating manual processes. For instance the requirement in author searches to match the author's name to the form of name in the data base in order to achieve a direct hit. Such systems are designed back-to-front. They fix existing practices and neglect to determine how the end-users actually conduct searches. At least some offer the opportunity to monitor catalogue use which may pave the way for more services input in future retrieval options.

TWO SYSTEMS

Two major systems are linked into ABN. CAVAL (Co-operative Action by Victorian Academic Libraries) is a local network in the State of Victoria. CAVAL encourages cooperation in a number of areas but its principal significance has been the creation of a regional data base and on-line catalogue. Established as a limited company with chief librarians as the principal directors CAVAL joined ABN in 1982. In large degree CAVAL was the facilitator of the transition from local shared cataloguing to full participation in ABN. But the creation of a regional data base and data access system to complement the services available from ABN continued to provide CAVAL with an independent role. Other systems of a similar kind include the Office of Library Co-operation in New South Wales and CLANN (College Libraries Activities Network) also in New South Wales.

The other major network which spans the country is CSIRONET. The Commonwealth Scientific and Industrial Research Organisation (CSIRO) is a government agency undertaking applied scientific research and is organised on decentralised basis with specialised institutes established in different centres around the country. CSIRONET is based on the organisation's Division of Computing Research facilities. Whilst providing bureau services it also provides a range of data bases, scientific, factual and bibliographic. CSIRONET was established as an autonomous unit only in 1984 providing service to appropriate external users as well as to users inside CSIRO itself and operating on a cost recovery basis. CSIRONET was recently connected to ABN. Even more recently the unit has established CSIRO Australis a new on-line information retrieval service. The system uses STAIRS software and includes CSIRO data bases, including an on-line version of the CSIRO Index, Australian data bases and some international data bases. The CSIRO Library catalogue is not at present available. The system has the potential for providing access to the results of the most significant Australian scientific research as well as identifying relevant researchers, research centres and research programmes.

MEDLINE has a rather more specialised clientele and is based on an arrangement between the National Library and the Commonwealth Department of Health and is the most long standing of the systems to be discussed here, being established in 1969 and becoming available on-line in 1976. The system makes available the medical information service MEDLARS, the machine-readable equivalent of Index Medicus, and some other health related files. Thus tapes obtained from the U.S. National Library of Medicine are loaded onto a national computer facility. For many years MEDLINE was provided as a "free" service to a community, the medical profession, which was coming under heavy public criticism for appearing to be more interested in making money than in providing a health care service. When a pricing structure was introduced in 1982 it did not attempt to reflect the real costs of providing the service which remained heavily subsidised. MEDLINE also has a message sending facility which is used for transmitting interlibrary loan requests.

The history of AUSINET is perhaps more instructive since it reflects well the changing history of approaches to providing online services in Australia and the recurring problems of proper management, both financial and otherwise. AUSINET was established in 1977 as a consortium between essentially Monash University Library in Victoria and the National Library of Australia. The original plans for AUSINET were to mount within Australia data bases like ERIC and CHEMABS in the same way MEDLINE mounted MEDLARS. The National Library supplied in machine-readable form the Australian National Bibliography and the Australian Public Affairs Information Service, an index to current affairs. The system was mounted by Australian Consolidated Industries (ACI) Ltd who entered into the consortium. In 1981 ACI announced its intention to assume proprietor status with regard to AUSINET a step which was taken "because an independent user co-operative has not emerged to fulfil a management role for AUSINET."[2] Accordingly ACI considered it necessary in the circumstances "to take steps to fill this management gap." From that date most overseas data bases ceased to be available through AUSINET.

More Data Bases

Over the last few years an increasing number of Australian data bases have been on the system which has expanded to prove itself a useful and viable commercial service. Data bases available now number 45 and include numeric data bases and full-text data bases as well as bibliographic data bases. A further restructuring took place in 1985. From that date two levels of service have been provided: the AUSINET Information Service which maintains access at a basic level for the low volume user with traditional research needs; requiring a low level of support and access only to the Australian text files: and the AUSINET Executive Information Service which provides a substantially higher level of support and advice and offers a wider range of information, including access to overseas business data bases. The division into two services has also resulted in a two tier pricing structure.

The increasingly commercial slant of AUSINET has been paralleled by the burgeoning of wholly commercial systems in the last few years. CLIRS for instance is an on-line system carrying legal information. Developed by Computerpower Ltd a subsidiary of Rupert Murdoch's News Ltd CLIRS recently was floated as a public company. The system includes the Commonwealth Attorney-General's data base of Commonwealth Statute, SCALE, and extended coverage to include also Victorian and New South Wales statute as well as a wide range of other materials especially relevant to lawyers including law reports mainly but also court lists and files of business and company names. As time goes on the legislation of other jurisdictions will be added to the service.

There is even some overcrowding in the business market. AUSINET includes STATEX in its Executive Service, being financial and share price information collected from the Sydney Stock Exchange. Money Watch is a service promoted by the media conglomerate John Fairfax and Sons, publishers of the Sydney Morning Herald: Australian Associated Press (AAP) has its Corporate Report and Elders' Farm Link. Agricultural information was the original commodity of AgriData now renamed Information Express and emphasizing a wider range of business and financial interests with its ShareTrack service. Information Express also includes general news and weather information. AAP has a range of information services available based on its extensive news gathering service and Newscan has been made available to federal parliamentarians through the Commonwealth Parliamentary Library. One development it remains to mention is VIATEL, Telecom Australia's videotex system which has been installed in some public libraries. Similar to the British PRESTEL and Canadian TELEDON systems VIATEL aims to provide a very wide range of information which can be readily accessed by the general user.

Overseas Databases

There is little point in enumerating the wide range and large number of overseas data bases accessed by Australian libraries. The giant DIALOG marched powerfully into Australia in the mid-1970s and created a new environment with which many are still only coming to grips. ORBIT was marketed less successfully but with BRS soon established a significant foothold. More recently European carriers have made a push and ESA and Pergamon-INFOLINE each have their customers. Aggressive marketing by Mead Data Corporation on behalf of LEXIS has taken place among members of the legal profession. And various specialised systems are accessed by those with special interests. One instance is POLIS the British House of Commons data base accessed by the parliamentary libraries: another, I.P. Sharp, the Canadian firm offers statistical data bases.

The ability to access overseas data bases is to be regarded positively. For it helps to overcome that tyranny of distance and isolation from which Australia has so long suffered. The opportunity to tap information at source as it is made available and not have to wait until hard copy arrives many months later by sea mail is a boon. And the value will grow as not only secondary sources are made available but even more so when full-text primary sources become available, as for example the American Chemical Society's making available its primary journals on-line. Curiously, dependence on large overseas systems has been seen in Australia at various times as a cause for concern. In the initial stages of the establishment of AUSINET it was seriously argued that overseas data bases should be mounted locally on the grounds that only then could access to the information be guaranteed under all circumstances. No longer do we seem to hear this argument however. A more genuine concern has been that Australian research is not included on overseas data bases and is thus overlooked by the rest of the world.[3] A further problem that has been highlighted is that Australian research can be overlooked on overseas data bases even where it exists because of variant usage of the English language: a knowledge of Australian English may be necessary to ensure that Australian information and research is picked up from international data bases. An interesting study on these problems concludes: "There is room for improvement in the coverage of Australian research by international data bases" and that "searchers can also produce better, more representative results by honing their sensitivity to language variations." Cultural imperialism has been seen as a significant risk: "The dominance of U.S. based data bases, their pro-American and anti-non-American biases and their natural use of American English can swamp smaller literatures."[4]

What can be done to redress some of the imbalance which clearly exists: to advise overseas enquirers of the existence of Australian information systems, to encourage their use overseas and indeed to facilitate their use—remains problematical. But Australian research that is lost to the world is that which appears in local publications and on local information systems. Both CSIRONET and AUSINET are available to overseas users but these and other systems have to be marketed more aggressively and their coverage extended. It is interesting to note that Chemical abstracts began as a result of disillusion with the coverage of American Chemical literature in European bibliographies. It may be of relevance to mention here the activity of the Australian Database Development Association and particularly its publication of a directory of Australian data bases.[5]

THE IMPACT OF ON-LINE SYSTEMS ON AUSTRALIAN LIBRARIES

Libraries, and Australian libraries are no different in this from any other libraries, have always interacted with the commercial world: even if the world of commerce was represented only by booksellers and publishers. One might assume that the extension of library information services beyond traditional print formats would be easily assimilated within existing organisational even philosophical or theoretical frameworks. Yet this has not occurred. And the reasons must include initial reluctance by reference librarians themselves to accessing on-line systems; the negative attitude to these services by many library managements; and the empire building of technical services departments which has tended to absorb funds earmarked for automation to the detriment of other services.

Few libraries in Australia have grasped the importance of on-line services in information delivery. Most academic libraries charge for services; while public libraries simply do not publicise their availability (even where they offer them). The great debate concerning charges which erupted when on-line services were first introduced has effectively been resolved by burying the idea of freely available service. (Interestingly at the same time fees began to be introduced into a variety of services including interlibrary loans.) Commercialisation was in the air. It has been observed:

> The question of funding information services has received considerable attention in Australia and elsewhere, particularly since the introduction of computerised information services. It has received further impetus with the increasing use of on-line services when institutions—in Australia mainly the libraries—were faced firstly, with sudden cash outflows that were difficult to budget beforehand, and secondly, with increasing demands on the part of funding authorities to recover cost from end users in order to reduce overall costs.[6]

The writer of the above claimed incidentally to be contributing to "discussion of the various 'market' factors that would be said

to govern the problem of funding modern information services.''
Most on-line systems have developed well away from any idea of being a public utility. AUSINET in order to develop had indeed to break free into the commercial environment as a service of ACI. And it is quite clear that the future for on-line systems now lies firmly in the market place. Systems are being targeted directly towards the end user; and are profit-based. While some librarians were quick to see the importance of computer applications to information services they have not been supported generally by the profession. As a result of this and the developments outlined above a number of serious questions have been raised for librarians to ponder.

Firstly the future of the Library as a non-profit institution providing a public information service endowed by public funds is now in doubt. Libraries have failed to convince their political masters that their continuing commitment to information services requires higher levels of funding. Willy-nilly they have dipped their toes into a commercial world (even the world of sponsorship) which they are ill equipped to deal with. Their most likely future is a retreat into their traditional passive role as book collectors and in due course irrelevance. Why there has been this failure must largely be answered in terms of the capacity of librarians as managers. The conservative nature of Australian library managers has caused them to fail to appreciate the potential of on-line services and the need to switch the attention of the library profession from the forms of information to the exploitation and dissemination of information content. Too many decisions result from a peer pressure which tends to reduce a question to its lowest common denominator. Library managers have failed to appreciate the needs of their clients and have failed to act decisively on their behalf. They have failed to articulate a vision for the future in which on-line systems will enhance information availability and improve document delivery in a country of great distances and at great distances from the principal sources of information supply. Concern about the ability of Australian library managers must even extend to doubt about the capacity of libraries to continue to manage the nonprofit information networks that do exist. This is not only a question of competence but also of funding needs and priorities: the two are inextricably intertwined. But there is for instance a very strong argument for ABN to separate from the National Library where it has been draining limited resources and to be established on a sound commercial footing as AUSINET was. The true value of ABN might then be determined. If not that then certainly the true cost.

Management failures in the end tend to bear hardest on the staff or employees. And it is undoubtedly true that the future of individual librarians is at greater stake as a result of failures at higher levels of decision-making. Concern about the future for librarians must inevitably exist where commercial systems direct themselves to the end-user: domestic users, managers, lawyers, farmers and researchers. The nature of the librarian's role (if there is any) as an intermediary between a client with an information problem and the information itself becomes more limited. Librarians have seen for a number of years that their traditional responsibility for information management via cataloguing systems has become not only less important but the preserve of systems analysts, computer programmers and clerical staff. Yet in trying to develop a new role based on being an "information professional" there have been few clear successes. While research has burgeoned as an industry creating vast numbers of jobs for research assistants and research officers, librarians have experienced only a diminishing of their role and in their prospects. Librarians have still a negative image. It is regrettable that there is so much justification for it.

CONCLUSION

This paper has I fear a rather gloomy character to it. It describes a trend in the provision of on-line information services in Australia away from library-based public utilities to commercial or commercially oriented systems. The failure by libraries having once taken the initiative to maintain the momentum may be ascribed to a number of factors: but significant among them have been the failure by library managements to operate them successfully; and slow professional recognition of the importance of such services. The future now seems to lie in the market place with systems directed to the end user.[7] On a more positive note it is hoped that this paper nevertheless alerts potential users to the existence of information systems within Australia of which they may not have been previously aware and encourages them to investigate and use them.

NOTES

1. Figures from the National Library of Australia's *Annual report* for 1984/85.
2. Statement from the chairman and secretary of the AUSINET Users Committee. *Australian academic and research libraries*, v.11, 1981, p. 288.
3. Byrne, Alex. "How to lose a nation's literature: database coverage of Australian research." *Database*, v. 6 no. 3, 1983, pp. 10-17.
4. Ibid.
5. The title of the directory is: *Directory of Australian databases* and copies can be obtained from: Australian Database Development Association, P.O. Box 53, Hawthorn, Victoria, Australia 3122.
6. Zwillenberg, H. "Funding of modern information services." *Australian academic and research libraries*, v.11, 1981, pp. 167-171.
7. Maguire, C. and Kench, R. "Online use of external databases in Australian manufacturing industry." *Aslib proceedings*, v.37, no.4, 1985, pp. 1-7.

UNITED KINGDOM

The International Component of Reference Work at the Science Reference and Information Service, The British Library

M. W. Hill

When the British Library was being set up in the very early 1970s, Lord Eccles, then the Minister responsible (and later first Chairman of the Board), said that it should not be called the National Library because it should be international in both scope and outlook. Indeed the exceptionally outward looking and service oriented character of the British Library will be well known to librarians familiar with the Document Supply Centre, Bibliographic Services Division and Research and Development Department, and by the fact that it earns over £12,000,000 about three quarters from Science, Technology and Industry. The same

---

The author is Director, The British Library Science Reference and Information Service, 25 Southampton Buildings, Chancery Lane, London WC2A 1AW England.

© 1987 by The Haworth Press, Inc. All rights reserved.   *155*

attitude has always been at the heart of that part of the British Library which was called the Science Reference Library but which, since December 1985, is now the Science Reference and Information Service (SRIS). This article will attempt to demonstrate the reality behind that claim. First, however, for those not familiar with the current organisational structure, here is a brief description of what SRIS is and its place in the British Library.

ORGANISATIONAL POSITION

Last Autumn, the British Library made a significant rearrangement of two of the three major functional Divisions. The Lending and Reference Divisions — a division by librarian's function — were regrouped into two client oriented divisions, one for Science, Technology and Industry (ST&I) and the other for Humanities and Social Sciences (H&SS). As a result the Science Reference Library, which had been part of the Reference Division, now became one wing of the ST&I, the other wing of it the former Lending Division (now Document Supply Centre). The diagram of the new structure illustrates what has happened. Physically nothing has moved but the reorganisation is not a cosmetic one. It signals a major change of emphasis in the Library's approach to customer needs. Perhaps it can best be seen as the modern version of Ranganathan's principle of "to every reader — his book." Less elegantly phrased perhaps it would now be "to every client problem — its information resource." Certainly it signals that the library's attitude is now that, whatever the client needs, all the relevant resources should be available wherever they may be housed. For science, technology, industry and commerce the combination of DSC and the SRIS must produce arguably the world's most outstanding coordinated resource of printed material.

The SRIS itself has been, since its original foundation under a quite different title, one of the great technical reference libraries of the world. Its origins lie in the foundation collections of the British Museum (one of them, that of Sir John Sloane, contained a high proportion of scientific works) and in the Patent Office Library. Today the library is probably unique in the world in presenting together a collection of something approaching 30 million patent specifications, all the other official industry property publications of the world, approximately 30 thousand current scientific, technical and commercial serials (to say nothing of many older ones, now ceased), about 300 thousand books, pamphlets, microforms and other monographic material plus the usual access to on-line data bases from a great many countries. Although our origins lie well back in the past our interest is in modern material — the historical material has largely been left to our colleagues at Bloomsbury.

Published literature and data bases are taken irrespective of language though nowadays, when acquisition funds are short, it has to be admitted that less foreign language material is acquired than used to be the case and since, despite our name, we are primarily concerned with supporting industry, technology and innovation there has been some much regretted cutting back on "pure" science literature from abroad. However, the essential basis of our reference service, the library's stock, is international in coverage. Further, as one wing of the new ST&I division we can also call upon the equally extensive multinational holdings of the Document Supply Service with which we have telefacsimile links if the urgency of the problem is such (and it often is) that next day delivery by post is inadequate.

Use of the SRIS is also international. That is not to say that we get many foreign visitors but those that know us tend to make a point of using the library whenever they visit Britain. Though I personally rarely nowadays get involved in actual enquiry work, I have recently been called upon to assist two such regular if infrequent users, one from Yugoslavia and one from India. Rather than visits though, use by people abroad takes one of two forms.

The most obvious is that the Library accepts enquiries from people in any country. The proportion we receive varies from year to year but the range is probably from 15 to 30%. In general the replies identify sources of the information sought but quite often the scientists on the staff (there are about 30 of them, i.e., 10% of the total SRIS staff) will give quite a lot of technical detail. In the case of the Business Information Service, most of the reference enquiries are handled by phone and the answers given are data extracted from the information sources, not references.

CLIENTELE

The second form arises from the clientele itself. A high proportion of the readers in the library are information brokers and information intermediaries of one sort or another. Many of them number overseas firms among their clientele. Others are from the UK units of multinational organisations and they too feed information back to their overseas units. Consultants are another category who make use of the library for clients who may be anywhere, certainly not just in the UK. All these people are undertaking reference and research work in a reference library and are almost as much a part of the library's services as the staff themselves.

Reference work often, of course, involves referral. In the international role this can work in both directions. Obviously, the SRIS helps enquirers from abroad by identifying for them suitable expert sources of information in the UK. In the other direction we can help UK enquirers either by using a colleague abroad to track for them information from other countries or by identifying expert sources of information which they can then contact for themselves. This we can do because not only many SRIS staff but also many members of other Departments get involved in international activities. There are few countries of the world in which one member or another of the BL has not got some official contact through whom information sources can be found.

Perhaps I should hasten to say, lest there be any misunderstanding, that such contacts are used only to identify sources of published or at least publicly available information and we always try to ensure that the source, once identified, is willing to give information to the enquirer. Perhaps it is the Library's long history of dealings in the patents world and the fact that several of the staff have worked in industrial firms that makes us very wary of becoming a channel for improper divulging of information.

Overseas contacts arise through participation in IFLA, IATUL and other similar bodies. We also participate in the work of the Commission of the European Communities (CEC), particularly DGXIII, Information Market and Innovation, and several other intergovernmental bodies. In all this we are ready to exchange experience of reference work with our colleagues in other libraries and information services in almost any other country. Sometimes the BL supplements this by setting up bilateral seminars (recent ones have been with the French and with NORDINFO), the initiative being taken by the Research and Development Department but staff from SRIS participate. SRIS also participates in many other international meetings such as Database '83 in Hungary, and the Mini and Microcomputers in Libraries conferences, the first in Israel, the second this year in Germany.

Last, two projects have recently been set up which are essentially international in character. Both spring from a combination of seeking to promote international use of the library's vast resources and from an appreciation of a growing need for a reference source in a particular sector.

The first of these is the Japan Information Service. The BL as a whole, not just the SRIS, has a large stock of publications from Japan. The scientific, technical and economic publications contain much useful information but, because of fear of the language and high cost of translations, people are unwilling to use it as readily as they would publications from the USA, France or Germany. The service, therefore, aims to assist people wanting to use the material and to increase awareness generally of ways of accessing it. In the patents field a service of identifying relevant specifications has been established which supplements the use of Derwent material by collaboration with INPADOC in Vienna. For general science and technology, links have been established with JICST in Tokyo. We have, of course, our own knowledge of how much is in fact published in English by the Japanese and of various sources of information about translations, not least the International Translations Centre in Delft. The CEC is also taking an initiative in this field and the SRIS has its usual contacts there. We are aware of similar initiatives in the USA and intend to see if collaboration would be to our mutual advantage.

NEW ACTIVITY

The second new activity is the European Biotechnology Information Project. Set up with support from the CEC, this project is exploring the need for information services in this subject throughout the twelve member states of the Common Market. To do this it is already providing reference services, including creating and mounting some specialised data bases, which are available to enquirers from any part of the European Community.

In common with all publicly-funded libraries, the SRIS does not have the resources it needs to provide all the material clients would ideally like or to mount all the services it should. There are two options: either to curtail the collections or services or both, since services usually depend on the collections; or to divert resources to exploit the superb collections even more and thus earn more revenue. It is the latter approach which appeals most and on which attention is being focused though, as said earlier, some inescapable curtailing of the collections has occurred. Marketing efforts will, not unnaturally, be directed to Western Europe, particularly as there is no combination of collections and services to compare with those of the Science, Technology and Information division but that is no way to imply that clients from other countries are not very, very welcome.

I trust that from this brief account it will be apparent that the SRIS interprets the term "reference work" very widely. To us, it includes giving information about publications and about other sources of information as well as providing information from publications. It includes promoting the use of published sources of information, both our own and those of other agencies and services. It includes also publishing guides to the literature and to sources of information generally.

The international component of this work is accepted and encouraged. The field in which the SRIS operates, science, technology and industry, innovation and industrial property, invention and commerce is international itself. National boundaries may from time to time create problems, different languages may create difficulties but these are things a reference service tries to take in its stride.

BBC Data As an Information Provider and Publisher

David Stoker

As the World's largest and most multifarious broadcasting and programme making organisation, the British Broadcasting Corporation has a voracious appetite for information on all subjects and in all forms. To satisfy the information needs of such an organisation (with a staff of 25,000) requires the employment of several hundred librarians, archivists, and other information and documentation staff, working in both highly specialised, and very general units, and dealing with a wide variety of media. This paper will not attempt to catalogue the full range of such services but rather to describe in detail the information and publishing work of BBC Data, the department which is responsible for providing the general reference and information services based on the written or printed word, whether from books, newspapers, on-line services, or from the Corporation's own working papers. To do this however, it is first necessary to describe the scale, and the information context within which the department and its customers work.

THE BBC AND ITS INFORMATION NEEDS

The BBC differs from many other comparable organisations in that it is both a programme maker and the operator of several

---

David Stoker (M.Phil., F.L.A.) is Radio Data Manager of BBC Data, and as such is responsible for the programme information and research services to domestic radio. He is at BBC Data, Broadcasting House, London W1A 1AA, England.

© 1987 by The Haworth Press, Inc. All rights reserved.

broadcasting networks. It is also responsible for providing three essentially different broadcasting services: (domestic) Radio, Television, and External (i.e., overseas broadcasting) Services. These three headings form the basis of the BBC's organisation, but also encompass a very wide range of educational, cultural, and entertainment activities related to programme making, as well as the associated technical and engineering services necessary for their being broadcast. For example, the BBC is by far the largest single patron of the arts in Britain, supporting six orchestras, two choirs, and producing many hundreds of hours of drama each year.

BBC Radio incorporates four national networks specialising in pop music, light music/sport, classical music, and the spoken word (current affairs, talks, documentaries, drama etc.). Scotland, Wales, and Northern Ireland, also have their own national Radio services which, at times, opt-out of the four networks and produce their own programmes. Specialist educational broadcasting to schools, as part of a programme of Continuing Education for adults, and to further education students of the "Open University" are also broadcast separately. Finally there is an, as yet incomplete, network of thirty-two local radio stations, broadcasting to specific communities within the U.K.

The Television Service, is responsible for two U.K.-wide channels, BBC1 and BBC2, but with opt-outs by Scotland, Northern Ireland and Wales for their own programmes. School and Open University programmes are broadcast on these channels during the day, together with major sporting events, although at present there are some gaps in the schedules. However, the Television Service is presently preparing to broadcast largely entertainment programming throughout the day on BBC1 with educational programmes and sporting events primarily on BBC2. At present the BBC is responsible for producing about 87.5% of its Television programming, the remainder being feature films, series or serials purchased from overseas.

External Services encompass the English language BBC *World Service*, thirty-four foreign language services ranging from Arabic (broadcasting 63 hours per week) to Nepali (1.5 hours per week), and an overseas Monitoring Service. The *World Service* also incorporates three other commercial services — the

Transcription Service, English by Radio and Television, and Topical Tapes, which sell complete programmes and programme materials to overseas broadcasters, including National Public Radio stations in the USA. The monitoring of overseas radio, and more recently television broadcasts, is also undertaken by the External Services on behalf of the British Government, and is carried out in conjunction with the United States Federal Broadcasting Information Service.

Domestic radio and television are financed from a compulsory licence fee payed by all owners of television sets, whereas the External Services are funded directly by the British Government. Expenditure during 1984/5 was £220m. on Radio, £555m. on Television, and £80m. on External Services. However, all services are to some small degree supported by a wide range of commercial activities, which together make a profit of £9m. Such commercial activities include the sale of radio and television programmes or tape and film footage, the publication of books, periodicals and course materials associated with broadcasting or particular programmes, or courses, the provision of engineering and training services, and the sale of library and information services.

It will be seen from the above, that the Corporation has many and varied information needs, and there are particular problems in providing an information service to meet them. The first of these is the range of library materials required, including film, videotape, videodiscs, stills, orchestral scores, audio tape, gramophone records, books, periodicals, news clippings, news agency and wire service materials, materials from on-line services etc. The next problem is one of physical dispersal. The Corporation is still largely centred in London, but even there it occupies some thirty buildings with separate headquarters for the three major functions situated some miles from each other. Radio and television also operate broadcasting centres in the capitals of Scotland, Wales and Northern Ireland, and Network Production Centres in four other major provincial cities in the United Kingdom. The output from these centres is not of merely local interest, and so their information needs are just as varied as those of the headquarters.

Information workers within the BBC therefore may have to

deal with any subject at virtually any level. Their customers might include a classical music producer preparing the introduction to a concert, a scriptwriter for a quiz, a research engineer involved in developments in satellite broadcasting, a researcher from a childrens' television programme, a monitor seeking to identify personalities or places mentioned in an overseas news broadcast, a lawyer preparing the defence of a libel action resulting from a broadcast, a statistician involved in audience research, or a journalist writing a news story; each of whom has radically different but equally important information needs. In aggregate, the clientele may be interested in information which is serious, entertaining, or trivial; in the durable and ephemeral; in the present, future, or past.

Most of our users however, are programme makers, who tend to be talented and creative people, each of whom regards his or her particular project as the most important ever undertaken, and many of whom seem incapable of planning their research until deadlines are imminent. They know that the British public tends to be vigilant for, and vociferous in their complaints against, factual inaccuracies in radio and television programmes, and so insist on the highest standards from their information services. They may have a particular area of subject expertise or merely the creative flair and technical knowledge to make entertaining programmes. They may have many years experience within the Corporation, and so understand the range and limitations of the information services available. Alternatively, they may have been employed on a temporary or freelance contract, in order to undertake a specific project, and consequently require considerable help, advice and patience from permanent staff.

Ideally, all the information needs of the Corporation's staff (or at least those in London) would be met under one roof, using integrated retrieval techniques, with co-ordinated subject headings. The idea of a single "resources supermarket" where the programme maker might find all the library materials required for his or her programme has often been put forward but is a long way from having been achieved. The three-way functional split between Radio, Television and External Services, results in the triplication of many functions, including libraries, but each with particular requirements and emphases designed to suit the needs of their users. Thus as there are three separate newsrooms, so there are three news clippings libraries to serve them, and whereas detailed press coverage of a foreign election might be of limited interest to the unit serving television, it would be essential within External Services. This degree of triplication of service unfortunately extends throughout the information field, including reference libraries, sheet music and gramophone record libraries and registries.

Certain library functions are primarily related to one of the three directorates—for example, the visual materials in the film and videotape libraries are of most interest to television producers, just as the audio tapes in the Sound Archives find their natural home within Radio. In such circumstances the libraries will be organised and managed within that directorate. Thus the collections of recorded sound within Radio (i.e., Gramophone Record Library, Sound Archives, Sound Effects, and Current Recordings) are the responsibility of a department named Recording Services Radio. However in other media—such as the printed word—the application is universal throughout the Corporation, and the information services are more efficiently managed on a cross-directorate basis. For this reason, the BBC's wide variety of library and information services are not fully integrated, even within individual directorates, although there is nevertheless a considerable degree of cooperation between information workers in all fields.

The Corporation's internal directory of libraries and information units therefore lists about 100 services and divides them into four categories: General Reference and Information Services, Libraries dealing with visual media, Libraries dealing with recorded sound, Music Libraries, and Libraries outside of London. BBC Data, and therefore the remainder of this article, is largely concerned with the services in the first of these categories.

BBC DATA AS AN INFORMATION PROVIDER

BBC Data provides a wide range of information and documentation services both within and outside the BBC based, on the written and printed word. In addition it is also responsible for one major stills library—the famous Hulton Picture Library—which will be dealt with separately. Approximately three-fifths of the department is concerned with providing programme research and information services based on a network of reference libraries, news information units (news clippings libraries), and a variety of small specialised information services (such as the Pronunciation Unit, or the Events Unit). The remaining staff are engaged on records management and documentation services, or else in various commercial activities which exploit the BBC information resources on behalf of external fee-paying customers.

As mentioned earlier, the department is organised and managed on a cross-directorate basis, whereas most of the BBC is run within the directorate structure. The particular needs and requirements of radio, television and external services are therefore represented by three Data Managers who run the information units specific to their directorates, who also have a liaison role between the department and the programme makers.

PROGRAMME RESEARCH AND INFORMATION SERVICES

In the BBC, the term "Reference" is something of a misnomer, when associated with libraries for they not only provide a quick reference and research service but also loan books as well. They are named thus only to differentiate them from other BBC libraries. BBC Data operates three such Reference Libraries in London, serving the three directorates, which together have a stock of about 200,000 volumes. They deal in both factual and pictorial information and aim to stock books, periodicals, pamphlets and reports of all kinds and in all subjects, as well as make use of a growing number of on-line services. The range of enquiries is enormous: the recipe for custard pies in comedy films; what song titles are connected with cars?; who wrote "the Gatling's jammed and the Colonel's dead"?; what furniture would be in the interior of a Welsh miner's cottage in the 1900s?; what clothes might be worn by a nineteenth century navvy?; what are the heights of the members of the Royal Family?; when did a particular politician last speak in the House of Commons on the subject of homelessness?, and many many others.

As mentioned earlier, our clientele are interested in material at all levels. To a programme maker, a Peanuts cartoon book, or a romantic novel might be of equal or more importance than a library full of more serious books, if that is what he requires at the time. Most of the stock is however aimed at the intelligent layman — the type of books found in most large public libraries — and the only specialised collection we have relates to the history and practice of broadcasting. Reference Library staff constantly make use of academic books and periodicals but in the main these are borrowed from other sources, as they could never hope to stock everything needed without the resources of a national library. They have therefore to operate a large Outside Loans Unit which is regularly called upon to trace and obtain books in London within a matter of hours, and occasionally experiences great difficulty in ensuring their prompt and safe return. The other unusual feature about the work is that the majority of it is done over the phone rather than in person, with books and other documents frequently delivered to offices by messengers. Producers will occasionally come in to browse however, as an element of serendipity can give rise to some excellent programmes.

Most enquiry staff have to be able to answer questions on any subject, but there are also a number of subject specialists who are capable of answering questions and offering advice and guidance to producers on possible lines to follow or potential contacts outside the BBC. At present there are four such specialists in the fields of Engineering, Industrial Affairs, Natural Resources and Energy, and the Life Sciences. The Reference Libraries also carry out a number of specialised services such as the checking of quiz scripts to ensure that the questions are unambiguous and the answers are verifiable, and the compilation of bibliographies for BBC publications and course materials.

Perhaps the most unusual service provided is Negative Checks — to ensure that names used in a fictional context are indeed truly fictional. Over the years there have been a number of accidental instances of libel in plays where the scriptwriters have used names which could be identified with real people, places, or things, as in Britain the libel laws are much stricter than in the United States. Sometimes trade names get absorbed into the language, like hoover, xerox, sellotape, or tannoy. Mostly the manufacturers are quite happy about this but if you broadcast a play in which people died in a hotel fire because the tannoy had broken down, then writs are likely to start flying. Similarly, if a real address is accidentally used in a police series to represent a brothel, the innocent occupants are likely to be extremely upset. Names, addresses, telephone and car numbers, names of companies, products, and anything else that will be named on the air in a fictional context, are now checked, and it is often much more difficult to prove that things don't exist than that they do.

Apart from the Directorate Reference Libraries, BBC Data is also responsible for some collections which perhaps more truly fit the usual ideas of a "special library." The Engineering Research Library, for example, relies mainly on periodicals, research reports, and on-line services in the fields of broadcasting electronics, accoustics, and information technology. The officer-in-charge is our Engineering Subject Specialist.

Similarly the Monitoring Service Reference Library at Caversham is open eighteen hours each day helping to identify people, places, and things heard on overseas broadcasts. For example, the monitor may be listening to Radio Morocco talking about a trade delegation to Poland. The Moroccan newsreader may not be very good at pronouncing Polish names, and in any event the reception is not good, and so the Monitor hears only a garbled name which he has somehow to identify. The Reference Library is there to help him find the correct answer using a host of home-grown information files, maps, and foreign directories. The Monitoring Reference Library is one of the few places outside the USSR which is able to provide not only a full list of members of the Supreme Soviet of the USSR but also biographical details of the majority of its members. Caversham is also frequently the first place in the West to hear of major political events such as coups, and so the staff have to know not only who is currently in power but also of any political enemies or insurgent groups. The Monitoring Service just coming to grips with the visual element in their work as Caversham now monitors Soviet Television broadcasts. It may be of supreme importance to be able to identify who is standing next to Mr. Gorbachev at a military parade in Red Square.

The second main library service is known as News Information, which is four clippings libraries serving Radio, External Services, Television News, and Television Current Affairs. The Radio Services unit for example, stocks nearly 20 million newspaper clippings in hard copy and microfiche together with indexed sets of radio news bulletins. It is open 24 hours a day, 365 days a year and last closed for a few hours in 1960 when it moved into a new building. Otherwise it has not closed since the 1940s. The unit is certainly the largest clippings library in Britain and probably also in Europe.

News Information exists primarily to fill the "information gap" of days, weeks, months, or years between the time events happen and are reported in the papers until the time when the information is retrievable from other printed sources. Indeed sometimes material which is published in newspapers is never available elsewhere. The four units serve, primarily, journalists working in news and current affairs, but also the producers of a host of other chat shows, magazine programmes and documentaries. They work by classifying clippings and filing multiple copies of daily and weekly newspapers and magazines and follow a fixed schedule so that the morning's clippings will be in the files by the afternoon. The clippings files are supplemented by information from indexed copies of the BBC's own news bulletins, and from various news data bases. The clippings are kept in hard copy for about 18 months but are then microfiched. News Information concentrates on the "quality" newspapers but will always cut the "popular" press looking for exclusive stories, "human interest" stories, or where there is a particular treatment of news stories.

In addition to the classification of newspaper articles, each News Information Unit is also responsible for the storage and indexing of the news bulletins issued by their respective directorates. At present all such indexing is still carried out manually, but as electronic newsroom systems are introduced over the next few years, such a function will be rendered largely unnecessary.

Journalists can be among the most difficult of all library customers to serve. They constantly search for new angles on stories thus defying traditional schemes for classifying information to produce the goods, they are very demanding and like to be spoonfed; they hate new technology, such as computer terminals, and even microfiche, and as likely as not will lose an irreplaceable clippings file once they have finished with it — if you allow them the chance. But, at the same time, a good journalist can see the germ of an investigation or story in the juxtaposition of a few otherwise diverse clippings. It is the task of news information to juxtapose them.

BBC Data's News Information Service provides an essentially pragmatic information system, and the main qualification for working for it is a deep knowledge of, and unflagging interest in news and current affairs. The breakdown of subjects in the thesaurus is not always logical, but it works, and truly reflects the needs of the users for both "hard news" and "offbeat" stories. The unit will be equally capable of providing details of the latest developments between the Contra and Sandinista forces in Nicaragua, stories of horseplay at public functions, political "banana skins," or sexual scandals. However unscientific it may seem at times, the News Information service, is extremely successful and, for example, the Radio unit is now answering more than two and a half times as many enquiries per year as in 1974 with only a minimal increase in staff. The fact that it also provides the major source for the answering of enquiries by the commercial BBC Data Enquiry Service also tends to indicate that it can provide information not readily available elsewhere.

In addition to the two major BBC Data library services, the department also operates a number of smaller specialised information units. The most famous of these is probably the BBC Pronunciation Unit. This exists to advise broadcasters about the pronunciation of English words — for example diphtheria rather than diptheria, Enoch Powell (rhyming with towel) but Anthony Powell (rhyming with pole) — and how foreign words and particularly names might best be pronounced by English language broadcasters. The unit is always busy at election times and preparing for major sporting events such as the Olympic games, but throughout the day they will answer a stream of enquiries from continuity announcers and newsreaders.

The Events Unit is another BBC Data unit which exists to provide details both of forthcoming events in order to assist the planning of news coverage, and also diaries and chronologies showing the anniversaries of personalities which form the basis of so many programmes. The International Briefing Unit is there to advise broadcasters planning to work overseas, on the conditions, regulations, and contacts necessary for their trip. It also produces a series of Feedback documents about different countries, where the advice and experience of previous BBC travellers can be collated for future use. Another unit, Programme Index, can provide a list of BBC Radio and Television programmes dealing with (e.g.) drug abuse, identify the dates when a given programme was broadcast, or advise on the number of times particular politicians have contributed to programmes in order to counter any allegations of political bias.

PAPER-KEEPING AND DOCUMENTATION SERVICES

These include a number of Registries and specialist filing services for the Corporation's working papers, a Records Management Centre providing low cost bulk storage of non-current materials, a Written Archives Centre for historical materials, and a Micrographics Unit, which caters for the remaining document storage needs.

There are a large number of Registries and filing units within the BBC, the largest of which are the responsibility of BBC Data. These include Registries which relate to wide areas of the Corporation's work—such as the Television Central Registry or the External Services Programme Registry, and others working closely with specialised areas such as the Programme Contracts, Radio Management, or Personnel Services Registry. Staff will gather, select, grade, and where appropriate index current working papers, contracts, scripts, and other programme documentation. As a unique record of BBC policy, activities and intent, as well as providing logical files for BBC staff, the Registry Service is the main source of material for the BBC's archival document collection. Where such a large scale filing operation is not appropriate, the service can also offer tailor-made filing systems within individual offices, or an advice and consultancy service about all aspects of paper management.

The BBC Records Management Centre is probably the largest records centre within the United Kingdom. It has recently moved to large newly converted warehouse several miles from the centre of London where accommodation costs are considerably lower. The Centre will accept, store, and where necessary retrieve any non-current documentation, thereby saving expensive office space. The staff do not rearrange material in any way. Where necessary they will restrict use of the papers to the originating department, and carry out periodic reviews with a view to permanent preservation or destruction.

The Written Archives Centre is the ultimate destination for any documents of permanent historical value. This Centre holds thousands of files, scripts, publicity materials and other documents principally relating to the first forty years of the Corporation's history, including correspondence with some of the most eminent statesmen, speakers, writers and artists of the twentieth century. These papers are listed, indexed and made available to BBC staff for use in solving administrative or legal queries about rights, ownership or copyright payments, and as research materials for programmes. Papers up to 1962 are also made available to academic researchers and are widely used for theses, books, and other projects. For example, the Centre's holdings of a large number of scripts and letters written by George Orwell during the years in which he worked for the Corporation have recently merited publication.

Finally, for those areas where hard-copy documentation storage is not economic, but destruction is not feasible, BBC Data operates a Micrographics Unit. This department can produce, process and duplicate roll film, microfiche and jacketed film to archival standards.

COMMERCIAL SERVICES

In the last decade the BBC has become more aware of the potential commercial value of the information services which have been built up for its own purposes. BBC Enterprises and BBC Publications have been operating as commercial operations and selling products and services created by the BBC and ploughing back their profits into the Corporation for many years. However, since the formation of BBC Data in 1982, one of its responsibilities has been to operate a commercial division to exploit the resources in its custody, and also to investigate other commercial possibilities from the sale of BBC information. Much of this is managed through the Data Enquiry Service which provides a personal research service, based on BBC Data and other libraries, to public relations companies, advertisers, bankers, industrialists and the media and other clients who need up-to-the-minute and accurate information. The service has grown steadily since its inception and has always met its stringent financial targets. It operates on an ad-hoc hourly rate or by annual subscription and can receive and deliver information by telephone, telex, letter or dispatch rider. Strict confidentiality is maintained as, frequently, several clients may be seeking the same information.

The Corporation also operates one major commercial picture library, which is unique among its information services in that the collection was not originally developed for broadcasting purposes. The Hulton Picture Library originated with the extensive collections of the *Picture Post* weekly magazine, and became a picture library following the magazine's closure in 1956. The library was eventually purchased by the BBC and although it ran at a loss for several years, it was retained because of the enormous potential value of the pictures. However, in 1979 responsibility for the library was transferred to the Department which was later to become BBC Data, with the requirement that it should become commercially viable. As such it became the exception to the rule that BBC Data was concerned with the written and printed word.

The financial objective has been achieved over the last five years. The range of the original collection has been greatly extended and brought up to date with a number of acquisitions including the London *Evening Standard* picture library. It now contains over ten million images, and is one of the largest picture libraries in Europe. It has also recently extended the range of its commercial services by developing a publishing arm and a postcard imprint. It has entered into an arrangement with the Bettmann Archive in the United States, so that both collections may call upon the resources of the other.

Through BBC Data Publications, there is now available a

range of specific information and research publications drawn largely from the information output of the department and other departments. Examples include a *Thesaurus of Terms* for use in news libraries, a *Bibliography of British Broadcasting*, and material from the corporation's Broadcasting Research Department. The extensive *Popular Music Index* is also now available for sale in microfiche format, and was produced by the Department's own Micrographics Unit which, in addition, carries out some commercial bureau work.

In 1983 BBC Data became involved with electronic publishing with the launch of the "World Reporter" news data base in conjunction with Datasolve Ltd. This includes the texts of the BBC's *Summary of World Broadcasts*, and External Services news items, among other British and American news publications. This is an example of BBC Data exploiting materials which were originally produced in machine-readable form for other purposes, and yet can be added to the database at comparatively little expense.

THE FUTURE

The future of BBC Data's programme research and information services will undoubtedly be determined by a host of unknown factors which may affect the future organisation, finance, and range of activities of the Corporation, which are all subject to public scrutiny.

The BBC has announced its intention of moving its central administration, and the Radio Directorate away from its present costly central London base, to a new and much larger site adjacent to the Television Centre in West London. This change in accommodation for a major studio complex and for some of the largest libraries, which will take place during the next decade, but it could provide the ideal opportunity for reducing the proliferation of libraries, either by integrating libraries using different media within the Radio Directorate, or else by combining similar operations currently serving Radio and Television programmes. In any event, however, there lies ahead a difficult time in which the Radio will be seeking to increase its output and reduce its overheads, whilst operating from inadequate accommodation.

In the field of picture libraries however, the BBC is already beginning to look at the possibility of combining and rationalising its resources, both for programme making and commercial purposes. Following the recent successful development of the *Hulton Picture Library*, a recent report has advocated the establishment of a central stills collection on one site incorporating the collections of the Hulton, with two other large, and several somewhat smaller stills collections. Together, such a collection would probably represent the World's largest single collection of images. The future management of such a collection is as yet undecided.

Computerisation has already begun to have an effect in the Reference Libraries, both for information retrieval and for housekeeping activities. The range of data bases used and the libraries' reliance upon them continues to grow, although the service will continue to be primarily based on traditional methods and materials for the foreseeable future. However the present computerised cataloguing system should shortly be extended to include an integrated book and periodical acquisition and circulation scheme. This has been no easy task because BBC Data is responsible for acquiring and distributing the newspapers and periodicals required not only for its libraries but also for the Corporation as a whole, and consequently operates on a very large scale in this area. Similarly microcomputers are gradually being introduced for a variety of housekeeping functions within the various Registry and Records Management services.

Nobody in the News Information Service thinks that the present intensive manual systems will always remain. In the past the service has looked closely at various computerised indexing and retrieval methods, and decided that none could cope with the volume, variety, and currency of enquiries handled each day. Automation of news information will come when all British newspapers are available in machine-readable form. This has always seemed a fairly distant prospect, but at the time of writing some fundamental changes taking place in the newspaper industry seem likely to bring about this state of affairs much sooner than was previously believed. Similarly the present manual indexing of news bulletins will shortly disappear as computerised newsrooms are introduced throughout the BBC.

The continuing introduction of automated methods for the production of a wide range of BBC materials, including scripts, news bulletins, research reports, catalogues, and all kinds of documentation, will provide BBC Data publications with an enormous field for developing their publishing activities, in hardcopy, micrographic, and electronic media. The department is only just beginning to show its real potential in this area.

Gradually there is developing throughout the Corporation an awareness of the cost, and above all the value of the enormous information resources which have been built up to support BBC programmes. If part of their commercial value can be realised, without prejudice to the Corporation's primary activity as a public service broadcaster, additional funds could be ploughed back into enhancing such services, and as a result, into improving the quality of programmes.

GERMANY

Automated Information Services for Supreme National Authorities: The Libraries' Contribution — The Example of the Federal Republic of Germany

Ernst Kohl

Parliamentary and administrative libraries, unlike public libraries, are not institutions of their own but part of the administrative organization of their authorities. Moreover, as a rule they are not the only organizational units which provide information to their authorities. In consequence, the standard of their services is permanently being exposed to a comparison by their users with the standard of services rendered by the other organizational units.

In these days the proliferation of informations, the ever widen-

---

Ministerial Counselor Dr. Ernst Kohl is Director of the Library Network of the Supreme Federal Authorities at the Deutscher Bundestag, Bundeshaus, 5300 Bonn 1, Federal Republic of Germany.

© 1987 by The Haworth Press, Inc. All rights reserved.

ing scope of Government and Parliamentary activities, and the impact of new technologies sum up to present a formidable challenge to all agencies with the task of collecting, indexing, and disseminating information. Different information materials suggest different solutions. The traditional library materials are less suited to highly advanced solutions than other kinds of materials. The nature of the challenge with which the Parliamentary and administrative libraries are faced as well as possible lines of response are illustrated by activities of the libraries of the supreme national authorities of the Federal Republic of Germany.

INFORMATION REQUIREMENTS OF SUPREME NATIONAL AUTHORITIES

Politicians, legislatures, governments, governmental bureaucracies, and party functionaries, require various kinds of published information: factual, statistical, legal information, news and commentaries, background information and surveys, scholarly studies. In most of the supreme authorities in the Federal Republic of Germany an organizational unit called press documentation is responsible for the procurement of the press releases of the news agencies and of news items, press commentaries, and newspaper articles in the press. Periodical articles, books—trade and non-trade publications including fugitive documents—looseleaf publications, which are particularly important, as most legal commentaries are published in loose-leaf form, communications of political parties as well as of special-interest groups, in particular of pressure groups or registered lobbies, official publications, especially Federal Government information and Parliamentary documents, are covered by the libraries. The documentation of legislative activities, in particular in the Parliamentary committees, is effected by the archive and record offices. The verbatim record of Parliamentary debates is indexed by a special section in the Administration of the Federal Parliament, called "subject and speaker indexes." With the advent of the computerized information data bases available on-line, information retrieval by skilled intermediaries was added to the range of information activities. In some of the Supreme Federal Authorities the data processing section is in charge of this service, in others this service is offered by the library.

It is characteristic of supreme national authorities that the information services of the various organizational units are required by politicians and the governmental bureaucracy ubiquitously. For a large part of the year there are no Parliamentary sittings, and Members of Parliament are away from the Federal Capital in their constituencies. As concerns the Government, Departmental Ministers, Ministers of State, and Parliamentary Secretaries of State as well as high ranking Civil Servants are often away from Bonn for negotiations or attending conferences or supervising public administration.

Before the computer age, all of the organizational units in charge of gathering, storing, and disseminating information in the Supreme Federal Authorities were organized according to the same pattern: the documents were shelved and made accessible through catalogues or finding lists with index entries to these documents. It is a distinctive trait of this method of organization of knowledge that both the documents and the indices to them are location-dependent. In consequence, the demand for ubiquity of information cannot be met by the traditional forms of organization of information services.

AUTOMATED DOCUMENTATIONS OF PRESS RELEASES – A CHALLENGE TO LIBRARIES

In the 1970s a radical improvement of information services through the use of computer technology was achieved by the Press and Information Office of the Federal Government (BPA), one of the 24 Supreme Federal Authorities of the Federal Republic of Germany, in automating its documentation of press releases. This very effective solution serves as a standard of comparison ever since. It is characteristic of the BPA solution strategy that data processing is made use of for both processing and information retrieval. As the press releases of the news agencies arrive in machine-readable form already, they can be input without any prior data preparation into the BPA's SIEMENS computer, resulting in full-text storage. At input the texts are indexed automatically by a software packet called PASSAT, also a product of SIEMENS, one of the leading German computer manufacturers. After input the press releases are immediately accessible by on-line searching.

Press releases are highly topical news. The up-to-dateness achieved through an imaginative implementation of computer technology could never have been effected by traditional methods of documentation. Full-automatic analysis of documents makes it also easier to cope with the steadily growing communication overload just by replacing the installed hardware by still mightier machinery, taking into account the downward trend of hardware prices. What is most important, however, is that a virtual ubiquity of both the documents and the index information to these documents is made possible by automation: wherever there is a terminal with on-line access to the data base, the documents can be searched and are made available on the terminal. Information services are no longer location-dependent.

To achieve a similar ubiquity of information for library materials through the use of computer technology is impossible, at least for the time being. The documents which the libraries of the Supreme Federal Authorities collect, are much more voluminous than press releases. Full-text storage and, as a result, a ubiquity of documents on a large scale are dreams of the future, which still may come true quite soon, if we take the prospects of electronic publishing and the storage capacities of optical disks into account. At present, however, for a universal availability of publications other solutions have to be sought.

As most of the library materials are not available in machine-readable form, input without editing, and automatic indexing are also unattainable solutions for libraries. In consequence, increases in the number of publications, if they cannot be met by corresponding increases in library staff, have to be met by other ingenious measures. Otherwise there is a permanent threat to libraries that they gradually become understaffed and as a result cannot even maintain any longer the present-day standard of their services.

As far as index information to documents is concerned, both bibliographic and subject access can be automated through the implementation of on-line catalogues thus effecting at least a ubiquity of index information to library materials.

THE RATIONALE OF AUTOMATING LIBRARIES IN SUPREME AUTHORITIES

Under these circumstances the libraries of the Supreme Federal Authorities devised a concept which is characterized by a combination of

— infrastructural measures
— organizational adjustments
— strategic management.

In this concept the most important infrastructural measure and prerequisite for the other two objectives is automation, resulting first and foremost in a cessation of a number of internal processing activities, e.g., the maintenance of in-process files, and in integrating others, e.g., cataloguing for acquisition purposes and for recording works in the catalogues. Automation, therefore, makes organizational adjustments possible which relieve library staff from a number of the traditional library routines. This helps the libraries of the Supreme Federal Authorities to cope with the increase of publications on the one hand and to improve the standard of cataloguing, indexing and abstracting, and, in consequence, the quality of their services, on the other.

As library materials are too voluminous for full-text storage, libraries should compensate for the presently unattainable ubiquity of primary information by offering abstracting information in addition to bibliographic and subject indexing information. Software to that end was, therefore, developed for the libraries of the Supreme Federal Authorities. Abstracts made available on-line, should be evaluated as the first step on the way towards a ubiquity of documents.

Automation is not the only infrastructural measure. Telecopying and telefacsimile are other present-day technologies to be introduced into the libraries. They are another step towards the same end. The contents of books can hardly be transmitted by these means to users who require the services of the libraries of the Supreme Federal Authorities when being away from Bonn. Periodical articles, however, might possibly be made available this way.

The Ubiquity of Catalog Information

The course has thus been set for the universal availability of libraries' collections, pending future technical developments. It must be admitted, however, that the standard which the Press and Information Office of the Federal Government set in automating its documentation of press releases, cannot be attained by the libraries at present. As concerns the indices to the primary information, libraries are in a better position. A universal availability of bibliographic and subject indexing information is enabled by data processing, which suggests that the catalogues of the libraries of the Supreme Federal Authorities be converted into data bases for on-line searching by users, including remote access.

The Press and Information Office of the Federal Government offers its data base for on-line searching expecting of the users that they acquaint themselves with an information retrieval system learning a special query language developed for the I&D community, GOLEM, again a product of SIEMENS, the German computer manufacturer. The data base search technologies of the on-line information retrieval systems are powerful, but make high demands on a user, viz:

— the technical mastery of the terminal functions
— the command of a query language
— an acquaintance with the data base structure, in particular with the indices
— a knowledge of the indentifyers for the access points
— the adoption of new search strategies

If we have the level of computer literacy of the adult population in mind, we can hardly classify these information retrieval systems as end-user systems. Instead, they require an information retrieval specialist as a professional intermediary between the data base and the end user. The ubiquity of index information brought about by data processing, is, therefore, impaired by these retrieval limitations.

The OPAC Concept

Libraries, on the other hand, have a long tradition of helping their users to help themselves to the information they require. The libraries of the Supreme Federal Authorities, therefore, looked for solutions to strengthen their users' self-reliance that they could continue to serve themselves in an automated library system. It is interesting to note that between 1980 and 1982 data base search technologies were devised by the libraries of the Supreme Federal Authorities which very much resemble those of the American on-line public access catalogues (OPACs), of which the Federal Authorities then had no knowledge. Their on-line catalogue is distinguished by the following characteristics:

- it is oriented to the traditional search strategies in library catalogues
- it is menu- and/or command-driven
- an *implicit* AND is the prevalent Boolean operator, without the user being aware of that
- it is to a large extent self-explanatory according to the German standard DIN 66 234 Teil 8
- it contains a knowledge acquisition component
- tutorial help is offered throughout the search.

The OPAC of the libraries of the Supreme Federal Authorities has recently been presented elsewhere in some length.[1] Therefore, only the increase in the quality of bibliographic and verbal subject access will be assessed here.

It is an evidence for the underlying system design principle of modelling the menus on the customary search strategies that a choice between two search displays is offered.

The display of Figure 1 (display 010), by and large, specifies access points for the traditional alphabetical catalogue whereas the display of Figure 3 (display 710) follows the pattern of a search in the verbal subject catalogue.

The improvement of bibliographic access by an on-line catalogue is demonstrated, first, by the number of access points of-

```
HEBIS-KAT                          V B B    Bundestagsbibliothek (101)
Titel'- Suchen/Eing.Suchwerte          KGRZ Frankfurt am Main    Bild 010
------
ISBN
ISSN
Wv-Nr.                              ZDBN
Vollstaendige Suchwerte mit einem Punkt abschliessen.
Sachtitel
1.Abteilung
weitere Abt.
                  Ab 3. Abt. Trennzeichen (/) verwenden
Person            Strauß, Franz Josef.
Urh. KAl-Nr
    oder Name    Witikobund.
Ort und
Verlag
Ersch.-Jahr
Bd.-Ang. AF
SEND = Interne Speicherung    PF07 bis PF09 = Vorlage- / Ansetzungsform
                                                         Neue Funktion:
```

FIGURE 1

fered which exceed the access points of the traditional card catalogue by far:

- numbers (ISBN, ISSN, national bibliography number (WV-Nr.), national union catalogue of periodicals number (ZDBN);
- titles (Sachtitel);
- names of persons;
- names of corporate bodies (Urheber);
- publishers and places of publication (Ort und Verlag); year of publication (Ersch.-Jahr);
- volume number (Bd.-Ang. AF).

Second, the on-line catalogue provides for a known item to be always accessed by its title, whereas in the conventional card catalogue such a search is successful only when the main or an added entry was made under the title. Third, the access points which according to DIN 66 234 Teil 8 are specified in plain language,[2] are internally coordinated by an implicit AND as a Boolean operator. By this means quite sophisticated searches can be made as is demonstrated by Figure 1. Many politicians have relations of one kind or other to a great many organizations, including special-interest groups and lobbies. A typical question, therefore, which the users often ask the libraries of the Supreme Federal Authorities, is whether there are any documented relations between a given politician and a given organization (Figures 1 and 2: between Franz Josef Strauss and the Witikobund). This question may well result in protracted searching in the traditional author/title catalogue as this catalogue can only file an author's works in the alphabetical order of their titles. For Franz Josef Strauss, one of the prominent politicians of post war Germany, some 450 titles are recorded in the catalogue of the Library of the Deutscher Bundestag, which means that a search like the one of Figure 1, which occurs quite often, takes a lot of time. The on-line catalogue of the libraries of the Supreme Federal Authorities enables a number of specific searches which take account of the peculiarities of political life, to overcome sequentially examining each entry under a person or corporate body in the traditional card catalogue.

```
H E B I S - K A T                              V B B     Bundestagsbibliothek (101)
Titel-Anzeige ISBD                                       KGRZ Frankfurt am Main      Bild 050
----------
Strauß, Franz Josef:
@Der@ Beitrag der Sudetendeutschen zur Freiheit
                          BF           KAT-NR. 000778710  STUFE 9
   @Der@ Beitrag der Sudetendeutschen zur Freiheit : Ansprache d. Vorsitzenden
       d. Christl.-Sozialen Union auf d. Jahrestagung d. Witikobundes am
       Sonntag, 9. Oktober 1977 in Kaufbeuren/Neugablonz
       München, 1978. - 31 S.

                                                                Neue Funktion:
```

FIGURE 2

The subject search display was, again, modelled on the customary search in the subject catalogue. As in the traditional library catalogue environment, the user is required to specify his search problem and translate it into individual search terms. The user is informed by the display about the individual classes of subject terms which he can select:

— topical subject terms (Sachbegriff)
— geographical and ethnographical terms (including territorial entities)
— corporate bodies, conferences (Koerpersch./Konferenz), and authorities (Behoerde) as subject headings
— persons as subject headings (Person)
— titles of works as subject headings (Werk)
— historical events (hist. Ereignis)
— form subdivisions (Formbegriff)
— subdivisions of period or time (Zeitbegriff)

Up to five single search terms can be keyed in, and are post-coordinated by an implicit AND as a Boolean operator, which cannot be matched by the traditional pre-coordinated indexing information of card catalogues. Figure 3 illustrates such a specific subject search in which studies on the foreign policy (s : Aussenpolitik) of the first Chancellor of the Federal Republic of Germany (p : Adenauer, Konrad) towards the Soviet Union (9 : Sowjetunion) during the Berlin Crisis of 1961/62 (h : Berlinkrise <1961 - 1962>) are asked for. It follows from the subject search strategy of the on-line catalogue that the corresponding method of indexing is coordinate indexing.

One of the major tasks of supreme national authorities is to initiate bills and pass laws as well as to amend them. Accordingly, the libraries of the Supreme Federal Authorities have to maintain extensive and detailed documentations on the individual laws, rules, orders, and regulations of the country as well as on all international treaties.

It is desirable to break down this documentation to the individual parts and paragraphs of the laws *etc*. To give an example, the amendment of the Federal law concerning the promotion of work (Arbeitsforderungsgesetz) was controversially debated in the

```
H E B I S - K A T ** Sachrecherche        V B B    Bundestagsbibliothek (101)
Suchkriterien: Schlagworte                     KGRZ Frankfurt am Main   Bild 710

Schlagwortkategorien: s=Sachbegriff  k=Koerpersch./Konferenz  p=Person  t=Werk
                     g=geogr.Begriff b=Behoerde f=Formbegriff h=hist. Ereignis
Bei -f-   T Kateg.(1): s : Außenpolitik.
vor der
Kategorie T Kateg.(2): p : Adenauer, Konrad.
erfolgt
die Suche T Kateg.(3): s : Sowjetunion.
ueb.den
Thesaurus T Kateg.(4): h : Berlinkrise <1961 - 1962>.

           Zeitbegriff : T h e s a u r u s b e z i e h u n g e n
      ------------------------------------------------------------------
           Aequivalenz * Zeit    * Hierarchie * Spezifizierung * Assoziation
       zu  int. extern * A B C D E F * OBG OB UBG UB* s.a. impl./spez.* s.a. aber:
       (1):   x  xxxxxx *  . . . . . . *  x   x   x   x *  x    x      *  x  x
       (2):   .  .      *  . . . . . . *  .   .   .   . *  .    .      *  .  .
       (3):   .  .      *  . . . . . . *  .   .   .   . *  .    *      *  .  .
       (4):   .  .      *  . . . . . . *  .   .   .   . *  .    .      *  .  .
       A/C=frueher B/D=spaeter  E=frueher und spaeter (Revertierung) F=zeitweise
      + bibliogr. Suchbegr.:     von: * bis:         Inhalt:
      PF3 =Sprung zu Relat.    PF4 =Anzeige/Auswahl der Relationen    Neue Funktion:
```

FIGURE 3

Federal Republic of Germany in 1985 and 1986. The controversy concentrated on one particular section, § 116. As it is the rule that the amendment of a law is restricted to a few sections only, Parliamentary and administrative libraries are often required to procure works on individual paragraphs. Sometimes also searches are required for works on the law as a whole plus all works on individual paragraphs of that law. In answering questions like these the on-line catalogue is superior to the card catalogue because of the truncation facility of the OPAC system. As illustrated by Figure 4 the uniform title of the law is filled in without a period as an end mark. The system then searches for works with this uniform title as a subject heading and for works the titles as subject headings of which begin with the uniform title of the law, e.g., "Arbeitsforderungsgesetz: § 116."

The on-line catalogue of the libraries of the Supreme Federal Authorities also enables combined searches with bibliographic access points of the alphabetical catalogue, e.g., the name of an author, and with subject access points. Figure 4 illustrates a typical search in the political field by which some one inquires whether the Federal Minister of Labour and Social Affairs, Norbert Blum, has written anything on the Arbeitsforderungsgesetz or one of its paragraphs. Multi-dimensional searches of this kind can never be offered by the traditional card catalogue. It follows from this search facility of the on-line catalogue that the headings for entities which may serve as bibliographic and also as subject access points must be constructed according to uniform rules. This concerns persons, non-territorial corporate bodies, geographic names, government officials, public corporations of various kinds, conferences, titles, in particular uniform titles, including collective titles. As the national cataloguing rules RAK (*Regeln fur die alphabetische Katalogisierung*) and subject indexing rules RSWK (*Regeln fur den Schlagwortkatalog*) differ to some extent in their rules concerning the construction of these headings, the libraries of the Supreme Federal Authorities had to elaborate an adaptation of the RAK which takes the requirements of subject indexing also into account.[3] As the RAK-PB contain uniform rules for the construction of headings for the access points mentioned above, they also lend themselves to the maintenance of dictionary catalogues. It is worthwhile taking note of

```
H E B I S - K A T ** Sachrecherche       V B B      Bundestagsbibliothek (101)
Suchkriterien: Schlagworte                  KGRZ Frankfurt am Main     Bild 710
-------------    Recherche in den u.a. Kategorien o h n e  Ergebnis -----------
Schlagwortkategorien: s=Sachbegriff  k=Koerpersch./Konferenz  p=Person  t=Werk
                     g=geogr.Begriff  b=Behoerde  f=Formbegriff  h=hist. Ereignis
Bei -T-      Kateg.(1): t : Arbeitsförderungsgesetz
vor der
Kategorie   T Kateg.(2):      :
erfolgt
die Suche   T Kateg.(3):      :
ueb.den
Thesaurus   T Kateg.(4):      :

             Zeitbegriff :
--------- T h e s a u r u s b e z i e h u n g e n ---------------
    Aequivalenz *  Zeit  .* Hierarchie * Spezifizierung * Assoziation
zu int. extern * A B C D E F * OBG OB UBG UB* s.a. impl./spez.* s.a. aber:
(1):  .  ....... *           *     *       *        *       *
(2):  .  ....... *           *     *       *        *       *
(3):  .  ....... *           *     *       *        *       *
(4):  .  ....... *           *     *       *        *       *
A/C=frueher  B/D=spaeter  E=frueher und spaeter (Revertierung)  F=zeitweise
+ bibliogr. Suchbegr.: lP von: 01 bis:   Inhalt: BLUEM NORBERT
PF3 =Sprung zu Relat.   PF4 =Anzeige/Auswahl der Relationen   Neue Funktion:
```

FIGURE 4

that, as the German catalogue tradition is based on separate alphabetical and verbal subject catalogues.

The Knowledge Acquisition Component

On-line catalogues should also have a knowledge acquisition component to assist users in searching. The maintenance of a thesaurus is a particularly powerful means to this end. The thesaurus POLIANTHES of the libraries of the Supreme Federal Authorities is based on international and national thesaurus standards, but contains more than the standardized relationships.[4]

The thesaurus relationships are indicated in the subject search display (Figures 3 and 5). Again, most of the relationships are self-explanatory according to DIN 66 234 Teil 8, an exception being the specification relationship which controls the linking of non-thesaurus index terms (e.g., political vogue words) to a thesaurus term. The equivalence, hierarchical, and associative relationships are the traditional thesaurus relationships of the International Standards ISO 2788 and ISO 5964. For a political thesaurus by which territorial entities are to be documented, the addition of the chronological relationship (Zeit) is a matter of course.

The users of the on-line catalogue are generally advised to mark the thesaurus relationships (by any character) in order to acquaint themselves with the index terms, and by doing so, improve their competence in handling subject searches.

The system answers the marking of relationships by display 711. At first the non-preferred terms are listed (Figure 5), prefixed by "benutzt fuer" (used for):

— synonyms
— quasi-synonyms
— abbreviations and acronyms
— more specific terms

The display of the latter terms is particularly important for ascertaining the scope of an index term. In order to reduce the number of index terms to an optimum, POLIANTHES often treats a number of more specific terms and a broader term as an

```
HEBIS - K A T ** Sachrecherche      V B B    Bundestagsbibliothek (101)
Relationen (Thesaurus:POLIANTHES)        KGRZ Frankfurt am Main    Bild 711
------    Begriffskategorie  S A C H B E G R I F F             --------

Außenpolitik.
    extern engl.     Foreign policy
    extern franz.    Politique exterieure
    benutzt fuer     Außenpolitikgeschichte
    benutzt fuer     Entspannungspolitik
    benutzt fuer     Europäische Politische Zusammenarbeit (EPZ)
    benutzt fuer     Gipfelkonferenzen
    benutzt fuer     Internationale Politik
    benutzt fuer     Sicherheitspolitik
  + UBG              Außenpolitik: Staatsbesuche
    UBG              Außenpolitiktheorie
    UBG              Außenpolitische Behörden
    UBG              Außenpolitische Behördenberichte
  + UBG              Außenpolitische Beziehungen
  + UBG              Außenpolitische Dokumente
  + UBG              Außenpolitische Dokumentensammlungen
  + UBG              Außenpolitische Koexistenz
    OB               Politik
  + UB               Diplomatie
Sollen Begriffe nicht mit in die Suchanfrage,dann  +  loeschen:
                                                           Neue Funktion:
```

FIGURE 5

equivalence set, the broader term thus functioning as the preferred term. The thesaurus standards refer to this technique as "upward posting." Whenever upward posting is employed by a thesaurus, the user is well advised to mark the equivalence relationship because it reveals to him the degree of specificity of subject analysis effected by the library.

An external equivalence is also implemented in the POLIANTHES thesaurus as is illustrated by Figure 5, too. Prefixed by "extern," English and French equivalents of the preferred term, taken from the EUROVOC thesaurus of the European Communities (EC), are displayed. The external equivalence relationship of POLIANTHES is indicative of the third objective, for which computer technologies are to be utilized, viz. a strategic information management. Terms in relationships other than the equivalence relationship can be included in the search by marking them by the + sign. Internally these terms are linked by an implicit OR as a Boolean operator. For the information retrieval systems of the I&D community the user has to learn Boolean logic; in the OPAC system of the libraries of the Supreme Federal Authorities Boolean logic is applied, too, but without the user being aware of it.

By the inclusion of terms in relationships to the search term powerful cluster searches can be operated, again an improvement over the card catalogue.

Through automation the individual library is put into a position to cope with the increase of publications on the one hand, and improve the standard of its services on the other.

In addition, data processing offers the opportunity of resource sharing.

NETWORK DEVELOPMENT

The Press and Information Office of the Federal Government was constituted as a Supreme Federal Authority to provide the Government with outside news and to inform the public on Government activities. The individual Ministries share the information gathered by the Federal Press and Information Office.

As concerns libraries, however, each Supreme Federal Authority has its own library. Although their collections overlap to some extent, by the establishment of an automated library network with a common data base they can procure much more information than if they stay alone.

The idea of a library network of the Supreme Federal Authorities of the legislative and executive branches was ventilated in the 1970s, and as it was substantially approved, a Network Development Office was instituted in 1980 at the Deutscher Bundestag, as the Library of the Deutscher Bundestag is by far the largest library among the libraries of the Supreme Federal Authorities.[5] The Network Development Office arranged for the library software system HEBIS-KAT of the Hessian network of university and public libraries, to be extended to conform to the requirements of the libraries of the Supreme Federal Authorities, major extensions being the OPAC component, including the POLIANTHES thesaurus and RAK-PB, the documentation of periodical articles, and the provision of abstracting facilities. The extended HEBIS is being tested at present, and the Library Network of the Supreme Federal Authorities is to become operational in 1987.

It may be surprising at first sight that authorities of the legislative and executive branches form a network. Therefore, a few words will have to be said about the political structure of the Federal Republic of Germany. If we take the two major types of constitutional democracy in the modern world into account, the Federal Republic of Germany is structured according to the parliamentary system like the United Kingdom as against the presidential system of the United States. Whereas in the presidential system the doctrine of separation of powers prevails leading to a distinction of the personnel of legislature and executive (with separate elections), the parliamentary system is characterized by the integration of legislature and executive.

The Federal Republic of Germany being a federation of states (German: Land, *pl*. Länder), the legislature is bicameral: The Deutscher Bundestag, corresponding to the House of Representatives, is chosen by direct vote of the electorate in each Land, the number of representatives allotted to each Land being based on population. The Deutscher Bundestag selects the Federal Government, most members of the Government (the Federal Chancellor and the Federal Ministers assisted by Ministers of State and Parliamentary Secretaries of State) being members of the Deutscher Bundestag (MdB). The second chamber, the Bundesrat, is constituted on different principles. It may be compared with the United States Senate before the 17th amendment to the Constitution provided for direct election of United States Senators in 1913. In the Bundesrat each Land is represented by between three and five members of the respective State Government (Landesregierung), depending on the population of the individual Land.

In a federation there are federal, state, and local divisions of power. In the Federal Republic of Germany, laws, rules, orders, and regulations are enacted on both the Federal and the Land levels, the legislatures of the Lander (Landtag) being mostly unicameral (with the exception of Bavaria). It is mostly the executive which initiates the legislation, and the executive also exercises delegated powers of legislation. To counteract any attempts at a fragmentation of power, the Constitution (Grundgesetz) of the Federal Republic of Germany provided for an interrelationship of the different levels of Parliaments and Governments.

Against this background a network of the legislative and executive branches of the Supreme Federal Authorities is no longer a constitutional surprise. The benefits resulting from resource sharing have always been undisputed.

The on-line catalogue, as pointed out above, effects a ubiquity of bibliographic and subject indexing information. In order to achieve the direct availability of the documents themselves, i.e., immediate document delivery to users (at least as long as they reside in Bonn), it is imperative for the Library Network of the Supreme Federal Authorities to have software for both electronic mailbox and interlibrary lending components.

Interlinking

Networking is an evidence for the opportunities of strategic information management offered by automation. Ad hoc interlinking with other automated library networks and, in addition, suppliers of information outside the library community is another.

In the Federal Republic of Germany, the interrelationship of the different levels of power provided for by the Grundgesetz, makes it necessary that the Supreme Federal Authorities take account of the activities of the Supreme Land Authorities and vice versa.

As far as the libraries of these supreme authorities are concerned they receive official documents on exchange or legal deposit bases. The growth rate of official documents in the Federal Republic of Germany is zooming up at present to an extent that Parliamentary and administrative libraries cannot keep pace with it. As a result some libraries are no longer in a position to record these documents as individual items in their catalogues.

To give a few examples, the Parliamentary documents of the Landtag of Lower Saxony increased from 1362 published by the 6th Landtag to 3533 of the 9th Landtag. In Bavaria, the increase was from 4163 documents of the 6th Landtag to 13,092 of the 9th Landtag, which corresponds to a growth rate of more than 200%.

It is, therefore, a goal for the Supreme Federal Authorities to encourage the Supreme Land Authorities to constitute networks of their libraries, and see to it that the networks of the supreme authorities will be interlinked. This would take the burden of indexing every individual official document of the Länder off the libraries of the Supreme Federal Authorities while they would still continue collecting and shelving them. Once the systems are interlinked, searches could be made in the data bases of the respective Land library network while immediate delivery of the relevant documents is ensured since they are stored in the libraries of the Supreme Federal Authorities.

On the other hand the integration of European states within the European Communities is advancing. Linking the utilities of the supreme authorities of the individual member states of the EC on the basis described for the interlinking of library networks of supreme authorities within the Federal Republic of Germany is, therefore, another goal. Interlinking on the EC level poses the problem of the language barrier. The Library Network of the Supreme Federal Authorities took the European dimension into account by implementing, as a first step, the external equivalence as a specific thesaurus relationship (see Figure 5).

As concerns the interlinking of library networks of supreme

authorities there is still a long way to go. Within Germany the Supreme Authorities of Hesse have been tentatively approached by the Supreme Federal Authorities, as the software system HEBIS-KAT originally was a Hessian venture. On the European level a start will be made by the Supreme Federal Authorities with the utilities offered by the European Communities themselves.

As concerns on-line bibliographic data bases offered for public access by commercial hosts, which since 1968 are gradually replacing the traditional bibliographic utilities, they form part of the strategic information management of the Library Network of the Supreme Federal Authorities. To illustrate this objective: in 1984, the Library of the Deutscher Bundestag acquired some 11,000 serials, but only 1380 were scanned for relevant periodical articles, which corresponds to not even 13%. Some 23,000 periodical articles, which compared with monographs provide the more up-to-date information, were entered into the catalogues as against 16,000 individually recorded monographs. In former years the ratio between periodical articles and monographs was 3:1, which is still the target for cataloguing and indexing.

Through access to the commercial bibliographic data bases this end will certainly be attained, and the libraries of the Supreme Federal Authorities need no longer index periodical articles which are adequately indexed and made available on-line by other institutions.

A third target for linking are the seven regional networks in Germany of university and public libraries.[6] In this case the Library Network of the Supreme Federal Authorities is not primarily interested in the bibliographic and indexing information which the libraries of these networks produce, because university and public libraries do not record periodical articles. Instead, the interest is in holding information. The rationale of linking is in this case that if, for instance, a Representative who is staying in his constituency retrieves information from the data base of the Library Network of the Supreme Federal Authorities by remote access, but cannot get hold of the documents stored in Bonn, he or she might be able via the interlinking facility to find the relevant documents in a library of the corresponding regional network. Interlinking with the regional networks of university and public libraries is, therefore, another step towards a universal availability of documents.

In summing up it should be pointed out once more that a major difference between university and public libraries on the one hand and the Parliamentary and administrative libraries of supreme authorities on the other lies in the fact that because of the particular user group they have to serve the services of the latter are required ubiquitously. Automation is the primary prerequisite for the libraries' coming up to these requirements. Through the use of computer technology the traditional location-dependent card catalogue has to be superseded by an on-line public access catalogue, with remote access to the data base to be provided. In addition, library automation must be complemented by a strategic information management including networking, interlinking of networks, and utilization of the bibliographic data bases of commercial hosts.

NOTES

1. Kohl, Ernst. The online union catalogue of parliamentary and governmental institutions in the Federal Republic of Germany. *The future of online catalogues*. Essen: Gesamthochschulbibliothek, 1986, pp. 287-338. ISBN 3-922602-09-6.

2. DIN 66 234 Teil 8. *Bildschirmarbeitsplätze – Grundsätze der Dialog-gestaltung*. Berlin: Beuth, 1984.

3. *Regeln für die alphabetische Katalogisierung in Parlaments – und Behördenbibliotheken:* RAK-PB/verantwortl.: Ernst Kohl. Arbeitsgemeinschaft der Parlaments-und Behördenbibliotheken. Bonn: Bibliothek des Deutschen Bundestages, 1985. ISSN 0518-2220.

4. Kohl, Ernst. Der Thesaurus POLIANTHES der Bibliothek des Deutschen Bundestages in Beziehung zu den Normen DIN 1463, ISO 2788 und ISO 5964. *Anwendungen in der Klassifikation*. Frankfurt/Main: INDEKS-Verlag, 1985, pp. 96-107. ISBN 3-88672-013-6.

5. Kohl, Ernst. Problems arising from the establishment of library and information networks for supreme national authorities. *Networks and networking in social science information. (FID Publication 606)*, 1984, pp. 87-96.

6. Kohl, Ernst. Library Networks and Network Planning in the Federal Republic of Germany. *Future of Library Networks*. Essen: Gesamthochschulbibliothek, 1982, pp. 15-42. ISBN 3-922602-04-5.

ISRAEL

Information Services in Industry: Difficulties in Less Developed and Small or Peripheral Countries

Beth Krevitt Eres

We live in an age where information is a commodity of value in international trade. And as is true of many commodities its value is set by market supply and demand. While the production of information products is largely based in the developed world with a preponderance of English-language material, the clientele for information is certainly international and multi-language in scope.

Less developed and small peripheral countries (including the newly industrialized countries as examples of the latter), have great difficulty in participating in the mainstream flow of information. Scientists, for example, in these countries tend to cite older material than their colleagues in the more developed countries and/or mainstream of science. The industrial librarian in the "peripheral" country faces particular difficulties in trying to op-

The author is at the Interdisciplinary Center for Technological Analysis and Forecasting, Tel-Aviv University, 69978 Ramat-Aviv, Tel-Aviv, Israel.

© 1987 by The Haworth Press, Inc. All rights reserved.

timize the service preferred. This paper cites the difficulties faced by industrial librarians and offers some solutions, on both a national and industrial level.

MANPOWER DIFFICULTIES

Information technologies are typified by a relatively short market life span while at the same time they require more complex technical skills. The library of today, in order to be efficient, is either strongly dependent on such information technologies as online searching, automated circulation, etc. or is simply not able to provide an adequate level of service. And, what is more, the required manpower proficiencies for maintaining this level of service should change but are doing so more slowly than the technologies. Librarians in the past have not been trained in understanding information technologies nor are the newly trained librarian's receiving a well rounded, technologically oriented education. Although industry often attracts the highest quality librarians (by paying the highest salaries and benefits), the field of librarianship does not enjoy a reputation which ensures high recompensation. Simply changing the name of the library to information center is not enough, as is discussed in greater detail below in the section on organizational structure. What is needed is a change in educational approach as one sees today, for example, in trends in the United States whereby information studies programs regard the training of information managers as their objective. And in proof, a new breed of "librarian" has entered the profession.

Assuming the information manager is both intellectually and technologically competent, the organizational structure of the industry often prevents the information center/library from providing the type of information services it would like. While in the past one saw data processing and office automation being handled separately, today they are usually combined. It is the rare industry, however, which recognizes that library-type information delivery is also related to the above. In general the library is understaffed and underfunded. And even when the central organization does recognize the library as part of the general data/

information processing needs of the organization, rarely are the information management skills of the librarian used outside the library whether or not the library is called an information center. Thus, often handled separately are activities such as archival records management, or maintaining competitor information files.

FINANCIAL DIFFICULTIES

While manpower and organizational difficulties exist in the more developed countries although to a lesser degree, financial difficulties are incomparable. The major information sources must be paid for in hard currency and hard currency is intentionally (because of national priorities) difficult to obtain. For example, in Israel, there exists a 15% tax on every foreign currency outlay, and for online information service, there is an additional (approximately) $30 an hour cost for using the national packet switching network (over and above the cost of using the online service and the international network to it and, of course, the 15% tax on foreign currency payments). What this means to industry is that they must even more carefully consider every book they buy and every search they do then would their counterparts in the more developed world.

The infrastructure refers to everything from telecommunication links to inter-industry interlibrary loan programs. With regard to the former, each country suffers from different levels of this problem. In Israel, for example, there still exist areas of the country which need to dial long distance to reach the packet switching networks. However, there are other countries with just as strong information needs but no telephones to speak of. Plus, we cannot forget that some countries cannot support the use of microcomputers because, even if the library and the librarian were perfectly trained, the infrastructure could not support the hardware breakdowns and software support, inherent in the microcomputer.

While the majority of information is generally transferred in English, it is not equally true that the majority of end users are English speakers. Libraries, in particular, must meet the information needs of their clientele as well as, is often the case, meet the formal or informal restrictions to provide information in native language. Since it is not uncommon to find an industry of 1,000 or even 8,000 employees with only 2-3 information specialists (i.e., librarians), one can see the limitations this imposes on any translation program.

DISCUSSION AND RECOMMENDATIONS

In small or peripheral countries and, of course, even more so in less developed countries, the problems facing industries themselves are difficult to surmount. The value of information and, in conjunction, the value of the library/information center is generally underevaluated. Training of librarians is often inadequate as are their salaries and status within the organization. Furthermore, infrastructural and financial problems create further barriers to the provision of adequate information service. What then can be done? After all, the needs of the industry are not only no less than those of their developed country counterparts, but are actually stronger due to the distances from informal information sources and technologies. The only solution is one of cooperation rather than competition; that is, the sharing of information sources. National policies supporting information sharing should be aimed at all levels of the library world from the public to the industrial.

LATIN AMERICA

The Most Useful Reference Sources on Latin America: Results of a Survey of Those Who Use Them Most

Edwin S. Gleaves

Twenty years ago John Gunther observed that, to most North Americans, South America is still terra incognita:

> To many in the United States the concept "South America" still prominently includes generals in white sombreros on mangy horses picking their teeth and shooting peasants at random, love in the hot sun, polo ponies, a peculiar capacity for disorganization, the philosophy of *mañanas*, cha-

---

A frequent visiting professor in Latin American universities, Edwin S. Gleaves is also Chair of the Department of Library and Information Science, Peabody College, Vanderbilt University, Nashville, Tennessee 37203. In addition to those who responded to his inquiry, he wishes to express special thanks to Paula Covington of the Vanderbilt University library for her advice on the selection of Latin American bibliographers, and to Nancy Gorman and Michael Hatchett for their assistance in the onerous task of bibliographical verification.

© 1987 by The Haworth Press, Inc. All rights reserved.

cha-cha, excessive edgy pride and sensitivity, gigolos drenched in eau de cologne, the overemotionalism of personal contacts, Indians squatting over dark pots of beans, *gauchos*, and fragile young women in black lace dresses with large red roses in their hair leaning over grilled balconies within range of a serenading guitar. . . . Timbuctoo is more familiar to most Americans, if only as a symbol, than thriving hemisphere cities like Medellín, Cordóba, or the new industrial complexes of Venezuela. Such a distinguished and otherwise cosmopolitan man of letters as Edmund Wilson makes a point of never having visited the continent or read its literature.[1]

Twenty years of instant electronic mass media and insular journalism have failed to improve the situation. Little from Latin America filters through the American press unless it bears tidings of bad news: natural disasters (an earthquake in Mexico, a volcano eruption in Colombia); wars (the showdown in the Falklands, the ongoing revolutions in El Salvador and Nicaragua), or major financial news that has a direct impact on the United States (the massive debts of Argentina, Brazil, Mexico, and Venezuela). The cocaine wars in the Andean countries, because they are related directly to drug problems on American streets, have caused our government to sit up and take notice; a drought in Brazil will affect our coffee prices; and an occasional turnover in government in the Caribbean will inconvenience American tourists. Beyond such events, the average American cannot recall the latest news from Argentina, Brazil, Colombia, Ecuador, Peru, or Uruguay, much less the smaller republics of Central America and the Caribbean.

The American college student is little better off when it comes to knowledge of Latin America, and even more ignorant of where to find information on the southern part of the western Hemisphere. I dare say that even librarians, custodians of knowledge, have their gaps when it comes to basic materials on Latin America. Example: name one Nobel laureate in literature from Latin America.

Need we be reminded of the importance of Latin America to the world and to our own country? At the current rate of growth, by the end of the century one person in ten of the world's population will live in Latin America; 30 million of them will live in the world's largest city, Mexico City, and Sao Paulo will not be far behind. Those living south of the border in this hemisphere will outnumber Americans and Canadians two to one. The United States is currently exporting over $30 billion in goods per annum to Latin America, while importing over $50 billion. We also provide over $2 billion in foreign aid to Latin America, much of it in the form of military assistance to Central American nations.

Although we tend to believe the old proverb that "Brazil is the land of the future — and always will be," for Brazil, and other Latin American nations as well, the future has arrived. The gross domestic product of Brazil exceeds $190 billion and Mexico has surpassed $160 billion. When we add the gross domestic products of Argentina, Chile, Colombia, Ecuador, Peru, and Venezuela, the total comes to over $500 billion.

Dry financial statistics, of course, only begin to reflect the importance of Latin America. In many areas, such as literature and the arts, these nations have been no less than prolific. Indeed, it could be said that the artist in Latin America is revered in a way not yet understood in the Anglo-American culture. The region has produced five Nobel laureates in literature, one as recently as 1983.

Latin America is a land of contrasts, both geographically and demographically. The extremes in elevation and rainfall make South America the most diversified of all the continents. The massive Andes, the longest mountain range in the world, "attains altitudes exceeding twenty thousand feet over an area of more than 3,500 miles; it forms a wall with few passes less than twelve thousand feet above sea level in the median sector."[2] Many of the mountains of South and Central America "have the odd feature of combining perpetual snow with endless heat."[3] The rain forests of western Colombia contrast sharply with the virtually rainless deserts of Peru and northern Chile.

South America, Central America, and the Caribbean are home to many ethnic and national groups, representing both indigenous populations and transported Europeans. Most of them live within two hundred miles of the Atlantic or Pacific Ocean. Unfortunately, extremes in economic conditions also exist, making Latin

America an area of political ferment which our country ignores at its peril.

ASKING THE EXPERTS: THE SURVEY

If the information gap on Latin America is to be bridged, where better to start than in our libraries? And where better to start in our libraries than with the reference collections? In order to arrive at a limited number of the most useful reference sources, I polled a select group of Latin American bibliographers and reference specialists, most of them librarians in research libraries and most of them members of the Seminar on the Acquisition of Latin American Library Materials (SALALM).

The survey-letter consisted of four questions:

1. What, in your judgement, are the ten (10) most useful reference tools on Latin America [including the Caribbean]? (I have in mind sources that cover more than one nation, but they may not necessarily cover the whole region.) Please indicate your choices *in order of preference* insofar as that is possible. Comments on the reasons for your choices will be welcomed.
2. What, in your judgement, are the three (3) most useful reference *series* on Latin America (excluding annuals or near-annuals such as the *Handbook of Latin American Studies*)? Again, your order of preference and your comments would be helpful.
3. Which of these titles, in your judgement, are overpriced? Underpriced (if possible)?
4. What reference works *need* to be published [on Latin America]? What kinds of works would be most helpful to you?

The intent of the survey was described in the paragraph that followed:

> From your responses and from other sources at my disposal, I plan to construct a bibliographical essay that will guide the

user through this jungle of information sources. I hope to include a fair sampling of bibliographies, indexes, and other reference works.

I also tried to clarify how the names of the respondents would be used:

> As part of my paper, I plan to list the names and institutional affiliation of all those who respond, using individual quotes without direct attribution. I trust that this will be acceptable to you; if not, simply let me know.

Of the 53 persons queried, 23 responded, three of whom indicated that they did not feel qualified to answer the questions. Since letters were sent to more than one person at some institutions, in two instances three respondents pooled their comments in one letter. Therefore, I received a total of 16 letters, representing 20 persons, providing the information I requested. Most of those responding were kind enough to provide the comments that I requested; some letters exceeded two single-spaced pages of lists and commentary. The names, titles, and addresses of those responding (either singly or in a group) appear at the end of this article.

By asking for the respondents' choices in order of preference, I hoped to get a sense of relative importance of the basic reference sources on Latin America, not by assigning any arithmetic value to the titles so much as by noting how many titles tended to be mentioned frequently and to rank high among most or all of the lists. Most of the respondents provided such ranked lists; two said that they did not feel comfortable with the idea and simply provided their "top ten" and "top three" in no particular order. Several of our experts also pointed out the importance of some general reference sources in providing information on Latin America.

My wording on the most useful reference series on Latin America, however, was sufficiently ambiguous to raise some questions concerning the *type* of series, a legitimate question. One respondent assumed that I was asking for bibliographies and reference sources. My intent was to determine the most useful *publishers'* series, some of which became evident from the responses. Some of the titles which appear in the first list are serial (e.g., *Handbook of Latin American Studies*).

A number of respondents declined to comment on prices, and comments on this question tended to be so general as to be of little use—except to note the divergence of opinion on the matter. Some felt that, given the work involved, none of the works was overpriced; others noted that most if not all of the publications (especially some from the United Kingdom) were overpriced.

As for the works that need to be published, the responses again varied from no suggestions to some who listed ten or more ideas for publication, some of them very specific. Unlike the basic reference sources, no strong core of titles-to-be-published emerged, indicating perhaps the broad range of needs for new publications on Latin America. Publishers would do well to take note of these suggestions.

Useful General Works

One of the early respondents sounded a warning about not overlooking some of the more general reference works:

> Presumably your article will touch upon some of the general serial reference works that are so useful for any part of the world, such as the *World of Learning*, which helps in identifying and locating universities, institutes, and the likes, *Statesman's Yearbook*, and the *MLA International Bibliography of Books and Articles on the Modern Languages and Literatures*. The *Handbook of Latin American Studies* and the *Hispanic American Periodicals Index* (HAPI) must also be mentioned.

The last two titles, as we shall soon see, became part of the standard list for most respondents, but more general titles were mentioned by the respondents: *Arts and Humanities Citation Index, Clements Encyclopedia of World Governments, Countries of the World and Their Leaders Yearbook, Directory of American Firms Operating in Foreign Countries, Dissertation Abstracts International, Encyclopedia of the Third World, Foreign*

Language Index, Index to International Statistics: IIS, National Newspaper Index, Public Affairs Information Service Bulletin (PAIS), *Readers' Guide to Periodical Literature,* and *Social Science Citation Index.* Two other respondents mentioned the *MLA International Bibliography* and one each mentioned *World of Learning* and *Statesman's Yearbook.*

These particular titles should be taken as little more than suggestive of the importance of a good general reference collection to support study and research in Latin America, beginning with the basic encyclopedias and almanacs. The more general periodical indexes will be useful for information about Latin America but they will rarely index the periodical literature emanating from that area of the world. Special care should be taken in selecting foreign-language encyclopedias that provide special insight into Latin America, ranging from the one-volume *Pequeno Larousse ilustrado* to the monumental multi-volume *Enciclopedia universal ilustrada europea-americana,* better known as the *Espasa Calpe.* Nor should one forget the Portuguese speaking part of Latin America (Brazil), represented by such general reference works as the 17-volume *Grand enciclopedia Delta Larousse.*

By the same token, as one respondent pointed out, each country has its own tools for research, and in the case of the larger nations such tools will be important for research in the larger public and research libraries. For the purpose of this study, however, we have concentrated on the most important reference sources that apply to the entire region.

REFERENCE SOURCES ON LATIN AMERICA: THE TOP 24 (OR SO) TITLES

Most of the respondents listed ten or more titles that they deemed most important; one listed six and another seven titles. In all, the 16 letters representing 20 respondents listed a total of 73 titles. No title was mentioned by all respondents. *HAPI: Hispanic American Periodical Index* was listed in the "top ten" in 10 letters and mentioned in still another, representing in all about two-thirds of the respondents. Two titles, *Handbook of Latin American Studies* and *Latin American and Caribbean Contempo-*

rary Record, were listed by seven, or nearly half, of the respondents. Two others, Gropp's *Bibliography of Latin American Bibliographies* (and its several supplements) and *Statistical Abstract of Latin America*, appeared 6 times. Four titles were mentioned in 5 responses, 3 in 4, 2 in 2, and 2 in 11, with the remaining 48 titles being mentioned only once. Thus a total of 12 titles were mentioned 4 or more times in the 16 responses received. Table 1 provides a listing of the 24 titles (groups of titles) that were mentioned two times or more. (It should be remembered that two letters represented the consensus of three persons each; these are counted as one response, not three.)

As requested, a number of the respondents shared their impressions of the Works which they recommended, some of which serve as fresh annotations of these important works. Following is a listing of the top 24 titles (those mentioned at least twice) order of frequency of mention, complete with appropriate bibliographical information. For the first 12 titles (those mentioned three times or more), I have added some comments of my own and/or have included a sampling of the respondents' comments. Prices (as of March 1986) are provided wherever possible and practical. In the case of serials, the price represents the latest edition, even though earlier editions may be available at different prices.

No. 1: Ten (10) Mentions
1. *HAPI: Hispanic American Periodical Index*. Los Angeles: University of California, Los Angeles, Latin American Center, 1975- . Annual. $225.00.

HAPI is the only periodicals index on Latin America currently being published. It is a comprehensive index by subject and author to approximately 250 major journals on and from Latin America, covering the major disciplines in the humanities and the social sciences. Latin American journals are indexed in full, others selectively. *HAPI* continues *Index to Latin American Periodicals: Humanities and Social Sciences* published by G. K. Hall, 1961-1970, which in turn updated the eight-volume *Index to Latin American Periodical Literature, 1929- 1960.* based on the holdings of the Columbus Memorial Library of the Pan American Union and published by G. K. Hall in 1962.

TABLE 1

THE MOST USEFUL REFERENCE TOOLS ON LATIN AMERICA:
A RANKING BASED ON A SURVEY OF LATIN AMERICAN
SPECIALISTS IN NORTH AMERICAN LIBRARIES

Rank	Title	Times Cited	% of Total	Cum. Freq.
1.	HAPI: Hispanic American Periodical Index	10	6.94	6.94
2.	Catalog of the Latin American Collection (Texas)/Bibliographic Guide to Latin American Studies	8	5.56	12.50
3.	Handbook of Latin American Studies	7	4.86	17.36
4.	Latin American and Caribbean Contemporary Record	7	4.86	22.22
5.	Gropp, Bibliography of Latin American Bibliographies (including supplements)	6	4.17	26.39
6.	Statistical Abstract of Latin America	6	4.17	30.56
7.	Encyclopedia of Latin America	5	3.47	34.03
8.	Handbook of Middle American Indians	5	3.47	37.50
9.	Index of Spanish American Collective Biography	5	3.47	40.97
10.	Cambridge Encyclopedia of Latin America and the Caribbean	4	2.78	43.75
11.	Latin America: A Guide to Historical Literature	4	2.78	46.53
12.	ISLA: Information Services on Latin America	4	2.78	49.31
13.	Manual del librero hispanoamericano	3	2.08	51.39
14.	Indexed Journals	2	1.39	52.78
15.	Fichero bibliográfico hispanoamericano	2	1.39	54.17
16.	Index of Anthologies of Latin American Literature in English Translation	2	1.39	55.56
17.	Grand enciclopedia portuguesa e brasileira	2	1.39	56.94
18.	Handbook of Latin American Art	2	1.39	58.33
19.	Handbook of South American Indians	2	1.39	59.72
20.	Women in Spanish America	2	1.39	61.11
21.	Latin America and the Caribbean: A Dissertation Bibliography	2	1.39	62.50
22.	Libros en venta en hispanoamérica y España	2	1.39	63.89
23.	Oxford Companion to American Literature	2	1.39	65.28
24.	South American Handbook	2	1.39	66.67
	All other titles	48	33.33	100.00
	TOTAL	144	100.00	

Comments:

This title along with the next two (*Handbook of Latin American Studies* and *Bibliographic Guide to Latin American Studies*) form the basic set of research tools in Latin American studies. Between the three of them you get extensive coverage of both the journal and the monographic literature.

Very usable, well-indexed source for articles from or about Latin America. Students tend to seek articles in English.

No. 2: Eight (8) Mentions
2. Texas. University at Austin. Library. Latin American Collection. *Catalog of the Latin American Collection.* 31 vols. and 4 supplements in 19 vols. Boston: G. K. Hall, 1969, 1971-1977. Basic set: $2950.00; suppl. 1: $550.00; suppl. 2: $340.00; suppl. 3: $930.00; suppl 4: $330.00.
    Bibliographic Guide to Latin American Studies. Bibliographic Guides. Boston: G. K. Hall, 1978-. Prepared cooperatively by the Library of Congress and the University of Texas at Austin. Annual. $350.00.

The *Bibliographic Guide* updates the massive *Catalog of the Latin American Collection* and its supplements. In its totality, this set provides the most complete record of books published in Latin America.
  Comments:
  > I use this a great deal, particularly since we have a very large backlog of uncataloged material which is listed only by title. It is the most comprehensive bibliography of Latin America-related books available anywhere.

  > I recommend that researchers use this tool in conjunction with HAPI and HLAS for a complete search. I will use it to find out if a work exists for subject areas in which we are weak.

Nos. 3-4: Seven (7) Mentions
3. *Handbook of Latin American Studies.* Austin: University of Texas Press, 1935- . (Formerly published by Harvard University Press and University of Florida Press) Annual. $65.00.

Beginning with volume 26, 1964, *HLAS* was divided into two parts: social sciences and humanities. Each part is published in alternate years as a separate volume. *HLAS* continues to be a model annotated bibliography in the field of Latin American studies, providing an excellent periodic overview of monographic and serial literature in a well organized and readable format. Coverage varies, but most volumes contain special articles on different aspects of Latin American life and culture.

Comments:
> Introductory section essays provide state-of-the-art analysis of treated disciplines.

> Because it publishes alternating subject volumes each year, other tools need to be used for more current information.

4. *Latin America and Caribbean Contemporary Record.* New York: Holmes and Meier, 1981- . $244.95.

The publisher claims, with good reason, that "this unique, comprehensive annual survey [provides] the *only* current, thoroughly documented, single-volume survey of Latin American and Caribbean affairs." Topics of the essays are timely and written by authorities in the fields. Country-by-country coverage of events and trends is excellent. Only the high price tag will keep this off the ready reference shelf of our smaller libraries.

Comments:
> It is hoped this will be an on-going publication. With index, book abstracts, documents, current essays, and arrangement by country under such headings as political affairs, social affairs, economic affairs, this work presents an up-to-date picture of Latin America and can be approached from different access points.

> Reliable, up-to-date, in English, easy to consult, indexed. Economic, social and political data.

> This will become a standard source as more volumes are published. Already, I refer students here for current background information on the region, by topic by country.

> This excellent new source for Latin American studies provides a wealth of information on many aspects of present-day Latin American affairs and reflects current developments.

Nos. 5-6: Six (6) Mentions:
5. Gropp, Arthur E. *A Bibliography of Latin American Bibliog-*

raphies. Metuchen, N.J.: Scarecrow Press, 1968. 515 p. $40.00. (o.p.)

Gropp, Arthur E. *A Bibliography of Latin American Bibliographies. Supplement*. Metuchen, N.J.: Scarecrow Press, 1971. 277 p. $10.00. (o.p.)

Piedracueva, Haydee. *Bibliography of Latin American Bibliographies, 1975-1979: Social Sciences and Humanities*. Metuchen, N.J.: Scarecrow Press, 1982. 313 p. $25.00.

Cordeiro, Daniel R. *A Bibliography of Latin American Bibliographies: Social Sciences and Humanities*. Metuchen, N.J.: Scarecrow Press, 1979. 272 p. $20.00.

Here is an idea that would not die. Gropp's original volume was based on a work by the same title compiled by C. K. Jones and published in 1942 (reprinted by Greenwood Press in 1969). Gropp added 4,000 new references to Jones's 2,900, covering items published through 1964. Gropp's first supplement (1971) added 1,400 items, and those by Cordeiro and Piedracueva, 1,750 and 2,122 respectively, updating coverage through 1979. Since the last volumes, the SALALM Committee on Bibliography has compiled and published annual supplements; a 5-year cumulation covering the years 1980-1984, edited by Lionel Lorona, is forthcoming under the title *Bibliography of Latin American and Caribbean Bibliographies.*

6. *Statistical Abstract of Latin America*. Los Angeles: University of California, Los Angeles, Latin American Center, 1955- . Annual (irregular). $100.00.

This is a useful source of statistical information on Latin American nations (English-speaking countries now excluded). Coverage varies.

Comments:
> This work is most useful for the frequent statistical questions that we receive. Of course, it doesn't answer all the requests, and we do have a variety of other statistical sources, but it is the best one stop source. It is especially useful for cross-country comparisons.

The single combined source for statistical data about Latin America. Includes essays on key current topics in quantitative historical research.

Nos. 7-9: Five (5) Mentions
7. *Encyclopedia of Latin America*. Edited by Helen Delpar. New York: McGraw-Hill, 1974. 651 p. $49.95. (o.p.)

This concise, one-volume encyclopedia provides information on the history, economy, politics, arts, and other aspects of Latin America. Treats the eighteen Spanish-speaking republics plus Brazil, Haiti, and Puerto Rico.
Comment:
This source is dated . . . but it is invaluable for information on Latin American figures and events through the mid-sixties.

8. *Handbook of Middle American Indians*. Edited by Robert Wauchope. Austin: University of Texas Press, 1964-1976. 16 v. Ca. $600.00.

This is an important set (or series) covering all aspects of the cultures and environments of Middle American Indians, made up of essays by specialists. Each volume has an extensive bibliography and index.
Comment:
Indispensable for ethnographic and anthropological research.

9. Mundo Lo, Sara de. *Index to Spanish American Collective Biography*. 6 vols. Reference Publications in Latin American Studies. Boston: G. K. Hall, 1981-85. Vol. 1, Andean Countries (1981): $62.50; vol. 2, Mexico (1982): $68.00; vol. 3, Central American and Caribbean Countries (1984): $75.00; vol. 4, The River Plate Countries (1985): $85.00. Volumes on Brazil and General Latin American Resources yet to be published.

This set serves as a guide to references in collective biographies of Spanish Americans which provides access to information not readily available in any other form.

Comment:
It is an example of what I see as a potentially useful tool. I have not had the occasion to use it, yet. I am amazed at how it covers people from many fields, and when finished will cover all of Spanish America.

Nos. 10-12: Four (4) Mentions
10. *Cambridge Encyclopedia of Latin America and the Caribbean*. Edited by Simon Collier, Harold Blakemore, and Thomas E. Skidmore. New York: Cambridge University Press, 1985. 456 p. $39.50.

Comments:

Valuable for quick, general orientation, although *Encyclopedia of Latin America* (1974) is still useful for covering certain topics.

If this work lives up to the expectation engendered by the calibre of its editors (Harold Blakemore, Thomas E. Skidmore, and Simon Collier), it could take the place of Helen Delpar's *Encyclopedia of Latin America* (New York: McGraw-Hill, 1974). The two works will undoubtedly supplement each other in many ways.

Although the format leaves much to be desired, this also provides recent and well-written articles on all aspects of Latin American studies.

11. Griffin, Charles C., ed. *Latin America: A Guide to Historical Literature*. 2 vols. Conference on Latin American History, Publication no. 4. Austin: University of Texas Press, 1971. 700 p. $25.00. (o.p.)

Comments:
Although this is obviously dated, it is still the classic source for standard historical information.

An excellent starting place for historical research.

12. *ISLA: Information Services on Latin America*. Oakland, Calif: Information Services on Latin America, 1970- . Monthly. $480.00.

Comments:
This serial compilation of reprinted newspaper articles is useful for dating and filling in details of events and trends since the early 1970s.

ISLA and *The Handbook of Latin American Art* are examples of useful reference sources [that are] more limited by discipline or period.

Invaluable for up-to-date information on current topics.

No. 13: Three (3) Mentions
13. Palau y Dulcet, Antonio. *Manual del hispanoamericano: Bibliografía general española e hispano-americana desde la invencíon de la imprenta hasta nuestros tiempos, con el valor comercial de los impresos*. Barcelona: Libreria Palau, 1948-1977. 28 v.

Nos. 14-24: Two (2) Mentions
14. Covington, Paula Haddox. *Indexed Journals: A Guide to Latin American Serials*. Seminar on the Acquisition of Latin American Library Materials, Bibliography and Reference Series, no. 8. Madison: Secretariat, Seminar on the Acquisition of Latin American Library Materials, University of Wisconsin-Madison, 1983.

15. *Fichero bibliográfico hispanoamericano*. New York and Buenos Aires: Bowker, 1961- . Quarterly; monthly, Oct. 1964- . $40.00 per year.

16. Freudenthal, Juan R., and Freudenthal, Patricia M., eds. and comps. *Index to Anthologies of Latin American Literature in English Translation*. Boston: G. K. Hall, 1977. 199 p. $20.00.

17. *Grand enciclopédia portuguesa e brasileira.* Lisbon: Editorial Enciclopedia, 1935-1958. 37 v.; Apêdice 3 v. _____. 2a parte: Brasil. In Progress.

18. *Handbook of Latin American Art/Manual de arte latinoamericano: A Bibliographic Compilation.* Edited by Joyce Waddell Bailey. Santa Barbara: ABC-Clio Information Services, 1984- . $75.00.

19. *Handbook of South American Indians.* Edited by Julian H. Steward. 6 vols. New York: Cooper Square Publishers, 1963. (As listed in Woods.)

20. Knaster, Meri. *Spanish America: An Annotated Bibliography from Pre-Conquest to Contemporary Times.* Boston: G. K. Hall, 1977. 696 p. $40.00. (o.p.)

21. *Latin America and the Caribbean: A Dissertation Bibliography.* Edited by Carl W. Deal. Ann Arbor: University Microfilms International, 1977. 164 p. Supplement, 1980.

22. *Libros en venta en Hispanoamérica y España.* 3rd ed. 2 vols. San Juan, Puerto Rico: Melcher Ediciones, 1985.

23. *Oxford Companion to Spanish Literature.* Edited by Philip Ward. Oxford: Clarendon Press, 1978. 629 p. $39.95.

24. *South American Handbook.* Bath, England: Trade and Travel Publications, 1924- . Annual. $25.00.

What have we missed? Are there other titles that some specialists—or generalists, for that matter—might consider indispensable? Of course there are, and always will be, other titles out there that could be very useful—48 more were mentioned once by the respondents as being in their "top ten" titles. Of those 48 titles, 14 ranked in the upper half of those who ranked their titles. One title ranked first and 4 of them ranked second. The first-ranked title is a vintage one:

Grismer, Raymond L. *A Reference Index to Twelve Thousand Spanish American Authors: A Guide to the Literature of Spanish America.* Inter-American Bibliographical and Library Association Publications, series III, vol. 1. New York: H. W. Wilson, 1939. 150 p. Reprinted, New York: B. Franklin, 1970. $19.00.

Those ranking second were the following:

Enciclopedia universal ilustrada europea-americana. Madrid: Espasa-Calpe, 1907-1930. 70 v. in 72, plus appendices and annual supplements.

Gropp, Arthur E. *Bibliography of Latin American Bibliographies Published in Periodicals.* 2 vols. Metuchen, N.J.: Scarecrow Press , 1976. 1031 p.

Ibero-Amerikanische Institut. *SchlagwortKatalog.* Berlin: Ibero-Amerikanische Institut. Boston: G. K. Hall, *Latin America and Caribbean.* Saffron, England: World of Information, 1980- $24.95. pa.

The Gropp bibliography is a classified listing of more than 9,700 items appearing in periodical literature covering the period 1929-1965.

Still other titles would be useful for the basic reference collection on Latin America, of which the following are a very few (the last title is a good place to start):

Bleznick, Donald. *A Sourcebook for Hispanic Literature and Language: A Selected and Annotated Guide to Spanish, Spanish-American, and Chicano Bibliography, Literature, Linguistics, Journals, and Other Source Materials.* 2d ed. Metuchen, N.J.: Scarecrow Press, 1983.

Block, David, and Karno, Howard L. *A Directory of Vendors of Latin American Library Materials.* 2d ed. Seminar on the Acquisition of Latin American Library Materials, Bibliography and Reference Series, no. 9. Madison: Secretariat, Seminar on the Acquisition of Latin American Library Materials, University of Wisconsin-Madison, 1986. 46 p. $12.00 pa.

Cambridge History of Latin America. Edited by Leslie

Bethell. 8 vols. Cambridge: Cambridge University Press, 1985- . Vol. 1 (1985): $65.00; vol. 2 (1985): $75.00; vol. 3 (1985): $80.00. Vols. 4-8 not yet published.

Chaney, Elsa M. *Women of the World: Latin America and the Caribbean*. Washington, DC: U.S. Department of Commerce, Bureau of the Census; U.S. Government Printing Office, 1984, $5.50. (o.p.)

Foster, David William, comp. *A Dictionary of Contemporary Latin American Authors*. Tempe: Center for Latin American Studies, Arizona State University, 1975. 110 p. $6.95 pa.

Foster, David William, and Foster, Virginia Ramos. *Modern Latin American Literature*. 2 vols. New York: Frederick Ungar, 1975. $120.00.

Guía a las reseñas de libros de y sobre Latinoamerica/Guide to Reviews of Books from and about Hispanic America. Blaine-Ethridge Books, 1960-1964 and 1972- . Annual.

Sable, Martin H. *The Latin American Studies Directory*. Detroit: Blaine Ethridge Books, 1981. 124 p. $16.50.

Werlich, David. *Research Tools for Latin American Historians: A Select, Annotated Bibliography*. Garland Reference Library of Social Science, vol. 60. New York: Garland, 1980. 269 p. $43.00.

Wilgus, A. Curtis. *Latin America: A Guide to Illustrations*. Metuchen, N.J.: Scarecrow Press, 1981. $20.00.

Woods, Richard D. *Hispanic First Names: A Comprehensive Dictionary of 250 Years of Mexican American Usage*. Bibliographies and Indexes in Anthropology. Westport, Conn.: Greenwood Press, 1984. 224 p. $35.00.

Woods, Richard D. *Reference Materials on Latin America in English: The Humanities*. Metuchen, N.J.: Scarecrow Press, 1980. 639 p. $40.00.

PUBLISHERS' SERIES TO LOOK (OUT) FOR

Despite the confusion over the term "series," the survey turned up some useful comments on important materials. Some of the sets appearing in the preceding list could be considered as series; certainly a number of them are serials. In addition to those works, respondents identified five publishers' series and one "authors' series" on Latin America. The author who was singled out by three respondents was David W. Foster, a prolific writer in the field of Latin American studies. Any public catalog of a research library will turn up a list of fifteen or more monographs. The special place accorded Mr. Foster can be seen in these two comments:

> David Foster's series of publications (e.g., *Mexican Literature*, *Cuban Literature*, etc.) would be a good candidate (his country bibliographies have been published by Scarecrow, Garland and Greenwood).

> The many excellent publications written by David William Foster. Although not published as a series per se, they form a collection of very high quality dictionaries, bibliographies, and sourcebooks on Latin American literature, culture, etc.

Of the publishers' series, one was mentioned five times, but not always in a favorable light: the Scarecrow Press "Latin American Historical Dictionaries" (1970-). Each book deals with a single Latin American country, providing, in alphabetical dictionary form, pertinent information about persons, places, events, geography, and political subdivisions. A bibliography is also included in each volume. Volumes 1-21 were edited by the late A. Curtis Wilgus. Volumes 22 and 23, now in preparation, will be edited by Karna S. Wilgus. Second editions of several volumes are in preparation under the direction of Laurence Hallewell.

The coverage of the series is impressive; to date the following titles have been published: 1. *Guatemala*, by Richard E. Moore (rev. ed., 1973); 2. *Panama*, by Basil C. and Anne K. Hedrick (1970); 3. *Venezuela*. by Donna K. and G. A. Rudolph (1971); 4. *Bolivia*, by Dwight B. Heath (1972); 5. *El Salvador*, by Philip F. Flemion (1972); 6. *Nicaragua*, by Harvey K. Meyer (1972); 7. *Chile*, by Salvatore Bizzarro (1972); 8. *Paraguay*, by Charles

J. Kolinsky (1973); 9. *Puerto Rico and the U. S. Virgin Islands*, by Kenneth R. Farr (1973); 10. *Ecuador*, by Albert W. Bork and Georg Maier (1973); 11. *Uruguay*, by Jean L. Willis (1974); 12. *The British Caribbean*, by William R. Lux (1975); 13. *Honduras*, by Robert H. Davis (1976); 14. *Colombia*, by Robert H. Davis (1977); 15. *Costa Rica*, by Theodore S. Creedman (1977); 17. *Argentina*, by Ione S. Wright and Lisa M. Nekhom (1978); 18. *French and Netherlands Antilles*, by Albert Gastmann (1978); 19. *Brazil*, by Robert M. Levine (1979); 20. *Peru*, by Marvin Alisky (1979); and 21. *Mexico*, by Donald C. Briggs and Marvin Alisky (1981). Volumes now in preparation include *Cuba*, by Jaime Suchlicki, and *Dominican Republic*. by Frank Moya Pons.

The dates alone of some of these titles suggest that, given the pace of events in Latin America, new editions are due. The unevenness of these dictionaries is reflected in the comments of several respondents. Two called it "highly variable" in coverage and quality. Two others had more lengthy comments on the series:

> I was very excited about this series when it first appeared. I use the different titles frequently for quick facts about people and events, but I have found that they vary greatly in coverage. You can't always find the same information; for example, some include chronologies and lists of rulers while others don't.
>
> We would also like to comment on what we consider to be the least useful series. It is the Historical Dictionary Series published by Scarecrow Press. We find the contents of these publications to be highly idiosyncratic. Apparently there are no systematic criteria for the types of information to be included. Often the information that is included is so minimal or fragmentary that it is useless, and entries that could reasonably be expected to be included are not to be found.

A much more favorable tone characterized the comments about another series mentioned by four respondents: the handbooks prepared by the Foreign Area Studies of the American

University, under the Country Studies/Area Handbook Program, and published by the U.S. Government Printing Office. Formerly published as "Area Handbooks," titles published since the late 1970s have each been subtitled "A Country Study." Each book in the series describes and analyzes a country's economic, national security, political, and social systems and how they are shaped by cultural factors. Each volume includes a full bibliography and a generous sprinkling of charts, graphs, and black-and-white photographs. The series is constantly being updated, with title pages indicating the month and year when research was completed. Some titles are simply reprinted.

The coverage of this series is worldwide (over 100 titles in all) and includes the following titles on nations of Latin America and the Caribbean (with series number and date of latest revision or reprint): 20. *Brazil* (1983); 26. *Colombia* (1977); 42. *Peru* (1981); 46. *Panama* (1981); 54. *Dominican Republic* (1974); 66. *Bolivia* (1979); 71. *Venezuela* (1977); 77. *Chile* (1982); 78. *Guatemala* (1984); 79. *Mexico* (1985); 82. *Guyana* (1980); 88. *Nicaragua* (1982); 90. *Costa Rica* (1984); 97. *Uruguay* (1976); 150. *El Salvador* (1971); 151. *Honduras* (1984); 152. *Cuba* (1985); 156. *Paraguay* (1972); 177. *Jamaica* (1976); and 178. *Trinidad and Tabago* (1976). Virtually all of the titles are still available from GPO at prices ranging from $11 to $16, clearly one of the best book bargains in the field.

Comments:
> The foreign area handbooks . . . are perhaps the best series of publications for up-to-date information on Latin American countries. The quality and currency vary with the editor and the revision cycles for the series.

> The reference series that we consider most useful are the Area Handbooks issued by the U. S. Government Printing Office, and the guides published by the Library of Congress entitled *A Guide to the Law and Legal Literature of* . . . within its Latin American Series.

> As far as the best series on Latin America, I believe [that] for my library the Area Handbook or Country series, put out by the U.S. government, is the best reference series.

The following series were each mentioned three times: "Latin American Serial Documents," edited by Rosa Quintero Mesa and published by University Microfilms International, and the SALALM "Bibliography and Reference Series." Mesa's series, subtitled "A Holdings List," consists of bibliographies of serial publications, with locations for as many documents as could be identified. This "holdings list" is based upon the collections of the University of Florida, former Farmington Plan participants, and other special collections of Latin American materials. Volumes in the series published thus far include the following: 1. *Colombia* (1968); 2. *Brazil* (1968); 3. *Cuba* (1969); 4. *Mexico* (1970); 5. *Argentina* (1971); 6. *Bolivia* (1972); 7. *Chile* (1973); 8. *Ecuador* (1973); 9. *Paraguay* (1973); 10. *Peru* (1973); 11. *Uruguay* (1973); and 12. *Venezuela* (1977). Future volumes are planned for the Dominican Republic and Haiti (one volume), Costa Rica, El Salvador, Guatemala, Honduras, Nicaragua, and Panama.

The SALALM "Bibliography Series" — continued by the "Bibliography and Reference Series" — has been helpful to librarians and Latin American bibliographers since its inception in 1969. Paula Covington's *Indexed Journals: A Guide to Latin American Serials*, already mentioned, forms part of this series. Other titles dealing with Latin America in general include *A Basic List of Latin American Materials in Spanish, Portuguese, and French*, ed. Hensley Woodbridge (1975); *Doctoral Dissertations in Hispanic-American Literature: A Bibliography of Dissertations Completed in the U.S., 1964-1974*, by Barbara J. Robinson (1979); and *Directory of Vendors of Latin American Library Materials*. ed. David Block and Howard L. Karno (1983, 2d ed., 1986). The annual updates to Lionel Lorona's *Bibliography of Latin Bibliographies*, also mentioned above, appear in the "Bibliography and Reference Series." SALALM also publishes its final reports and working papers, along with other publications on Latin America. SALALM publications are difficult to find in the standard book trade bibliographies; for information write directly to the SALALM Secretariat, Memorial Library, University of Wisconsin-Madison, Madison, WI 53706.

Comments:
This series contains a wide variety of publications which range from very specific to broad appeal. A sampling of recent titles includes a bibliography on Eva Peron as well as a guide to where Latin American journals are indexed. Beginning in 1984 the annual update to the *Bibliography of Latin American Bibliographies* appears in this series.

One other publishers' series mentioned was G. K. Hall's "Reference Publications in Latin American Studies," edited by William Vernon Jackson. Sara de Mundo Lo's *Index of Spanish American Collective Biography*, mentioned above, appears in this series. Selected titles in this series, most of them focusing on specific countries or regions, include the following: *Chilean Literature: A Working Bibliography of Secondary Sources*, by David William Foster (1978); *The Catholic Left in Latin America: A Comprehensive Bibliography*, by Therrin C. Dallin, Gary P. Gillum, and Mark L. Grover (1981); *The Mexican Revolution: An Annotated Guide to Recent Scholarship*, by W. Dirk Raat (1982); *The English-Speaking Caribbean: A Bibliography of Bibliographies*, by Alma Jordan and Barbara and Commissiong (1984); and *Petroleum in Venezuela: A Bibliography*, by William M. Sullivan and Brian S. McBeth (1985).

Another G. K. Hall series, the "Reference Publications in International Historical Statistics," edited by Oliver Pollak, while not limited to Latin America, has thus far produced very useful publications on two Latin American nations: Brazil and Cuba.

DESIDERATA:
WHAT ELSE WE NEED ON LATIN AMERICA

The apparently simple questions asking Latin American library specialists what reference works are needed drew the most varied response at all, so varied that even with more than 40 different suggestions, there was little overlap. Some suggestions were global:

Your question 4 could take several pages since just about every reference book that is reliable, up-to-date and easy to use (has indexes) has yet to be published with revised editions.

Another respondent is even less sanguine about the state of affairs with bibliographers:

In general, there is a need for better reference sources than the ones that we have currently available, especially for sources that are systematically and scientifically compiled. Amateurish bibliographers would get better results by consulting or working in cooperation with bibliographers of established reputation before and during the production of their works.

That state of affairs seems to suggest that, while a number of major publications on Latin America have appeared over the past decade, we still have a way to go. The following list is distilled from the many suggestions and comments on the need for new publications; quotes are used when deemed appropriate.

1. A basic guide to research on Latin America and the Caribbean. "The project which Paula Covington has been planning for the publication of a research guide to the study of Latin America and the Caribbean is one example of a reference work that is needed."

2. An on-line version of the *Handbook for Latin American Studies* and *Hispanic American Periodical Index*, preferably available through DIALOG.

3. A guide to specialized subject collections in the U.S. and Canada on Latin America, similar to Lee Ash's *Subject Collections*.

4. A selective, annotated guide to serials on and from Latin America, updating Irene Zimmerman's *Guide to Current Latin American Periodicals*. Such a project is now under way by Barbara Valk. "There are actually two types of works that I would like to see in this area. One would be an update to Alexander S. Birkos, *Latin American Studies* which was part of the series *Academic Writer's Guide to*

Periodicals. The other would be a Spanish/Portuguese language version of Katz's *Magazines for Libraries*. What I am looking for is something that will give descriptions of magazines from both the writer's point of view and the reader's."

5. A periodical index for Spanish and Portuguese journals, many of which relate to Latin America.

6. "A magazine index for general Spanish/Portuguese language magazines, similar to *Magazine Index*. There is a lot of valuable information in these magazines which is difficult to get at because it isn't indexed. The type of magazine I am referring to is not as scholarly as those indexed in HAPI or even in *Contents of Periodicals on Latin America*. For news events, you can get the date and follow through from there, but this doesn't work for other types of stories, such as cultural and sports."

7. Reference bibliographies that provide comprehensive subject coverage of the larger countries such as Argentina, Brazil, and Chile.

8. A current encyclopedia on Latin America more extensive than the one-volume *Encyclopedia of Latin America* (1974); (e.g., *Cambridge Encyclopedia of Latin America and the Caribbean*).

9. More reference tools for art, music, medicine, science/technology (including computer science), folklore.

10. A guide to art and architecture in Latin America and the Caribbean.

11. An update of Irene Zimmerman's *Current National Bibliographies of Latin America* (1971). "Up-to-date and complete national bibliographies are [also] sorely needed, but that is like asking for pie in the sky."

12. An update of or supplement to Charles Griffin's *Guide to Historical Literature* (1971).

13. More bibliographies of literature and criticism by country, along the lines of those done by David W. Foster on Mexico and Cuba.

14. Other up-to-date bibliographies by country, such as the *Honduras Bibliography and Research Guide* published by CAMINO in Cambridge, Mass.

15. Research guides by country, such as the *Guia bibliográfica para el estudio de la historia ecuatoriana* (University of Texas, 1978).

16. An historical guide to land ownership in Latin America.

17. A guide to the literature on immigration to Latin America.

18. An updated version of *Who Is Who in Latin America* or another good biographical dictionary.

19. An updated version of *Latin American Studies Directory*.

20. An updated acronyms dictionary. "A question that can cause trouble is what the full name for an acronym [is]. The only tool that we have (UNECLA's *Latin American Initialisms Acronyms*) is out of date. If the organization publishes, the LC name authority file on OCLC can often supply the information."

21. Current list of political/government officials. "We also need something that would give us up-to-date information on government officials in Latin America."

22. Sports information. "I have had several questions regarding sports in Latin America for which I wasn't able to find an answer. The general sports reference tools mention soccer and the World Cup and that is it. I have been unable to identify any tool which gives basic information about which sports are played where, let alone information on records, etc."

23. Indexes to leading newspapers of Latin America, similar to the *New York Times*.

24. An ongoing bibliography of dissertations on Latin America, which include as many universities as possible, not just those whose dissertations are microfilmed by University Microfilms.

25. "Almost anything" on official publications.

26. Additional dictionaries or encyclopedias of Latin American Literature, including both new and older writers. "A single work, necessarily in multiple volumes, combining the basic facts and bibliographical keys to works by and about writers, would be enormously helpful to librarians

and their clientele alike. Such a tool would be particularly useful to those who have not specialized in literature."

27. A special gazetteer for Latin America and a good dictionary of old and new Latin American place names.

28. Guides to Latin American government agencies with descriptions of their activities.

29. Guides to research centers in Latin America with descriptions of their activities and publications.

30. Guides to picture resources in the various countries, similar to one in progress, Martha Davidson's *Guide to Mexican Picture Resources*.

31. Up-to-date language dictionaries for the various countries.

32. Book reviews on a current basis.

33. Translation lists (Spanish/Portuguese to English and vice versa).

34. More current reference works for non-book materials.

35. Good reference works on Central American republics. "Central America is poorly covered by reference works."

TENTATIVE CONCLUSIONS – AND ONE MORE LIST (FOR THE SMALL AND MEDIUM-SIZED LIBRARY)

This survey of Latin American bibliographers and reference specialists in North American libraries underscores the difficulty of arriving at consensus on the outstanding reference titles on Latin America. Some respondents pointed out, first of all, that some of the tried-and-true general reference works are a good place to start for information on Latin America. In any case, of the 73 titles listed among the "top ten" or so titles by the respondents, a basic core emerged based not only on the number of times each title was mentioned but on the comments of the respondents. The price range among these titles, however, is enormous, and suggests very strongly that not all libraries can afford to purchase the *crème de la crème*. Some of the reference works consist of large and expensive sets; others consist of series which, while excellent for the research library, are beyond the means of most small and medium-sized libraries. Even with all this publishing activity, the specialists had no trouble whatsoever in pointing out the lagunae—the many types of reference publications that are needed on Latin America.

And now, one more list—my own selection of titles for a basic reference collection on Latin America in the small and medium-sized public library. This list passes over some of our more expensive publishing jewels, but provides representative publications among bibliographies and other reference works. It may not be the ideal list, but it is an affordable one. All of these items are in print at this writing.

1. For a basic list of reference works on Latin America in the English language: Woods, *Reference Materials on Latin America in English: The Humanities*.

2. For travel information: *South American Handbook*.

3. For a periodic overview of publications on Latin America: *Handbook of Latin America Studies*.

4. For basic factual information: *Cambridge Encyclopedia of Latin America and the Caribbean*.

5. For factual information on Spanish and Spanish American literature: *Oxford Companion to Spanish Literature*.

6. For language information and basic facts (in Spanish): *Pequeño Larousse ilustrado*.

7. For an authoritative history of Latin America: *Cambridge History of Latin America* (moderately expensive).

8. For up-to-date information on specific countries in Latin America and the Caribbean: selected Area Handbooks/Country Studies.

9. For books in print in Spanish: *Libros en venta en Hispanoamérica y España*.

10. For an ongoing list of publications in Spanish: *Fichero bibliográfico hispanoamericano*.

And the list goes on. . . .

LATIN AMERICAN SPECIALISTS WHO RESPONDED TO THE SURVEY

1. Ana Maria Cobos
   Manager, *BorderLine*
   Latin American Center
   University of California, Los Angeles
   Los Angeles, CA 90024

2. Paula Anne Covington
   Latin American and Iberian Bibliographer
   Jean and Alexander Heard Library
   Vanderbilt University
   Nashville, TN 37203

3. Oscar E. Delepiani
   Librarian
   Benson Latin American Collection
   Sid Richardson Hall 1.206
   University of Texas at Austin
   Austin, TX 78712-7330

4. Enid F. D'Oyley
   Bibliographer/Book Selector for Spain,
   Portugal and Latin America
   University of Toronto Library/Latin American Studies
   University of Toronto
   Toronto, Ontario, Canada M5S 1A5

5. Russ Davidson
   Coordinator, Latin American Collections Development
   General Library
   University of New Mexico
   Albuquerque, NM 87131

6. Jane Garner
   Archivist
   Nettie Lee Benson Latin American Collection
   University of Texas at Austin General Libraries
   Austin, TX 78713-7330

7. Donald Gibbs
   Latin American Studies Bibliographer
   Nettie Lee Benson Latin American Collection
   University of Texas at Austin
   Austin, TX 78713-7330

8. Mina Jane Grothey
   Ibero-American Reference Librarian
   General Library
   University of New Mexico
   Albuquerque, NM 87131

9. Mark L. Grover
   Latin American Studies Bibliographer
   Harold B. Lee Library
   Brigham Young University
   Provo, UT 84602

10. Ann Hartness-Kane
    Assistant Head Librarian
    Nettie Lee Benson Latin American Collection
    University of Texas at Austin
    Austin, TX 78713-7330

11. Suzanne Hodgman
    Bibliographer for Ibero-American Studies
    Memorial Library
    University of Wisconsin-Madison
    Madison, WI 53706

12. Maria Segura Hoopes
    Reference Librarian
    University Library
    University of Arizona
    Tucson, AZ 85721

13. Mary Ellis Kahler
    Senior Bibliographer
    Hispanic Division

Library of Congress
Washington, DC 20540

14. Everette E. Larson
    Reference Librarian
    Hispanic Division
    Library of Congress
    Washington, DC 20540

15. Ludwig Lauerhass, Jr.
    Latin American Bibliographer
    University Research Library
    University of California, Los Angeles
    Los Angeles, CA 90024

16. Karen J. Lindvall
    Latin American Bibliographer
    The University Library
    University of California, San Diego
    San Diego, CA 92093

17. Sara de Mundo Lo
    Modern Languages and Linguistics Librarian
    University of Illinois at Urbana-Champaign
    Urbana, IL 61801

18. David Null
    Social Sciences Coordinator
    General Library
    University of New Mexico
    Albuquerque, NM 87131

19. Barbara Valk
    Coordinator, Bibliographic Development
    Latin American Center
    University of California, Los Angeles
    Los Angeles, CA 90024

20. David S. Zubatsky
   Dean of Library and Media Services
   Helen A. Ganser Library
   Millersville University of Pennsylvania
   Millersville, PA 17551

NOTES

1. Gunther, John. *Inside South America*. New York: Harper and Row, 1966, pp. xiii-xiv.

2. Dorst, Jean. *South America and Central America: A natural history*. New York: Random House, 1967, p. 7.

3. Tannenbaum, Frank. *Ten keys to Latin America*. New York: Vintage Books, 1960, p. 6.

Foreign Trade & Econ Abstracts Measures Up Internationally

R. A. J. Van Loen

The Dutch have always been known as "the traders of the world." For centuries they have been involved in international trade and they still do. Today, the importance of trade to the Netherlands is exemplified by the fact that Rotterdam is the largest seaport in the world, and that Amsterdam International Airport is one of the major air cargo handling centers on the European continent.

The Netherlands are a gateway to Europe. Besides that, over sixty percent of the Dutch gross national income is earned through exports! It is for this reason that the Dutch government strongly supports Dutch export activities, among others by supplying information. In doing so, the "fourth production factor" business information, has become a major tool to Dutch industries.

One of Holland's most important institutions to apply to for business information is the Netherlands Foreign Trade Agency (NFTA), a subsidiary of the Dutch Ministry for Economic Affairs. On the next few pages the on-line data base that is produced by the Library Division of the NFTA is discussed, a data base with a worldwide coverage of market information.

The author is at the Netherlands Foreign Trade Agency, Ministry of Economic Affairs, Documentation and Library Branch, 151 Bezuidenhoutseweg, 2594 AG The Hague, Netherlands.

© 1987 by The Haworth Press, Inc. All rights reserved.

LIBRARY DIVISION

This year the Netherlands Foreign Trade Agency celebrates its 50th anniversary. The library division was founded long before the NFTA even existed, in 1903! After the economic recession of the thirties the NFTA started to supply Dutch industries with market information. In those days the present library division was added to the NFTA. Or, to be more exact, the NFTA was added to the library! Let's have a closer look at this very old library that still is the largest of its kind in the Netherlands.

The library division is subdivided into different departments, a documentation department, a literature research department, a reference library and a statistical department.

The *documentation department* is the very heart of the library system. Here the international literature is scanned and abstracted for inclusion in the data base. All the people working in this department are specialists and have a fluent command of four languages to be able to do their jobs properly. The data base they create is a multilingual file so a sound working knowledge of different languages is absolutely necessary. Together they produce over 10,000 abstracts every year.

The *literature research department* is working on the output side of the system; a well trained staff tries to find an answer to over 40,000 questions put by visitors, which is the estimated annual average. Of course they use terminals, connected to the Dutch State Computer Center, for accessing the data base. Further, they instruct people how to use the microfiche readers as a copy of the data base is available on microfiches in the library. Access to other on-line data bases is possible too. On demand, market surveys are produced by a small staff that is highly specialized in on-line information retrieval.

Quite a unique collection of reference works is available in the *reference library*. Over 3500 volumes on the shelves ready for immediate access! Need an address of a trading company in Oman? The answer is there. Who is selling paperweights in Malaysia? The answer is there. Needless to say that this department is of vital importance to anyone involved in international trade.

The *statistical department* covers a world of figures! Statistical surveys in the field of international trade are drawn from over

1400 different statistical sourcebooks from all over the world. The collection of the entire library is updated almost every day.

Online

The library division collected over two million articles, books, etc. on international trade, after having been incorporated with the NFTA. Up till the early seventies this huge amount of information was accessible by a manual system, which of course was highly inefficient regarding the ever increasing demand for information. So, in 1972 it was decided to create on-line facilities to improve the services rendered.

Within two years the data base was there, being the first file in the field of international trade in the Netherlands. Only a few years later international access was accomplished thru Dialog Information Services in the U.S. Later on, two European vendors took care of on-line distribution too, Data-Star and Belindis.

Foreign Trade & Econ Abstracts (FT&EA)

FT&EA originates with the Library division of the Netherlands Foreign Trade Agency. As was explained earlier it was created to meet the information needs of executives and managers in business and industry. Over the years it became one of the major sources for business information with special emphasis on foreign markets and international trade.

FT&EA provides the user with both current and retrospective information on a variety of business, economic and country specific topics. Foreign Trade & Econ Abstracts was formerly known as Economics Abstracts International. Currently FT&EA contains some 170,000 records with an annual increase of 12,000 approximately. Each record in the data base contains full bibliographic information and an abstract in the source language. Update tapes are run on a biweekly basis and are airmailed to the vendors abroad. They update either monthly or biweekly.

Sources

Some 1800 different periodicals are scanned extensively. Further, monographs, reports, market studies, annual (company) reports and development bank publications are selected for inclusion into the data base. Being part of a government institution the Library division closely cooperates with the economic departments of Dutch embassies and consulates abroad to keep its collection up-to-date. Of course, embassies and consulates have good access to their local information markets! Special attention is given to the acquisition of market related information. This know-how is transferred to the NFTA's Library division, the spider in the web!

Further, the library management keeps track of developments in international trade, product innovations and market opportunities. Flexibility in thinking and in acquiring the best possible information have top-priority in the organization. Within the NFTA-offices high speed information channels are created to keep ahead of information flows, thus enabling the Library division to adapt to the ever changing information demand. As the NFTA participates in over 250 trade-shows annually, a lot of information from workers in the field is coming in. So, traditional library sources are supplemented by a wide range of less traditional information channels.

SUBJECT COVERAGE

A full description of all the subjects covered would be quite impossible. However, three major areas can be distinguished.

- economics and business information
- country, and
- industry information

Within the *economics and business* information areas, comprehensive coverage includes,

- economic development
- industrial development
- investment climates
- economic policy
- international trade

- company profiles
- export business
- management and marketing

Country specific information can be retrieved on almost all the topics dealt with in the data base. It ranges from country profiles, i.e., general information on the political situation or the business climate, to more specific information such as market opportunities for certain products or services. Just to give an idea of the regional coverage of the information available, the following table is illustrative:

— Western-Europe	45%
— Eastern-Europe	5%
— North-America	14%
— Middle-America	2.5%
— South-America	4.5%
— Africa	8%
— Middle-East	4%
— Far-East	12%
— Australia	4%

From this table it should be clear that the major industrial powers are better represented than lesser developed countries. Notwithstanding that, much effort is put in covering ldc's as well. It should be mentioned that international cooperation between countries, such as by the EC- or ASEAN-countries, can be used in searching thus covering certain economic regions in one search statement.

The third major area, *industry information*, highlights the developments in different industrial sectors together with their products. Some areas of interest include energy, offshore, telecommunication, (micro)electronics, banking, (petro)chemical industry and so forth.

These three major areas of interest are just a glance of what the Foreign Trade & Econ Abstracts data base can provide to its users. To get a clearer picture of its contents it is highly recommended to use the FT&EA-Thesaurus which gives a listing of all the keywords used. Scanning all possible subjects is more easy then. Later on, the structure and use of the thesaurus will be discussed in greater detail. First, we will have a look at article selection procedures and at abstracting/indexing procedures.

ARTICLE SELECTION

Approximately 80 percent of the records included in the data base refer to periodical articles. The selection criteria that is used by the editorial staff guarantees, that every article entered contains a meaningful contribution to the data base. Articles' contents, therefore, are judged on their lasting rather than passing value. This is one of the major reasons that newspaper articles are not included, excepting those which give a lengthy discussion of an important topic. Further the length of the articles is taken into account, resulting in the storage only, of articles with a minimum length of two pages.

One of the extra features of the FT&EA-data base is that it distinguishes the so called "grade level" of the information included. The majority of the records are of a "popular" grade level, which means that an average user should be able to understand the information provided. This is by no means a judgement of the user's capabilities but rather an extra possibility to limit search results, thus avoiding too much noise. For instance, academic users could limit their searches to "university grade level" information only. The same applies to the business user, who most of the time needs information of a more practical kind.

ABSTRACTING AND INDEXING PROCEDURES

Every article or document to be included in the data base is abstracted and indexed. A full bibliographic description precedes the abstract. Abstracts are written in the original language of the document of which 65 percent are in English and the balance is in French, German and Dutch. All keywords assigned are in English only. Abstracts can be either descriptive or informative, depending on the source material. It should be mentioned however, that a gradual shift to more informative abstracts is pursued since early 1985. Informative abstracts may contain percentages and trends to improve their usefulness.

Besides keywords, every abstract will contain as many searchable terms as possible in order to make free-text searching viable. From all the periodicals scanned about 650 are frequently represented in the data base. The remainder is of less importance and is used occasionally for inclusion. Further, a core list of 250 periodicals approximately is microfilmed cover-to-cover, to secure maximum availability of the information. Abstracting and indexing soon becomes some kind of routine, especially to those people that are well experienced.

To avoid that routine interferes with the quality of abstracting and indexing, the documentation department has a responsibility too for the acquisition of new publications. The result of this extra assignment is that new subscriptions to periodicals are added almost every day to the existing 1800. The same applies to the scanning of terms to be included in the thesaurus. These procedures guarantee that the library system is kept up-to-date and gives a true picture of information in the ever changing field of international trade.

Thesaurus

Keywords assigned are drawn from a controlled vocabulary or thesaurus, consisting of two sections. The first section is the alphabetical listing of keywords which provides the user with approximately 2600 terms used in business and economics literature. It is by no means an exhaustive listing of all terms, but it will prove useful in pinpointing a majority of subjects. The alphabetical listing is presented as a KWIC-index. Further, every keyword has got its own numerical description, i.e., UDC-codes are added to uniquely describe the keyword. The second section provides a listing of subjects according to the UDC-codes. These codes are, by their origin, embedded in a hierarchical structure which enables the user to truncate codes, thus implying related subjects in a single search statement.

When the basic UDC-code is not fit to represent the full description of a subject, it is extended by as many extra digits as needed, the maximum being three. When two or more UDC-codes are combined to represent a compound term, the codes are connected by a colon which should be substituted by a question mark in searching, to avoid confusion with the Dialog colon operator. Normally, it is preferable to use keywords, either with or without the /DE-delimiter, than UDC-codes. Keywords are easier to handle in searching and yield the same amount of relevant postings as would have resulted from using codes.

COOPERATION

So far some of the features of Foreign Trade & Econ Abstracts were discussed. The international scope of the information stored is one of the most important items. As was mentioned earlier FT&EA originates with the Netherlands Foreign Trade Agency. Within the NFTA-offices certain information channels have been established to improve the information output to (Dutch) industries. Two major divisions of the NFTA need some further explanation.

The "foreign markets division" of the NFTA is a powerful source of information both to FT&EA and to industries. The main task of this division is to help industries in penetrating new markets abroad or to secure an existing marketshare. Their large staff collected a vast amount of information by frequent visits to their markets abroad and by accompanying firms to trade shows all over the world. Of course this information is transferred to the Library division. A second major division working in the field is the 'consultancy division.' They act in close cooperation with the foreign market and Library divisions. Their main task is to screen the Dutch export potential and to stimulate and coordinate new market penetrations. Here company and product information is collected. It must be clear, by now, that the Foreign Trade & Econ Abstracts data base by no means is an ordinary library product. It is based, as was explained, on a variety of information channels that together are responsible for producing another exportable product, i.e., international trade information!

Besides a well established cooperation among NFTA-divisions, external sources are being screened for inclusion into the network.

Currently research is carried out to broaden the scope of information gathering and distribution. Both the national and international Chambers of Commerce are about to enter the network. When accomplished a full picture of Dutch industries will be available. It may take some time, however, to have this information available on-line. The same applies to the incorporation of more fiscal documentation and trade regulations.

FUTURE

Since its inception in 1974 Foreign Trade & Econ Abstracts has been a so called bibliographic file. Over the last few years a tremendous increase in data bases and data banks was realized. So, one might wonder if a bibliographic file like FT&EA still can be of any importance to the business enduser. The answer to this question is twofold, yes and no! One of the major reasons to keep bibliographic files alive is, that a lot of desk research is still carried out. Despite a lack of numerical information these files provide the necessary background information for desk research. Especially in the field of international trade the availability of a variety of sources becomes in handy then.

Regarding FT&EA, it should be mentioned that its coverage is worldwide, though emphasizing Western-Europe, and that it is a multilingual file. Most of the files are of US origin and have a poorer coverage of non-English sources. Here the multilingual approach of FT&EA automatically fills in a gap. Although FT&EA does not provide translations, it does offer a low-cost document delivery service to its users ($.35 per page airmail included). So the language gap can be easily overcome by having the original document sent over and have it translated.

So, the answer is yes, despite the lack of numerical information and a multilingual approach. The answer must be "no" when a bibliographic file does not have the flexibility to adapt itself to the changes in information demand. This simple statement is very true but flexibility is a bit more than just a word.

To add numerical information to a bibliographic file most of time requires the creation of a completely new file. Record layout, software and so forth have to be redesigned to create a useful tool in information transfer. FT&EA introduced some modifications to make the file more attractive to its users. In the near future it will be decided if, and what kind of new files will be added to FT&EA.

CONCLUSION

This short introduction to Foreign Trade & Econ Abstracts is meant to inform mainly American users, that online data bases originating from Western-Europe can be a tool in satisfying certain information needs. The multilinguism of Western-Europe is reflected in the data bases that are produced in the Old World. Especially in the field of international trade multilinguism can cause a language gap, which for a few dollars more, can be easily overcome. The willingness of European data base producers to advertise their products in the US is exemplified by the fact that they are represented at US Online Meetings. Over the last two years FT&EA participated in four major on-line meetings in the U.S. The first opportunity to get better acquainted with Foreign Trade & Econ Abstracts will be at the forthcoming National On-line Meeting in New York City, to be held in May. For those not able to come to New York more information on FT&EA can be obtained at the NFTA-offices (P.O. Box 20101, 2594 AG The Hague, Holland).

For Product Safety Concerns and Information please contact our EU representative GPSR@taylorandfrancis.com
Taylor & Francis Verlag GmbH, Kaufingerstraße 24, 80331 München, Germany

www.ingramcontent.com/pod-product-compliance
Lightning Source LLC
Chambersburg PA
CBHW071823300426
44116CB00009B/1417